SANDPLAY – SILENT WORKSHOP OF THE PSYCHE

Sandplay is a growing field of interest for Jungian and other psychotherapists. *Sandplay – Silent Workshop of the Psyche* by Kay Bradway and Barbara McCoard provides an introduction to sandplay as well as extensive new material for those already using this form of therapy. Based on the authors' wide-ranging clinical work, it includes in-depth discussion of sandplay processes with material from a wide range of clients, both adults and children. These case studies are extensively documented with over ninety illustrations in black and white and color. There is an examination of symbols they have researched and collected in their work and a discussion of the use of symbolic concepts in sandplay.

Clearly written and soundly based in theory, this book provides a historical background for understanding sandplay and notes on the establishment of sandplay as an international therapy. The text goes on to discuss how sandplay works in practice.

Kay Bradway and Barbara McCoard bring their indispensable personal experience of clinical and seminar work to the subject. They stress the healing potential of sandplay throughout and reflect on the nature of a therapy where the psyche works largely in silence.

Kay Bradway is a Jungian analyst and founding member of the C.G. Jung Institute of San Francisco, the International Society for Sandplay Therapy and of Sandplay Therapists of America. **Barbara McCoard** is a Jungian-oriented psychiatrist in private practice and a consulting editor of the *Journal of Sandplay Therapy*.

SANDPLAY – SILENT WORKSHOP OF THE PSYCHE

Kay Bradway and Barbara McCoard

London and New York

First published 1997
by Routledge
11 New Fetter Lane, London EC4P 4EE

Simultaneously published in the USA and Canada
by Routledge
29 West 35th Street, New York, NY 10001

Reprinted 1999

Routledge is an imprint of the Taylor & Francis Group

Typeset in Times by Florencetype Limited, Stoodleigh, Devon

Printed and bound in Great Britain by
Butler & Tanner Ltd, Frome and London

British Library Cataloguing in Publication Data
A catalogue record for this book is available from the British Library

Library of Congress Cataloguing in Publication Data
Bradway, Kay

Sandplay : silent workshop of the psyche / Kay Bradway and Barbara McCoard.
Includes bibliographical references and index.
1. Sandplay – Therapeutic use. 2. Sandplay – Therapeutic use – Case studies.
McCoard, Barbara 1944– II. Title.
RC489.S25B73 1997
616.89'165–dc20 96–16802

ISBN 0–415–15074–4(hbk)
0–415–15075–2(pbk)

Contents

List of plates

List of figures

Foreword

This book is about a healing process – more specifically, about a way Kay Bradway has found in sandplay to contain and further the process of her clients. What makes this book stand apart from so many others in humanistic psychology that have emphasized the importance of individual process in personal healing and growth is that it focuses not just on a stream of feeling that must be listened to respectfully, empathically, and without judgment if it is to flow in its own unique way toward the goal of greater human expression, but on a spontaneously selected sequence of images that give material, symbolic density to the stages of the course. In this, Dr. Bradway's emphasis is Jungian, because she believes just as much in image as in affect when she writes of the current of life energy that psychologists call process. But unlike many, if not most Jungian analysts, Bradway is not an interpreter of archetypal images, bent on developing an effective hermeneutics of unconscious imagery. Her approach, rather, is to value and to hold the image that appears in the sand, selected by the client from a universe of possible objects to express a feeling state, and to let that image have its way with her and her client with a minimum of commentary. Her interest seems to be above all in honoring the fact that this image and no other is there in the tray and thus has become part of the fate of the person seeking orientation to the purposes of the psyche by means of the sandplay work. Although the resultant image could be used either for diagnosis or as a springboard for various kinds of creative therapeutic intervention, Dr. Bradway's overall technique, as she explains it with Dr. McCoard in their section called "Reflections," is a method of "appreciation," and it is her rare capacity to appreciate the symbolic process of other people that gives this book its special glow.

Depth psychology has already entered a new era of its being by the end of its first full century of therapeutic application. This era could be characterized as one of respect for the choices of the Self. The client who turns to a shelf of objects and selects and arranges a few to give tangible meaning to the somctimes abstract notion of self-object is telling us that just these figures – this turtle or bridge, that witch or well, or the animal to drink from a pool of water scooped out by hand – are essential accretions of the Self. Bradway and McCoard write as if our field has always known this fact, which self psychology has struggled so hard to articulate to a clinical discipline more used to regarding symbolic choices as defensive, compensatory, or neurotic acts not at all deserving of anything but the most meticulous unmasking. Like C.G. Jung and Dora Kalff, Kay Bradway is there to let symbolic things happen. One gets the sense that she really enjoys learning from her patients, and perhaps that is why it is so instructive to learn from her.

John Beebe

Preface

The "I" throughout the book is Kay's voice. Barbara focuses on the clarity and aesthetics of its expression. She is behind the scenes – questioning and commenting, rearranging and revising, remodelling paragraphs and fine-tuning sentences. The "I" is happy to admit that the book would not be in existence without our working together. We jointly accept responsibility for the completed whole.

A word about "then" and "now." It is not unusual to find that I contradict myself. Certainly, I view sandplay in a different way now than I did when I learned it from Dora Kalff and first started to use it in the 1960s. I initially used sandplay as a part of my diagnostic evaluations of children. Later, when I started to use it in therapy, I talked much more than I would now – just as I did in verbal therapy. I asked questions about and commented on objects after the scene was completed – as I would in dream analysis. I reviewed the scenes with the sandplayer earlier than I would now, often while the process was still in progress. I interpreted more. In most instances I have changed the text of my earlier writings to conform with my more recent and, I hope, more helpful ways of using sandplay, but not always. And I am sure I am still changing – I hope so. This means that each time I review what I have said, I always make additions or corrections. My ideas and my recommendations continue to develop. We are all still learning from our own experiences and from each other.

Another note about the earlier use of sandplay. Some of the first sandplay scenes discussed in the book were done in a square red tray without any sign of blue on the sides of the tray. Later I learned that it was not the official Dora Kalff size and I changed to a rectangular blond tray with the now familiar dimensions of 19.5 by 28.5 by 2.75 inches. The floor of the tray was the specified blue, but the sides were not. Still later, when I started to use trays with the sides also painted blue, I found that the scenes more frequently had a three-dimensional quality.

I was fortunate when I started to work with sandplay to have the use of the sandplay room at the C.G. Jung Institute of San Francisco with its collection of miniatures. Acquiring my own collection was a further step in my commitment to sandplay. And I found that it *does* make a difference to have the sandplayer use items personally chosen by the therapist.

Since we had to limit the number of illustrations which we could include in the book, we have resorted to verbal descriptions of some of the sandplay scenes. We chose this alternative instead of deleting individual cases altogether, which would have allowed us to include illustrations of all the scenes in the remaining cases. Some of the case studies in Part III have been published previously in earlier versions with more complete visual records; these can be located through the Acknowledgements and Bibliography. Additionally, in those instances in which scenes were used in more than one chapter, we have referred to illustrations in previous chapters when discussing a particular scene. This is particularly true for "Jim" and "Ursula."

The use of colored plates permits a more satisfactory reproduction of a sand scene, but also necessitates placing the illustrations some pages from the accompanying text. We hope, we trust, that our readers will adjust to such inconveniences and applaud our publishers as we do for including such a large number of illustrations – more than have appeared in any previous publication on sandplay.

Acknowledgements

One looks forward to finally being able to acknowledge the help one has had in preparing a book. Then it becomes apparent that it is not possible to acknowledge all those whose thought and support have made a contribution to the completed product. Sometimes a single sentence in a conversation can contribute as much as an entire series of lectures.

First and foremost I want to express my deep gratitude to my sandplay teacher and friend, Dora Kalff, not just for her words, but also for her attitude toward my work. She was always encouraging me and respecting my attempts to clarify my own thinking, at the same time that she was sharing her wisdom and experience with me.

The colleagues who have been helpful are innumerable, some specifically with this book, and others with some of the material that has been used in the book. I will name a few, realizing that I am inevitably leaving some out. A special gratitude goes to Estelle Weinrib who never tired of looking at my, and sharing her, sandplay "pictures" with me. Whenever we had some time together, one of us would ask, "Can we look at some pictures?" And out would come the projector and screen and we would look and talk.

I want to express my deep appreciation to the other International Society for Sandplay Therapy (ISST) founding members besides Estelle with whom I was privileged to meet for several successive summers at Dora Kalff's where we showed slides of sandplay processes to each other. These include: Cecil Burney, Paola Carducci, Kazumiko Higuchi, Martin Kalff, Hayao Kawai, Kaspar Kiepenheuer, Chonita Larsen, Sigrid Löwen-Seifert, Andreina Navone, Joel Ryce-Menuhin and Yashuhiro Yamanaka.

Other colleagues who have been helpful in many ways include Kate Amatruda, Ruth Ammann, Nessie Bayley, Ann Bernhardt, Lauren Cunningham, Lucia Chambers, Harriet Friedman, Florence Grossenbacher, John Hood-Williams, June Matthews, Bonnie McLean, Karen Signell, Janet Tatum, Barbara Weller.

I am happily indebted to Paula Kimbro who has graciously produced several videos of my sandplay presentations which I have later incorporated into the book.

My numerous consultations with Michael Flanagin (ARAS) and Marianne Morgan (Library) at the C.G. Jung Institute of San Francisco helped me in preparing the list of references. They were always optimistically cheerful. And my thanks go to the Scholarship Committee of the Institute for giving me a generous grant to process the many illustrations.

I am also deeply grateful to John Beebe for his continued and warm encouragement from the time I first voiced the possibility of writing such a book to its completion.

Portions or edited versions of some of my previously published articles have been used in this book. I want to acknowledge my appreciation to the publishers for giving me permission to include the revised material: C.G. Jung Institute of San Francisco for *Sandplay Bridges and the Transcendent Function* and for two chapters in *Sandplay Studies: Origins, Theory and Practice* including "A woman's individuation through sandplay" ("Ida" in this book) and "Developmental stages in children's sandworlds;" *Archives of Sandplay Therapy* for "Sandplay journey of a forty-five year old woman" ("Ilsa"); *Art Psychotherapy* for "Sandplay in Psychotherapy" ("Irene"); *Journal of Sandplay Therapy* for "Transference and countertransference in sandplay therapy" ("Co-transference" and "Emmy"), "Sandplay in preparing to die" ("Debbie"), "Sun and moon in sandplay," and "Sandplay toriis and experiences of transformation;" and Daimon Verlag for "What makes it work" in *Archetypes of Shadow in a Split World.*

Acknowledgements are also due to the publishers of the following works for permission to quote extensively from them: Estelle Weinrib (1983) *Images of the Self* (Boston, MA: Sigo); Joel Ryce-Menuhin (1992) *Jungian Sandplay: the Wonderful Therapy* (London: Routledge); Ruth Ammann (1991) *Healing and Transformation in Sandplay* (Chicago: Open Court).

Permission was granted by Princeton University Press to include several quotations from the *Collected Works of C.G. Jung;* by Jack Rudloe to include passages from his book, *Time of the Turtle*; and by Yasuhiro Yamanaka to include his photo of the founding ISST members.

My heartfelt gratitude goes to the many persons who have done sandplay with me. They have been my teachers. And to the many who have given me permission to use their sandplay material in research and publications. This book could not exist without their contribution. They give it its life. I want to deeply thank each of them.

Finally I have the pleasure of thanking Brad, my husband of sixty years, who has encouraged me and supported me in all of my projects. For this book he was "in charge" of the illustrations, getting them organized and offering general and specific recommendations. But he has contributed in many more ways, in ways that I could never have done without.

Introduction

I was initially attracted to both Jungian psychology and sandplay therapy because of what I sensed as an accepting and valuing of individual differences rather than an emphasis on the judging of people. I had been taught in traditional American psychology to emphasize testing, which evaluates a person as better or worse than other people in various dimensions. So I was comforted by Jung's only test, the word association test, which simply identifies what complexes a person has without judging whether they are good or bad complexes. Moreover, his theory of typology is based on the principle that people naturally differ from one another in personality type and does not place a premium on one type over another.

I first encountered Dora Kalff's sandplay at her presentation for a joint conference of Jungian analysts in San Francisco in 1962. She showed photographs, with minimal comment, of sandplay scenes made by a child. The scenes "spoke for themselves." I don't remember the case but I do remember my impression of relief. Here was a therapeutic method where the therapist largely stayed out of the process and let the self-healing take place, guided by the child's psyche rather than by the therapist.

This was the beginning of my viewing sandplay as a place where the psyche works. I came to think of it as "playwork." We speak of homework, office work, why not playwork? Work in play.

The concept is at first easier to connect with children. After all, sandplay originated when a father observed that his two sons "worked out" their problems while at play with miniatures. Play as a form of therapy for children was easily accepted when it was first introduced fifty-plus years ago. But play as therapy for adults?! Most adults push it aside as not very serious. In fact, sandplay in its early form was used only for children. I do not think that Margaret Lowenfeld ever used it with adults. And the first edition of Dora Kalff's book on sandplay carried the secondary title, *Mirror of a Child's Mind*.

When adults came to my office for the first time and saw my sandplay set up, they often remarked, "Oh, you see children." It was difficult for them to take me seriously when I explained that adult patients used this setup also.

But when adults do sandplay themselves, they no longer have such wonderment. They experience that sandplay works. It works largely in silence. And I think we are learning that it is the psyche that does the work.

This book is based on presentations about sandplay which I have made orally or in writing since the mid-1970s. My earliest presentation, a comparison of the sandtrays made by "home" and "career" women, was made at one of Dora Kalff's Monday morning seminars at her home in Zollikon in 1975. I had shown her some of the pictures from this study during a consultation hour. Her encouragement freed me to work up something, which she later invited me to present. She gave me the same free and protected space that is a hallmark of her sandplay therapy.

The book is divided into three parts. Part I presents some of my historical reminiscences about how sandplay first came into being, and attempts to get at what makes sandplay work. I had no doubt both from my own personal process and from witnessing the processes of many others that sandplay did work but, being a curious type, I want to know both why and how. At the same time I keep in mind a dream I once had:

> I was carrying hundreds of little sandplay miniatures in my spread-out skirt from a darkened place where I couldn't see them to a place of light. As I moved toward the light, objects kept falling out of my skirt, until finally I had none left to look at.

There is some magic in our therapeutic work that cannot be brought completely into consciousness.

Part II presents my understanding of a few of the symbols we see in sandplay including three specific figures that I have "researched" more extensively than others: the turtle, the bridge, and the torii or Japanese sacred gate. It also discusses two more abstract symbolic concepts that can be useful ways of looking at sandplay scenes: differences between "Hestia" women who work primarily at home and "Athena" women who work primarily in the outside world; and differences in stages of development among children of different ages.

Part III presents ten in-depth studies of individuals. Earlier versions of some of these case studies have been published elsewhere. They have all been extensively revised for this book. I think this is the most important section in the book. Dora Kalff taught by leisurely presenting sandplay scenes of individuals with an emphasis on what was being experienced. This is the way I learned sandplay. It is the way I still learn.

A word about the Appendix. "What I look for in final case reports" is added here because therapists who are writing their final case reports often ask what readers look for when evaluating their write-ups. Over a period of years, I have made and revised lists of what I personally think is important. It is no way official. And the final lines are something I wrote for myself when I was in the early years of my own analysis.

Part I

Background and reflections

Chapter 1

Introduction to background and reflections

This first part opens with a chapter on what makes sandplay work. The second chapter reviews how sandplay began and how I started using it myself, together with my personal remembrances of the founding of the international and American sandplay societies. The third chapter extracts quotes that I especially value from what three other authors have had to say about the theory and practice of sandplay in their recent books and compares them side by side. The fourth chapter looks at some of the similarities and differences between Jungian analysis and sandplay therapy. And the fifth chapter explains why I prefer the word "co-transference" to the less precise "transference-countertransference."

The next several chapters are best described as my "from-time-to-time" reflections on different aspects of sandplay, including chapters on sandplay language and sandplay appreciation.

The final chapters of Part I present my more "how-to" thoughts on the role of the therapist and the process of sandplay, with an emphasis on empathy. Part I ends with a chapter on four key areas that I keep in mind when I am trying to understand sandplay scenes: levels, stages, sequences and themes.

Chapter 2

What makes sandplay work?

What is there about sandplay that causes both patient and therapist alike to experience it as having such power? What is there about sand in a 19.5 by 28.5 inch tray with blue base and sides, a supply of water, a collection of miniatures and the instructions "Do what you want in the sand" that is so effective in promoting both healing and growth?

Sandplay is a form of active imagination, but the images used in sandplay are concrete and tangible rather than invisible and intangible. Like dream scenes, sandplay scenes are a series of figures and actions. But, unlike dreams which must first be remembered by the patient, then reported to the therapist and then visualized internally by the therapist, sandtrays are immediately seen by both patient and therapist. And sandplay is, of course, play. But, unlike spontaneous play, it occurs within specified boundaries of time and space.

Even a single sandtray can have healing power. A few days before I left for a month's vacation, a young man I had been seeing for several months came in and went directly into the sandplay room. He put his fingers into the sand down to the blue base and circled with them through the sand making the largest oval shape the rectangular box permitted. He ended up with an oval island in the center of the tray. He piled more sand on the island from the edges and proceeded to pat the sand down hard, adding water occasionally, and stroking and re-stroking the sand into a smooth, and smoother, hard surface. He said nothing until about half the time was up and then he asked me how much more time he had. When I told him, he heaved a sigh of relief and settled in. He spent the rest of the time smoothing and patting the oval island, sometimes with one hand and sometimes with both hands, circling it with his finger or fingers, and clearing the sand away from the blue so that there was a clear blue space around the hard central mound of sand.

I found myself relaxing with the rhythm of his movements. I had been feeling harassed with last-minute preparations for my trip. This hour put me in a centered space. He also seemed to enter a new place. I silently thanked this man. Later, I learned that for him, too, this had been a healing experience, and had prepared him for this interruption of his therapy. Words did not have to be spoken. No amplification, no interpretation, no verbal exchanges were necessary.

Sandplay has parallels in alchemy, which Jung found so helpful in describing the process of individuation. The chaotic placing of a multitude of objects which often occurs in beginning sandplay scenes is like the *prima materia* of alchemy. "It provides a glimpse of the . . . chaos prior to the operation of the world-creating Logos" (Edinger 1985: 12). In a sandplay process, one can often see order emerging from the chaos of earlier trays.

In the alchemical process of *calcinatio*, matter is burned into a white powder. Edinger refers to the ash that has survived calcinatio as the "white earth." I liken this to the sand in the sandtray, even to the whiteness of it. And, of course, the alchemical operation of *solutio* refers to water, represented in the sandtray by both the blueness of the bottom and the water that can literally be poured into the tray.

But it is Edinger's description of the alchemical procedure of *coagulatio* that most alerted me to the parallels between sandplay and alchemy. He states,

> Concepts and abstractions don't coagulate. . . . The images of dreams and active imagination do coagulate. They connect the outer world with the inner world . . . and thus coagulate soul-stuff. Moods and affects toss us about wildly until they coagulate into something visible and tangible; then we can relate to them objectively.
>
> (Edinger 1985: 100)

Sandplay offers an opportunity for such coagulation. Emotions and moods are experienced concretely in the use of sand and water with, or even without, miniatures.

Dieckmann writes,

> If the individual is concerned with consciousness, he will become acquainted with this unknown thing that is growing in him; if he is concerned not only to know *that* it is, but also to experience *what* it is, then he attempts to give form to the unformed, to speak the unspeakable, and to shape the chaos that is bubbling up.
>
> (Dieckmann 1986: 101)

It is the experiencing of molding the sand, of adding water in sprinkles or by cupfuls, of placing the objects, of burying them, of letting something happen, be it felt as creative or destructive, and of honoring whatever process takes over, that is healing. In watching patients work, I sometimes feel that they enter a near-trance state.

The sandplay therapist typically avoids intruding upon the patient's experience of this concretization, or coagulation, in the sandtray. It is out there in front, to be seen, to be felt with the hands, to be changed with the hands. But therapists do provide the necessary container or *temenos*. Kalff's phrase, "free and protected space," describes it best (Kalff 1980: 39). The holding container of the co-transference, a term I like to use for the transference-countertransference, is always there. It is an essential part of the therapy.

Both negative and positive transference may be depicted in the sand scenes. Sometimes the patient specifically identifies a figure as the therapist. This is more likely to happen in early scenes. As the sandplay process progresses, it tends to be accompanied by reduced consciousness, often verbalized by such remarks as "I don't know what I am making" or "I don't know why I am putting this in." It is at this time that archetypal symbols are most likely to be used.

Intrusive or premature interpretations may interrupt the only partially conscious processes of sandplay. Several psychoanalysts at Mount Zion Psychiatric Center in San Francisco designed a study (Gassner *et al.* 1982) to investigate Freud's early theory, which assumed that analysts had to interpret repressed mental contents in order to make those contents conscious. What they found did not support this theory. Repressed contents typically emerged without the analysts having made any prior interpretations that were relevant to the repressed contents.

The Mount Zion group found, however, that the lifting of defenses against the repressed contents did depend upon the therapist passing what they called the "transference test." When the patient feels safe in trusting the therapist, feels held in a safe *temenos*, then the material can flow.

This therapeutic safety, Kalff's "protected space," is akin to what Goodheart calls the "secure container" or "secured-symbolizing field" (Goodheart 1980: 8–9). And Kalff's "giving the patient freedom to do what he or she wants to do" in sandplay can be translated into Goodheart's phrase, "respect for the patient." He sees this secured-symbolizing field as one of three fields that occur in therapy. In this state, the therapist is aligned with unconscious forces within both the therapist and the patient. According to Goodheart, the therapist's most important job is to provide for and maintain such a space (Goodheart 1980: 12).

Winnicott calls this field the "transitional play space" and the "area of illusion" (Winnicott 1971: 95). He writes, "It exists as a resting place for . . . keeping inner and outer reality separate, yet interrelated" (Winnicott 1971: 11). Gordon refers to this space as the "third area" or "area of experience." She adds,

> when deintegrates emerge out of the self, they are at first crude. . . They are archetypal. However, if they can become contents of the third area, if they can be experienced and experimented with . . . they become "digestible" for integration into the ego.
>
> (Gordon 1993: 304)

This third area, this area of illusion or area of experience, is exactly the place where the sandplay process occurs. It is the place where inner and outer reality come together, sometimes more of one and sometimes more of the other. In the early trays, the contents are usually dictated more by outer reality. As the sandplayer gets deeper into the process, the making of the scene is often influenced more by inner reality. When the sandplayer says such things as "I don't know what I'm doing" we can conclude that the inner process has mostly taken over the making of the tray.

Gordon feels that Winnicott's theory of the third area provides analysts with a theoretical foundation for their practice and experience (Gordon 1993: 304–5). And, I would add, a theoretical foundation for sandplay.

Many therapists now appreciate the hazards of the therapist intruding into this space. Langs (1981), for example, ranks silence as the primary form of intervention.

Delaying or avoiding amplification and interpretation during the sandplay process does not, however, lessen the sandplay therapist's responsibility to become familiar with the cultural and archetypal dimensions of the available objects, and to try to understand through both feeling *and* thinking what is going on as the process unfolds. Understanding and empathy are both essential, although they need not always be voiced. As O'Connell writes, "Silent amplification nourishes and expands the container. . . . There is meaning in the not-saying, in the conscious use of silent incubation, an inner witnessing" (O'Connell 1986: 123). And with this witnessing, sandplay therapists often find themselves deeply moved.

For me the power of sandplay has to do with the coagulative potential of working with actual sand and water and miniatures, and with the freedom to do whatever one wants with these media while feeling protected by a non-intruding, wise therapist whom one trusts. It seems so simple: a combination of sand and water, shelves of miniatures, freedom and protection. But this combination holds the potential both for healing and for transformation.

Chapter 3

Beginnings

BEGINNINGS OF SANDPLAY AND OF MY USING IT

Sandplay did not emerge fully formed. It has a long tap root. In the early part of the twentieth century, a father observed his two sons playing on the floor with miniature figures and noticed how they were working out their problems with each other and with the rest of the family (Wells 1911 and 1975).

Twenty years later, a child psychiatrist was looking for a method she could use to help children "express the inexpressible." She recalled reading about the father's experience with his sons and decided to add miniatures to the play room in her clinic. The first child to see them took them to the sandbox in the room and started to play with them in the sand. And thus what she called the "World Technique" was born (Lowenfeld 1979).

Then a child therapist studying with C.G. Jung heard about the work in England. With Jung's encouragement, she went to London and studied under Lowenfeld. She realized that the technique not only allowed for the expression of the fears and angers and secret thoughts of children but also encouraged the individuation process, which she had been studying with Jung. This woman was Dora Kalff. (For a discerning and detailed account of the beginnings and development of sandplay, see Mitchell and Friedman's (1994) book *Sandplay: Past, Present and Future*.)

Kalff introduced the technique which she called "sandplay" at a conference of Jungian Analysts in California in 1962. It was there that I first learned about sandplay and, soon afterwards, I had my initial sandplay experience with Renee Brand, the first American student of Dora Kalff.

As a psychologist, I was frequently involved in the evaluation of children, so it was in that way that I first used sandplay. I found it a helpful supplement to the battery of tests that I typically administered. But a little 8-year-old girl who was referred to me for therapy taught me to bypass evaluation and to instead incorporate sandplay directly into my play therapy with children. Kathy had had all the "testing" she could tolerate. She was dyslexic and had been through several batteries of tests to help psychologists understand why such a seemingly bright youngster was having so much difficulty in school. So I used no tests with her, but she took to the sandtray and started to use it the first time she came to me.

Kathy taught me much that supplemented what I was learning from Dora Kalff, who was supervising me during the time I saw Kathy. My work with her was the basis for my deeper understanding of sandplay: the significance of the initial tray; the role of transference-countertransference (what I call "co-transference"); the importance of the appearance of the Self; the imprinting of an important tray on the sandplayer's mind so that a subsequent tray practically duplicates the previous tray; the appearance of several recurrent themes in the sandplay process.

But perhaps the most important experience I had with Kathy was the power of self-healing without interpretation. Kathy did not want to talk about her father, who had recently died. She did not want to talk about her problems with her mother, or with her siblings, or in school. She worked all this out in the sandtray without discussion. And, most importantly for her immediate needs, she worked on her visual-motor problems in the tray, "practicing" visual-motor coordination skills on the figure of the flower plot with its removable flowers. She used me as she needed to: as an enemy in one tray where we shot guns back and forth at each other over a ridge of sand; and as a co-worker in the final tray to help her construct a castle.

I had my longest delayed review with Kathy. When I was contacting people who had done sandplay with me to secure permission to use their material for teaching and publication, I called Kathy's mother to find out how I could locate her. I learned that she was away but would be home for Christmas. So I called her and made an appointment to review her trays. It had been twenty years. I was taken aback when I came to the waiting room and saw this grown-up woman waiting for me. I must say I felt resentful that she had replaced the little girl I had loved. But she turned out to be charming in her adult form, too. And the contact was a rewarding one. I learned much that I had never known about her during the time I was seeing her for therapy. And I learned that you cannot really know what is in the trays until the delayed review. Kathy was the last child I saw "in the sand," as we began to say. But she was one of my most important teachers.

FOUNDING OF ISST AND STA

In February of 1982, eleven of us in five different countries, all but three being Jungian analysts, received the following letter from Dora Kalff:

Dear ——

I am happy to inform you that from September 10–17, 1982 I organize a meeting with a few representatives of Sandplay therapists of various parts of the world. This letter is to extend an invitation to you to participate in this meeting in order to share experiences which you have undergone in the field of Sandplay therapy.

The purpose of this meeting should be:

1 An attempt to define the essential characteristics of Sandplay understood within a Jungian framework.
2 To communicate what we feel is essential in this therapy. Therefore I suggest that we all present a case and a short paper where we define what we estimate as the essential point.
3 To integrate and draw conclusions of the variety of different views of what has been said.
4 To establish an organization of Sandplay therapists to meet periodically to further the study and practice of Sandplay.

The need for such a forum was born out of concern to establish a solid base for this type of therapy. During the meeting there should be ample time for the participants to exchange views among themselves, to discuss case material outside the formal sessions. In the hope that you will be able to participate I expect your reply.

With cordial greetings

(signed: Dora Kalff)

All but one of the eleven persons receiving this letter appeared in the Kalff living room in Zollikon seven months later. Few of us knew each other. I had never met the other two from America, Estelle Weinrib and Chonita Larsen. The others coming for that initial meeting were: from England, Joel Ryce-Menuhin; from Italy, Paola Carducci and Andreina Navone; from Japan, Hayao Kawai and Yasuhiro Yamanaka; from Switzerland, Kaspar Kiepenheuer and Martin Kalff. Kazumiko Higuchi from Japan could not be with us at that time. Two others from Japan who were in the area were invited to join us for that first meeting: I. Ankei and Takao Oda.

Dora arranged for a reception in the afternoon of 10 September for us to meet each other, and for us to attend a Tai Chi performance by Al Huang that evening. The pace for the presentations the rest of the week was leisurely with one-and-one-half to two-and-one-half hours for each presentation with discussion, and four hours for lunch and rest. The presentations focused on a diverse set of subjects: bridge phobia; a warning

Figure 3.1

about too much explanation; the triangle as a symbol of the heart; psychosomatics; anorexia; the cannon and the crown as symbols; nature play. Some of us shared personal dreams.

On the next to the last day Dora had a surprise for us, a journey to Bollingen to visit C.G. Jung's Tower. While we were there we were invited to sign the guest book under the heading, "First Annual Congress of the International Sandplay Society."

We met each of the succeeding two summers at Zollikon and worked on forming an international society. We continued the same format for these meetings; each of us always presented a case, despite the time and energy we were expending on working out the numerous details of a formal society. The official founding of the International Society for Sandplay Therapy (ISST) was August 1985. By this time, Cecil Burney from America had also joined. A photograph of the twelve members assisting Dora in founding the Society is reproduced in Figure 3.1 (standing, left to right: Kazumiko Higuchi, Kaspar Kiepenheuer, Martin Kalff, Chonita Larsen, Estelle Weinrib, Kay Bradway, Joel Ryce-Menuhin, Hayao Kawai; sitting, left to right: Yasuhiro Yamanaka, Andreina Navone, Dora Kalff, Cecil Burney, Paola Carducci). Tragically, Cecil died the following year. Sigrid Löwen-Seifert was invited to come in later to represent Germany and became the final official founding member.

After the founding of ISST, Estelle and Chonita and I proceeded to form an affiliated society in America. We used the ISST guidelines, whose principles have changed very little in the intervening years. There were eight additional Americans eligible to join ISST and the affiliated American group by 1987. Our initial meeting was in my home that year in Sausalito, California. Dora Kalff joined us in the afternoon and we discussed the steps we needed to take to form an official society. The following year the group met again in Sausalito and we were ready to choose a name, the Sandplay Therapists of America (STA). The Minutes of the 1988 meeting show that the founding group consisted of eleven people: Kate Amatruda, Linda Bath, Kay Bradway, Lucia Chambers, Lauren Cunningham, Harriet Friedman, Chonita Larsen, Susan Macnofsky, Mary Jane Markell, Estelle Weinrib and Barbara Weller. Jungian analysts June Matthews and Louis Stewart, who were pioneer followers of Dora Kalff, have joined since.

The beginnings are not far behind us, but membership and activities have expanded exponentially. By the end of 1995, ten years after its founding, ISST membership topped one hundred. There are now affiliate groups in Canada, the UK, Germany, Israel, Italy, Japan, Switzerland, and the USA, all actively engaged in training other sandplay therapists.

As of January 1996, there were fifty-two members in STA from fourteen different states, plus Canada. Two California members were residing outside of California, one in Amsterdam, the other in Japan. The society had sponsored a national conference every three years; the first three conferences were held in Minnesota, California, and Washington. The *Journal for Sandplay Therapy*, first published by the Society in 1991 under the editorship of Lauren Cunningham, was in its fifth year of publication. And the circle of people interested in sandplay continues to grow.

Chapter 4

Comparison of three authors

A number of publications and books on sandplay have appeared since Dora Kalff's seminal book, *Sandplay, a Psychotherapeutic Approach to the Psyche*, was published in 1980 (revision of her 1971 *Sandplay: Mirror of a Child's Psyche*). Three books on the theory and practice of sandplay, published between 1983 and 1992, are authored by members of the International Society for Sandplay Therapy (founder: Dora Kalff) who are also Jungian analysts: *Images of the Self: The Sandplay Therapy Process* by Estelle Weinrib; *Healing and Transformation in Sandplay* by Ruth Ammann; and *Jungian Sandplay: The Wonderful Therapy* by Joel Ryce-Menuhin. All three authors studied with Dora Kalff during the 1970s and 1980s. All have made significant contributions to the understanding of sandplay in a Jungian context.

As I was rereading these three books to prepare a summary of their ideas on the theory and practice of sandplay for this book, I found myself selecting a number of complete quotations that I especially liked from each of them. I wanted to preserve many of them in full rather than trying to paraphrase or summarize them. Then I saw that they could be collected together in a few key categories which coincide with many concerns frequently voiced by therapists interested in doing sandplay. And I found that juxtaposing the quotations from each of the three authors under these headings facilitated the highlighting of their similarities and differences. So I decided to share these quotations with the reader in this way, adding just a few of my own comments. I like letting the authors speak in their own words.

As I was comparing the writings of these authors, I was reassured to find how much they agree about many specific aspects of sandplay. There is a large area of commonality among them, as well as individual differences and unique contributions to the study of sandplay. One can sense that sandplay has a solid foundation out of which it can grow.

PROCESSES IN SANDPLAY

Weinrib distinguishes two processes going on in sandplay: (1) "*healing*," and (2) "*expansion of consciousness*." These are related but not identical.

> Healing implies first that there has been a wounding and possible impairment of natural organic function, and second, that the wound has then been remedied and natural function has been restored. Consciousness implies awareness of what one is feeling, thinking and doing and the capacity to make choices in one's actions and communications that are relatively free of control by complexes. Expanded consciousness, while it may contribute to healing, does not ensure it. On the other hand, healing, by restoring the psyche to its natural functioning, creates a condition out of which the insight and consciousness that are natural to the human personality will evolve organically.
>
> (Weinrib 1983: 21–2)

Ammann also differentiates between two processes in sandplay: (1) the "*healing process*," and (2) the "*transformation of the personal world view*." In describing the healing process that goes on in her patients, Ammann says,

> These people suffer from a so-called disturbance of the primary relationship with the mother or mother figure which makes it impossible for them to grow up with a healthy trust in the world or in their own life process . . . the therapeutic process leads into the deep-seated layers of experiences of early childhood. These layers are beyond consciousness and verbalization. Psychic energy then flows back until it reaches the healthy core of the psyche. The pictures and powers of undisturbed wholeness are animated and become effective through sandplay and a healthy foundation is formed on which the new structure of the personality is built.
>
> (Ammann 1991: 4)

Ammann describes the process of transformation, on the other hand, as occurring

> with persons who have a fundamentally healthy foundation in life and a stable ego, but whose world view is too narrow, one-sided or disturbing. They sense something is wrong with them . . . and enter the process consciously, not simply driven by unconscious suffering. The process of transformation includes, for example, confrontations with the Shadow, transformation of the feminine, encounter with the Self as an image of God, and so forth. Such psychic transformations which change the basic world view of a person presuppose a healthy ego consciousness and feelings of self-worth. They represent steps in individuation.
>
> (Ammann 1991: 5)

By contrast, Ryce-Menuhin does not differentiate between two separate processes in sandplay therapy. He characterizes all sandplay as a "healing therapy". According to him,

> [The] symbolic attitude refers to a contact between the ego and inner psychic contents that in sandplay may lead to a *healing process*. This *transformation* can be brought by the ego towards the self in an approach which has the 'as-if' symbolic quality. [emphasis added]
>
> (Ryce-Menuhin 1992: 20)

Here he seems to equate healing with transformation.

Along with Weinrib and Ammann, I also see two processes going on in sandplay. I identify them as: (1) "*healing*" and (2) "*growth*." In both verbal analysis and sandplay therapy, these twin urges for healing and growth are simultaneously activated if an appropriate atmosphere is provided by the therapist. In sandplay we identify this atmosphere as freedom, space, protection and empathy.

I do, however, depart from Ammann in her more definitive separation between healing and transformation. Some training institutes similarly distinguish between a personal analysis and a training analysis. This distinction is based on the assumption that those who come for training already have a fundamentally healthy ego and do not require the kind of analysis offered to those who come as patients. Other institutes, however, believe that there is value in treating each analysand as one who has been wounded and in letting analysands go at their own pace in the analysis.

I see an overlap between the two processes in sandplay: what I call the "healing" that is akin to Weinrib's "healing" and Ammann's "healing process;" and what I call the "growth" or individuation that is akin to Weinrib's "expanded consciousness" and Ammann's "process of transformation." I take my paradigm or model from nature. A tree that is injured will generally heal if protected; growth is usually impaired if healing does not occur. But the two may occur together. The acorn has within it the blueprint for the growth and repairing of the tree, just as the unconscious guides the growth and healing of the individual. Jung says, "Life has always seemed to me like a plant that lives on a rhizome. Its true life is invisible, hidden in the rhizome" (Jung 1961: 4).

SANDPLAY AND VERBAL ANALYSIS

All three authors favor the concurrent use of sandplay and Jungian analysis. Weinrib speaks of their taking place simultaneously, with "insights garnered from the sand pictures [used] in the analytical sessions just as ideas gained analytically shed light on the meaning of the pictures" (Weinrib 1983: 15). She adds, "in some cases, the interaction between sandplay and verbal analysis appears to have a synergistic effect" (Weinrib 1983: 82).

Ammann similarly sees analysis and sandplay therapy as going on together. She says,

> During my analytic work I use both verbal analysis and sandplay simultaneously. But it can happen that an analysand first expresses himself through sandplay and then, later, after working through the sand pictures analytically, continues with dream analysis. Another possibility is that an analysand alternates between verbal analysis and sandplay. He may perhaps create especially important stations of his process in a sand picture or treat specific or especially difficult themes or transitions in the sand.
>
> (Ammann 1991: XVII)

According to Ryce-Menuhin, his "own preference is to use sandplay in conjunction with a long, deep verbal Jungian analysis of many years" (Ryce-Menuhin 1992: 33). In one of the cases he presents in his book, however, he uses sandplay without other ongoing analysis. And he points out that his experience corroborates Kalff's experience that results from the sandplay method by itself can be deeply impressive.

I, too, have found that verbal analysis and sandplay usually occur concurrently, but sometimes one is emphasized more than the other, and sometimes they are done with different therapists. Often verbal analysis takes center stage and sandplay remains an adjunct to the verbal analysis. At other times, sandplay is the main mode of therapy and verbal analysis is clearly an adjunct to the sandplay, which is how Dora Kalff used sandplay. And, occasionally, analysts who do not use sandplay themselves have referred their patients to me for sandplay which went on in tandem with their regular verbal analysis.

REGRESSION

All three authors believe the regression which sandplay encourages is an essential ingredient of the healing process. Weinrib notes that whereas verbal analysis encourages progression and the thrust toward consciousness, "sandplay encourages a creative regression that enables healing precisely because of delayed interpretation and the deliberate discouragement of directed thinking" (Weinrib 1983: 22). In this way, "sandplay therapy attempts to repair damage to the archetypal mother image by metaphorically reconstructing the disturbed mother–child unity" (Weinrib 1983: 35).

Ammann also values the regression that is fostered by sandplay (Ammann 1991: XVII) and observes that the sandplayer often goes back to earlier childhood experiences, especially to the mother–child relationship, but this time with the therapist.

> Here he can relive the vital primal mother–child relationship, but this time with the therapist. This, however, will succeed only if the therapist can fully accept, protect and guide the child during the regression and accompany him in the subsequent reconstruction of his personality.
>
> (Ammann 1991: 86)

Ryce-Menuhin adds,

> Atmospheres of childhood are more non-verbal in memory than adult life usually is and the medium of sand can sometimes release more quickly the hidden, repressed content of early memory and begin to reconstruct the past. . . . Sandplay facilitates the return of early memory and can lead on to valuable work in the reconstruction and repair of a traumatic childhood.
>
> (Ryce-Menuhin 1992: 105)

MATRIARCHAL AND PATRIARCHAL ELEMENTS

Weinrib differentiates between the masculine logos of verbal analysis and the feminine container of sandplay. Verbal analysis

> is the analytical interpretation of concrete daily life events, as well as unconscious material such as dreams, fantasies and active imagination in the thrust toward increased consciousness. [On the other hand,] the making of sand pictures is a deliberate regression into the pre-conscious pre-verbal matriarchal level of the psyche.
>
> (Weinrib's introduction to a paper she presented on 21 September 1991)

> The aim [in sandplay] is to provide a maternal space or psychological womb, an emotional metaphor for the uroboric mother–child unit. In this safe "space" healing of the inner psychological wound can occur, the Self can be constellated and the inner child re-discovered, with all of its potentiality for creativity and renewal.
>
> (Weinrib 1983: 28)

Later, stages of the individuation process

> continue in the more cerebral and sensate way that is characteristic of the patriarchal level of consciousness hypothesized by Neumann – one more corroboration of his concepts.
>
> (Weinrib 1983: 88)

Ammann distinguishes between the quiet period of making the picture in the sand during which the attention of both analyst and analysand are directed to the inner world of the analysand and the subsequent interpretive period during which the analyst and analysand become partners in trying to understand the meaning in the pictures so that they become more connected to the experience of the analysand. She identifies these two periods as representing two distinct therapeutic attitudes of the analyst: first maternal or matriarchal and then paternal or patriarchal. To avoid evoking gender-specific roles, however, she prefers to use the terminology of the cerebral hemispheres. According to Ammann,

> The right hemisphere . . . works with holistic, nonverbal images and plays a large role in the processing of emotional information. It seems to me to be significant that the body image is located in the right hemisphere. The left hemisphere . . . is language-oriented and connects with logical and goal-oriented thinking. This hemisphere works rationally and analytically. The two therapeutic attitudes involve the two hemispheres of the brain alternately.
>
> (Ammann 1991: 6–7)

Similarly, Ryce-Menuhin says,

> There is a sense in which wordless ritual of the sandplay is a way, whether for men or women, to the feminine principle. In the universal sense of the feminine, sandplay shares the activity of accepting a conception and carrying knowledge to assimilate it while allowing a ripening to occur. This takes time and needs an allowance for submitting to something which is an unforced happening. No effort of will is required as the masculine tends to feel it a necessity to habitually draw from psyche . . . however, when the masculine is expressed in sandplay, it sharpens its definition precisely because it is seen against this feminine, unforced "earthy" background. Masculinity can have a very full range of expression; its battlegrounds, its hero's journeys, its phallic pride . . . its forceful power, its childlike omnipotence, its search for love, its demonic aggression, its genius and its love of God.
>
> (Ryce-Menuhin 1992: 31)

BODY AND SPIRIT

All three authors emphasize the value of connecting both with the body and with the spiritual through sandplay. Weinrib reviews Kalff's beliefs that the material elements of sandplay act as a "kind of metaphor for the body." Kalff noted that patients who were physically ill sometimes made pictorial representations in the sand of diseased organs whose shape they did not know (Kalff's seminar at the University of California in Santa Cruz, March 1979). At the same time, the appearance of symbols of totality in the sand pictures, and the numinosity of the patients' deeply felt experiences, led Kalff to the idea that sandplay is a way to the spirit (Weinrib 1983: 40).

According to Ammann,

> Both the spiritual and psychological dimensions are not merely constellated [but are] given physical form by the person's hands. Sandplay creates a common field within which spirit and body can mutually influence each other. Such direct interplay between psyche and matter is not known, at least in this form, in classical verbal analysis.
>
> (Ammann 1991: XV)

Ryce-Menuhin points out that "The earth quality of sand pulls the psyche towards body expression" (Ryce-Menuhin 1992: 104). Yet it also evokes spiritual expression. He says,

> the "awake dream" of sandplay creation often contains a rich and varied working through of a patient's spiritual religious dilemma. Many objects representing gods and goddesses are available together with shrines, retreats, churches, temples, cathedrals and chapels. . . . Many agnostics and atheists have discovered through sandplay the unconscious release of integrative archetypal material which consciously enables them to contact the God-image within their own psyche.
>
> (Ryce-Menuhin 1992: 104)

SELF-HEALING

Weinrib emphasizes the role of self-healing in sandplay. She observes, "A basic postulate of sandplay therapy is that deep in the unconscious there is an autonomous tendency, given the proper conditions, for the psyche to heal itself" (Weinrib 1983: 1). For the patient who experiences this,

> There is almost invariably a sense of awe and surprise at the richness within him. A new relationship with his own imagination and inner being is born, and he gains a new sense of his worth and strength because he literally sees it. Based on his own experience, he begins to sense that there really is a healing and organizing factor within that transcends his ego-consciousness and that it can be trusted.
>
> (Weinrib 1983: 77–8)

Ammann also feels that

> Sandplay heals not by being acted upon by another, but rather by the analysand's own action. Through the analysand's creations and attitudes the energies at work within him are made externally visible. We can speak of each sand picture as being an actual act of birth.
>
> (Ammann 1991: 121)

Ryce-Menuhin generally seems to take a more authoritative role in the sandplay process than the other two authors do. Like them, however, he also refers to the therapist as "a silent observing companion" (Ryce-Menuhin 1992: 32) who primarily is there to witness the ritual of sandplay. Within this silence, "The intuition of patients, which is related to an inward and non-rational impulse, can flow into the sandplay unreservedly" (Ryce-Menuhin 1992: 28).

THE THERAPIST

These authors all agree that the therapist needs to be a relatively silent supportive presence and also to understand within themselves as deeply as possible what is going on in the sandplay. According to Weinrib, "The therapist listens, observes, and participates empathically and cognitively, with as little verbalization as possible" (Weinrib 1983: 12). Further, "the sandplay therapist must discipline his urge to find ready answers to unclear questions" (Weinrib 1983: 16).

> [Yet] without understanding on the part of the therapist of these [developmental] stages and their symbolic representations, the process is only minimally effective. This understanding enables an unspoken rapport between therapist and patient . . . the therapist knows consciously what the patient knows unconsciously.
>
> (Weinrib 1983: 29)

Weinrib describes what the therapist needs to do in order to become worthy of the trust that the patient places in him.

> He should have had a deep analysis himself and adequate clinical training, including extensive knowledge of archetypal symbolism. He should have had a meaningful personal experience doing sandplay as a patient himself. He should be familiar with the stages of development as they manifest in the process, and he should have studied and compared many sand pictures, which is the only way to learn to read them. As the carrier of the process, he should have achieved rootedness in himself.
>
> (Weinrib 1983: 29)

Ammann specifies that "what is required of the analyst is restraint and fine sensibility" (Ammann 1991: 121). The task of the therapist

> consists in recognizing what is going on in the analysand, in protecting and supporting this process, in intervening in an emergency, but first and foremost, his task is just to add only so much commentary that the process in the analysand is kept going.
>
> (Ammann 1991: 4)

Although, she says a certain amount of "intellectual explication" is necessary to grasp the underlying sense of pictures, "the essential point about them is being gripped and stirred while viewing them!" (Ammann 1991:

57). The analyst follows the client's work "with one joyful and one watchful eye" (Ammann 1991: 31).

Ryce-Menuhin points out that the sandplay therapist does not immediately screen the image for meanings but is just being there patiently awaiting developments. Like the other two authors, however, Ryce-Menuhin also at times does make verbal comments.

> The therapist brings interpretation (where suitable) of the symbolic meaning, both one-pointed and in amplification where useful. This is given back to the patient, who, in being a sandplayer, may be re-connected to the child archetype and the archaic existential wisdom of other archetypal images which self chooses to let flow into sandplay.
>
> (Ryce-Menuhin 1992: 36).

AFTER THE SAND SCENE IS COMPLETED

I see the most differences between the three authors in their discussion of what follows after the completion of a scene. Weinrib strongly insists that "sandplay pictures created by the clients are NOT, repeat NOT, interpreted at the time they are made" (Weinrib's introduction to paper given 21 September 1992). But,

> After the picture is finished, the therapist may ask the patient to tell the story of the picture, or may ask relevant questions or elicit the patient's comments and associations regarding the pictures, or speak of matters suggested by them. The therapist does not press for associations or confront the patient in any way. . . . To press for associations would be to encourage cerebral activity, which is not desirable here except in its most spontaneous exercise.
>
> (Weinrib 1983: 13)

She does, however,

> make occasional exceptions to this practice. If the patient does not enjoy doing sandplay and is skeptical of its value, I comment on some aspect of the early picture to assure him that his pictures are, in fact, communicating his unspoken feeling . . . (or) if a particular theme has urgent significance; or if a patient is acutely anxious and needs the reassurance of cognitive understanding.
>
> (Weinrib 1983: 13)

Ammann apparently treats her patients differently depending on whether they are in the first or second phase of their sandplay process. In the healing phase, the analysand is led away from the rational into an activation of the sense of touch. And, in general after making a sandtray, Ammann feels that

> the analysand takes the picture of . . . *his world*, inwardly with him. There it will produce an emotional after-effect which lasts till the next

> hour. . . . It would not be correct to interpret the sand picture immediately after its creation. The danger lies in fixing the picture's interpretation intellectually, which interrupts the flow of emotions and feelings attending and following its creation.
>
> (Ammann 1991: 3)

During the transformation phase, however, sandplay scenes may be discussed and interpreted at the time they are made with analysands who have a stable ego (Amman 1991: 4–6). She adds that an analysand who is in the phase of transformation "will try to come to understand each of his sand pictures, and work out and make conscious their meaning" (Ammann 1991: 5).

Ryce-Menuhin feels that it is important to talk with sandplayers to find out what a symbol means to them. But he also recognizes that the sandplayer does not need to be conscious of other symbolic meanings that the therapist may be thinking about (Ryce-Menuhin 1992: 4–5).

Like these authors, I avoid discussion of the sand scene at the time it is created; but, as they do, I recognize that there are times for exceptions – perhaps less frequently than any of these three.

REVIEW AND INTERPRETATION

All three authors take photographs or slides after the completion of each scene, and review them at some time with the patient. Weinrib delays the review until after she feels that the Self has been constellated and "the ego has become strong enough to integrate the material properly" (Weinrib 1983: 14). She continues,

> At this time explanations, amplifications and interpretations may be given and questions answered. Often little needs to be said even then, for the slides themselves seem to speak directly to the patient, as he literally sees pictures of his own developmental process.
>
> (Weinrib 1983: 14)

Ammann also reviews the patient's slides. She says,

> After the process has ended it seems to me to be important in these cases [analysands with stable ego] carefully to work through the slides . . . .
>
> [But] the logical or interpretive discussion of images is not even necessary in certain cases, if they affect the early, elementary layers of human life in which the physiological and psychological to a large extent are united.
>
> (Ammann 1991: 6 and 46)

Ryce-Menuhin quotes Jung who says, "There are cases where I can let interpretation go as a therapeutic requirement" (Ryce-Menuhin 1922: 33).

But Ryce-Menuhin goes on to urge caution.

> To let a patient go into life, after experiencing sandplay, but not interpreting it, is rather like seeing that someone's broken ankle is mended (technically) but that when the cast is taken away, the wounded person is not helped to learn to walk again. . . . what symbolic interpretation does is raise possibilities that strengthen the patient's ego and raise its differentiation further from unconsciousness.
>
> (Ryce-Menuhin 1992: 34 and 89)

I differ from these authors in that I do not feel the therapist always needs to interpret the slides while going over them with the patient after the process is completed. So I speak of delayed "review" rather than delayed "interpretation". I feel that even when the mutual looking at the trays is postponed until some time after the trays are done, interpretation by the therapist still takes a back seat to insights arrived at together. I like to wait until the non-verbal process has had time to "work" and attitudes and behavior have had time to catch up with what was going on in the sandplay process. This may be five years or more.

UNIQUE CONTRIBUTIONS

Each of these authors brings unique contributions to the field of sandplay therapy from their own experiences. Weinrib is the only one who specifically presents a belief that sandplay can bypass some of the stages which normally occur in Jungian analysis. According to her, "Sandplay therapy accelerates the individuation process since . . . it seems to move in a more direct line toward the constellation of the Self and the renewal of the ego" (Weinrib 1983: 87).

Weinrib also spells out the several stages of a sandplay process. She includes in her sequence: first realistic scenes; then scenes from deeper levels including the shadow; the touching of the Self; emergence of the reborn ego; differentiation of the masculine–feminine; and finally the appearance of spiritual figures or abstract religious symbols (Weinrib 1983: 76–9).

Ammann makes a detailed comparison of sandplay and alchemy and points out that "in both methods the imaginative activity follows from the interplay of the material and physical with the psychic components" (Ammann 1991: 13–15). As an architect as well as a therapist she effectively uses the house and garden as metaphors for the psyche. She also discusses the question of why the rectangular sandtray is preferable to a square or circular one.

> Because of the inequality of measurements, the rectangular space creates tension, unrest, and a desire for movement, a desire to go forward. The square or circular space, however, creates balance, rest,

> and concentration towards the center. It is possible to compare the analytic process with a constant search for the center in uncentered space.
>
> (Ammann 1991: 18)

Both Ammann and Ryce-Menuhin use "mapping" of the sandtray as an aid to understanding the meaning of objects placed in different locations in the tray. Their systems, however, do not coincide. Perhaps there is a difference in how sandplay is experienced by persons living in a mountainous country surrounded by land and those living in a more-or-less flat country surrounded by water. This, I think, confirms my doubts about using the map of the sandtray developed by someone else. If you are going to use such a system, I think it is preferable to develop your own method out of your own experience.

Ryce-Menuhin emphasizes the need for ritual in sandplay.

> When one is initiated to a new relationship to self, one needs ritual to contain the powerful transformation of understanding involved. . . . For the atmospheric quality of ritual happenings to occur and recur in a progression, a special place of initiation is required.
>
> (Ryce-Menuhin 1992: 28–9)

Ryce-Menuhin also discusses specifically who should come into sandplay therapy and who should not. He wisely concludes, "Sandplay is not a panacea or a cure-all" (Ryce-Menuhin 1992: 34–6).

I particularly appreciate Ryce-Menuhin's recognition that sandplay therapists have much to learn. As he says, "the state of the art and the science of sandplay interpretation is yet in its first sixty years. Patient and therapist discover together" (Ryce-Menuhin 1992: 32).

Chapter 5

Jungian analysis and sandplay

In my practice as a Jungian analyst, I have used sandplay in three different ways over the twenty years that I included sandplay in my work:

1 with analysis as the primary therapy and sandplay as the adjunct
2 with sandplay as the principal therapy and verbal therapy or analysis as the adjunct
3 with sandplay and analysis going on concurrently with two different analysts or therapists.

Most analysts use sandplay in the first way, as an adjunct to verbal analysis. Some see it as a parallel to, or even sometimes as a substitute for, dream analysis. In this context, the therapist may ask the sandplayer about the tray – what certain objects mean to them or what their associations are – and then may "interpret" the scene; that is, connect it with the patient's past history, current problems, or the transference. At first I also used sandplay in this way as an adjunct to verbal analysis, with the immediate interpretation that is common in dream analysis. Later I saw the benefits of delaying the interpretation.

Ida is an example of doing it in both ways. For the first forty-four of her seventy-one trays, we spent most of the time after she made a scene talking about the tray. Then there was a shift; after each of the last twenty-seven scenes were made, we talked about her everyday life and dreams and did not refer to the tray itself at all. This paralleled a shift in the depth of her process, and more evidence of improvement in her condition. This, along with other experiences, made a deep impression on me.

Using sandplay in the second way, as the principal form of therapy, was the way Dora Kalff taught it. Unfortunately the second edition of her book on sandplay had an error on the back cover which stated, "Sandplay is *not* a method of therapy in and of itself." Dora was tremendously upset to see this error on the back of her book. The statement should read: "Sandplay is a method of therapy in and of itself." That was Dora's point, although she did also emphasize that in addition to the sandplay therapy there should be time for discussing everyday problems and important dreams (Kalff 1991:14).

The third method of using sandplay as a process that goes on separately from the patient's verbal therapy is perhaps the most controversial. I first experimented with it when an analyst colleague, who had a sandplay setup in his office but did not feel he was sufficiently trained to use it, asked me if I would see a particular patient for sandplay while he was seeing her for analysis. I was somewhat hesitant to try this because of the possible transference split. We established certain "rules." The analysand would delay talking with the primary analyst about the sandplay process until after it was completed; the analyst and I would have no contact with each other; and several months after the sandplay process was completed, the three of us would meet and review the slides of the trays together. At the conclusion of the experiment, all three of us felt that this system had worked.

After that, I felt free to use it in several other instances. When one of my sandplay colleagues questioned me, however, about prohibiting the patient from talking with her analyst about something important in her life, I took it to heart. I asked a few of the analysts with whom I had engaged in this dual therapy about their experiences during the time I was seeing their patients. None of them felt they had had any difficulty with it. One said that she was very relieved to have me taking care of the symbolic side of therapy since she and her patient seemed to be focusing mostly on the "nitty gritty" of life. Another analyst said that he was not even aware that he was not supposed to talk with the analysand about the sandplay! Yet it had come up only once, when the sandplay picture was an extension of a dream that the patient had discussed in his office. So I was satisfied at that time, at least, that it was not a problem to separate out the two kinds of therapy.

Sandplay therapists bring different expectations or "sets" to sandplay, depending on which professional affiliation they come from. Social Workers and Marriage, Family and Child Counselors have been trained to pay close attention to the details of family inter-relationships and to have the freedom to interview collaterals, both family members and teachers. And sometimes they look at sandplay pictures as another way of clarifying their understanding of these family inter-relationships. Psychologists and psychiatrists have been trained to focus on diagnosis and sometimes tend to use sandplay as an evaluative technique. Both may use a sand picture to confirm or correct their impressions of pathology in the patient.

All of these ways of using sandplay are valuable. I feel, however, that using it mainly for these purposes may mean that the *unique* contribution of sandplay is missed. Over and over again I find myself saying, "Sandplay is meant for healing, *not* for diagnosis." The unique healing quality of sandplay is activated primarily by empathy. When the patient experiences the therapist or "witness" of the sandplay process not only as agreeing with their feelings (sympathy) but also as feeling *into* their feelings (empathy), the twin urges for healing and growth can be constellated within them.

Sandplay provides a way of "dropping" into the pre-verbal, matriarchal areas of the psyche. Verbalization, with its demand for conscious articulation, may interfere with this. Most of the adults I saw in therapy were so much in their heads that the very experience of "playing" and getting connected with unconscious material was valuable in and of itself.

I do also believe, however, with Estelle Weinrib, that "delayed interpretation," as she calls it, is essential. In my experience it may be best if the delay is five years or more. I suppose we all are highly influenced by our own therapeutic experience. For me, the delay was ten years. The sandplay process had been working all that time without my being consciously aware of it. When Dora Kalff and I went over my slides ten years later, it was a profound experience. And when I go over a series of slides with people I was seeing five or ten years ago, I do not think of it as interpretation. I think of it as a mutual coming to understand what happened during and what has happened since the process. There are mutual insights and mutual "aha!" and "wow!" experiences.

All therapists find the methods which best work for them and there is no reason we should all do therapy in the same way. The way our own personalities enter into the co-transference is so important that we each need to develop our individual style that is most natural or compatible.

At the same time, I have thought of comparing sandplay with a musical instrument which has capabilities that are not always used. When therapists use it as they would other techniques with which they are familiar, its essence and full range may be missed. It is not easy to learn its full use. When we are accustomed to "talk therapy" it is not easy to follow the admonition I heard early on in my experience, "Don't just say something, sit there!" It is not easy when one sees a clear-cut connection in a sandtray – with other sandtrays or dreams, co-transference, past history, or present concerns – to use the connection silently to enhance one's empathy rather than to use it out loud as one does in most other therapies to help bring something from the patient's unconscious up into their consciousness. In sandplay we can just let the connections "work;" we can let them remain at an unconscious level where they can do their work. Early interpretation, or consciously making connections (a phrase I prefer to the word "interpretation"), can rob the patient. Gains have not incubated. They have to do some work in the unconscious first.

This emphasis on empathy and "staying out of the process," however, certainly does not mean that the therapist can get along with a minimum of training and experience. Far from it. In addition to empathy we need to have the backup of good, solid clinical knowledge and experience. We cannot depend on intuition alone, no matter how good, to carry us along. Sandplay therapists sometimes ask why it is necessary for them to know about symbols, know about pathology, know about co-transference, know about family constellations. Of course it is important to know as much as possible about the psyche. I do not think that we can function well as therapists without this knowledge. It is essential for developing true empathy. It is on reserve, an absolutely essential reserve, to use when indicated. And the knowledge of when to use it is also vital.

I sometimes think of sandplay as akin to sailing. It is good to let it be natural and unencumbered. If, however, the boat gets away from us, or the wind gets too strong or ceases completely, we need to have the protection of a motor, a good reliable motor that will get us out of danger spots. That is where the know-how, the long experience, the self-confidence, the close attention to all that has been happening, provides the protection which is needed in emergencies or when crucial decisions must be made as to direction and route.

Chapter 6

Co-transference

The term "transference," as used by Dora Kalff, refers primarily to the "free and protected space" which is the hallmark of her therapy. In the introduction to her book, she says that she tries through the transference to protect the child's Self when it is constellated in the therapy (Kalff 1980: 29). People who worked with Dora Kalff found that her very presence freed them to be what they truly were and protected them so that they could do whatever they needed to do. This is what the transference meant to her. She was more concerned with the experience of current feelings than she was with the transference of past feelings into the present situation.

Most references to transference and countertransference made at sandplay conferences similarly allude to this current relationship between therapist and client and each person's experiencing of it without regard for the pre-determinants of that relationship.

Yet all relationships must necessarily contain elements of all previous relationships. In the classical analytic literature, transference refers primarily to this carrying over of past feelings into the present. Freud first used the term transference to describe what went on when his women patients fell in love with him. He realized that his patients were repeating impulses and feelings they had experienced earlier, usually in their relationships with parental figures, in their relationship with him. Freud viewed these feelings as always sexual in nature, and warned physicians to avoid countertransference, by which he meant the doctors also falling in love with their patients (Freud 1915: 97 and 157).

Jung found alchemy helpful in understanding both transference and countertransference. He saw transference as an activation of the archetype of the alchemical mystic marriage or *coniunctio*. The doctor's task was to help the patient become conscious of the archetypal significance of this experience. This, he felt, would then bring about a re-integration of the personality and further the individuation process (Jung 1954b: 163–321).

According to Fordham (1978), when a patient transfers or projects the image of a significant figure from the past onto the therapist, the therapist often identifies with that projection. This "projective identification" enables the therapist "to put himself inside and feel along with his patient or experience in himself what it is like to be his patient," and helps the therapist to further his/her understanding of the patient (Fordham 1978: 91).

Kohut, founder of the school of self-psychology, emphasized the need for an atmosphere of empathy which would foster what he called a "self-object" transference to the analyst. This transference would then be periodically disrupted by an unintentional failure of empathy on the part of the analyst. If the therapist could accept the patient's negative reaction to the empathic failure, and could help them understand how it was in part a reactivation of childhood experiences, this could become a source of healing (Kohut 1984: 206).

The term transference has also generally been used in sandplay to refer primarily to positive feelings rather than to both positive and negative feelings. In Kalff's book, it is almost exclusively the positive feelings that receive attention. Generally a person's negative feelings are not even mentioned. When a child patient threw darts at the freshly painted walls in her house, Kalff emphasized her feeling that letting him throw the darts gave him the assurance that she wanted to help him, not that he might be acting out negative feelings towards her (Kalff 1980: 67). Throughout her book, Kalff also refers to her own feelings primarily in positive ways: "I felt sorry for him." "I was glad for him." "I was greatly touched." She reports at one point on a child who says to her, "Isn't that nice? I love you and you love me" (Kalff 1980: 129). This is the atmosphere that Kalff created. It is akin to what Winnicott described between mother and infant as the falling in love with each other.

With subsequent clinical experience, however, we have learned that both positive and negative feelings can have significant impact on the course of sandplay. Hayao Kawai and others at the International Society meetings have talked about the extent to which their feelings as a therapist, whether bad *or* good (both are judging), about a particular tray influences the making of the following tray. And for patients such as Emmy, for example, the expression of negative transference feelings in the sandtray can help them to release their capacity for strength.

It can be extremely difficult to control transference reactions. One of my first supervisors had red hair, the color of my mother's hair. Even though I did not think their personalities were actually very much alike, I could not get over seeing my mother in her no matter how much I tried.

If our projections are conscious, however, we do have semi-control over them. I am still struck by an incident that a young therapist told me about years ago. Halfway through the third session of marital counseling with an older couple, she stood up and said with finality, "I am sorry I can't work with you any longer; you remind me too much of my parents!" Although the young therapist could not control her feelings, she could recognize them. And her recognition of them led to a conscious act instead of an unconscious projection which could have been damaging to the patient.

As therapists, we have to be especially alert to cues that we are projecting, both negatively and positively, and we have to work on raising our projections into consciousness. This takes constant vigilance.

In the sandtray, clients may specify that a particular figure represents the therapist. Sometimes they do this when they are making the scene. Sometimes they recognize this only later while the scenes are being reviewed. Often a child may engage the therapist to enact a particular role in the sandplay. Kathy arranged for the two of us to stand on opposite sides of the tray and shoot sandplay cannons at each other. She was shooting at me, and I was shooting at her. The negative transference was out in the open, but non-destructive.

Many of us, moreover, have become aware of the importance of the physical position of the therapist in the room in understanding what is happening in a sand scene. In my own work, I have noted that the orientation of the scene or the placement of significant figures in the tray may be related to where I am sitting. A journey may be directed towards that corner or a gun may be aimed in my direction.

As Kiepenheuer pointed out at an early meeting, the collection of sandplay objects is itself a kind of extension of the therapist. And a client's reaction to the objects in our collection is often suggestive of their feelings towards us at the moment. Someone may complain that necessary items are not on the shelves or compare our collection with others and find ours less adequate. On other days, perhaps the very next session, the same person may praise our collection or become enthusiastic about finding just what is needed. They are feeling better towards us.

Often a therapist feels an unexpected inner reaction to such criticism or praise. Sometimes I have even verbally defended my collection. I accept these feelings of mine as natural. What is important is that we keep aware of our responses to the criticism and to the praise. Therapists are participants as well as observers. Use of the tray may facilitate being in the observer role but it does not eliminate being a participant. Perhaps I become less defensive in response to criticism of my sandtray objects than I do to criticism of my person, but I may still feel defensive, *very* defensive!

It helps, too, to recognize the naturalness of a person's negative feelings towards us, even when we are not obviously slipping up. After all, we do take vacations, we do charge fees, we do control the time.

A few years ago, I found that I was avoiding the use of the term countertransference. I preferred instead the word co-transference, which indicates to me a feeling *with* ("co"), rather than a feeling *against* ("counter"). I use the term co-transference to designate the therapeutic feeling relationship between therapist and patient. These inter-feelings seem to take place almost simultaneously, rather than sequentially as the composite term transference-countertransference suggests.

These feelings are, I believe, necessarily determined by both earlier and current happenings. And it is not just the person coming for therapy who projects; the therapist does also. Both may find hooks in the other on which to hang, or project, the unused or repressed parts of themselves, or personal memories from the past, or archetypal images. And both respond to these projections. One cannot help but be affected by the projections of significant others. Moreover, both projections and responses are often entirely at an unconscious level. The therapeutic relationship is a mix, a complex mix, a valuable mix. It is this mix that I am referring to when I use the term co-transference.

Chapter 7

Rorschach and Rogers

When I first started to use sandplay with children, I was still doing diagnostic work for schools and clinics. So I included sandplay in the battery of material I used for assessment, much like the Rorschach. And I found it useful. But I discovered that I could not use it for evaluation with a child whom I was then going to see in therapy. When I did, the child had already had to "perform" for me. And I had already been set up as the judge of the child. So they could never be completely free in their subsequent therapeutic sandplay.

Using sandplay for evaluation is a little like using a violin to prop up a table which is missing one leg. It will work, but it may hurt the violin, and then it can no longer be used to play the music that could accompany our tea or lunch. Far better that we find a box or a piece of lumber to support the table and preserve the violin for making music.

If sandplay is used to evaluate people, they may sense that they are being critically assessed even when this is not overtly communicated to them. There is certainly much evidence that communication goes on unconsciously between persons who are intimately related, like mother and child, or lovers, or therapist and patient. If a therapist is looking at a tray and thinking, "This shows a latent schizophrenia," or "This person is narcissistic," or "This indicates hostility," their judgmental stance may be communicated subliminally to the patient. It is better instead to look at the scenes as the person's way of coping in the moment with their problems or wounds or conflicts, both outer and inner.

Some therapists who use the Rorschach for evaluation tend to "interpret" the sandplay scene as a projective test just as they would a Rorschach. I remember one psychologist, for example, who saw images of food in a tray as an indication that the sandplayer was hungry and "needy" instead of as an indication that the sandplayer was actively doing something, right then and there, to "feed" himself. Clients can actually provide themselves symbolically with what they need in the sandtray, whether it be food, a caring mother, or energy to combat a hostile figure.

If a person can ask directly for what they need in their life outside of the therapy, they may not have to give it to themselves in the sandtray. I remember a woman who had a long history of agoraphobia. She had resolved it intellectually, but the habit of being fearful still persisted. A day came when her infant daughter had to be rushed to the hospital. She was the only one who could take the baby. She drove the car, which she had not been able to drive for two years, to the hospital with her infant and her 5-year-old son. As she drove, she repeatedly asked her son to "tell me I am a good mother." He did. And she was able to perform the task. The habit of fear was broken.

This giving of nourishment to oneself either in life or in the sandtray is often necessary first before one can perform a task which requires extra strength. Ilsa put a fawn drinking out of a pool in one tray. In the following tray she could for the first time face her long denied wound represented by the open pit in the scene.

The trend toward less evaluating and less interpreting and more empathic mirroring in therapy, like the mother who mirrors her infant as a necessary part of its growth, is not new. Carl Rogers introduced what he called "client-centered therapy" based on reflecting feeling as a way of doing therapy in the 1940s (Rogers 1942: 144). It was my first exposure to a way of doing therapy and I embraced it and found that it helped me to honor the person's process. I tried to avoid saying anything that was not a reflection of their feeling unless I had a reason to do so. I took to heart Rogers' statement that even "The use of silence may, curiously enough, be one such technique [for mirroring]" (Rogers 1942: 165). Later, he adds, "insight cannot be gained from being talked to; it is an experience which the client achieves" (Rogers 1942: 179).

Sandplay, too, is a form of mirroring. It can, like Rogers' empathically reflecting therapist, function as "a mirror which shows the client his real self" (Rogers 1942: 144).

Chapter 8

Expression vs. experience

In "sandtray" work *expression* is emphasized, whereas in "sandplay" therapy *experience* is emphasized. Margaret Lowenfeld, who first developed the therapeutic use of sandtrays in her clinic, chose to provide the children with this medium specifically because she felt that it allowed them to "express the inexpressible" to their therapists. They could say something they had not been able to communicate to anyone before because of its emotional impact. This is akin to catharsis, which is the "grandfather" of all modern therapies. John Hood-Williams later adapted Lowenfeld's work and brought it to the USA, teaching many followers of Lowenfeld's work who continued to see the sandtray primarily as an expression rather than as an experience.

Dora Kalff, on the other hand, emphasized the importance of the experience that clients actually have when they make a sand scene. She brought this to my attention most impressively when she corrected my sentence, "In using the bridge the child was showing a potential for making a connection between the opposites." Kalff said, "The client is in the actual attempt of making the connection." I have tried ever since then to see sand scenes in terms of the immediacy of the lived experience itself rather than merely as expressions or as potentials for experience. In sandplay, it is what the client is experiencing for themselves that is important, not what the therapist thinks the client is expressing to the therapist.

I once had a client who just left the tray as it was rather than making a scene. When I showed a photo of the blank tray to a student and asked what it meant to her she answered, "The client is trying to tell me how empty he/she feels."

I think this answer, which is in terms of what the client is trying to express to the therapist, is only part of it. According to Jung, "It's only in the state of complete abandonment and loneliness that we experience the helpful powers of our own natures" (Jung 1969a: 342). By contemplating the blank tray, without interfering inferences made by the therapist either aloud or silently, the client had the opportunity not only to express but also to actually experience both her emptiness and the healing powers of her own nature.

Chapter 9

Judging

Judging is built in to our life experience; it seems to be universal in humans. It begins at birth as soon as the infant emerges from the mother. The baby is immediately inspected to determine whether it is a boy or a girl. At that moment, it is judged. In some cultures being a girl is such a negative "attribute" that the baby is killed. The next judgments are measurements: what does it weigh? How long is it? New techniques now permit pre-natal judging. It is no longer put off until birth. In utero the foetus can be evaluated. Will it be a boy or a girl? Are there pathologies?

Only the mother of the newborn is non-judgmental. The baby is put to her breast and is nourished regardless of its gender or its weight or its length. The baby sees beauty in the mother, and the mother sees beauty in the baby. They "fall in love," the expression used by Winnicott to describe this bonding between mother and infant. There is no judging; there is only empathy. They fit together.

In therapeutic work there is also often a stage of "mothering" which is characterized by what we call "unconditional love," a total acceptance. Later a time comes when this is not sufficient for the growing person. As one patient said to me, "I don't want you to love me for *myself*, anymore. I want you to love me for what I can *do*." And our relationship changed. I found myself evaluating her performance in her schoolwork, her job-getting, her love relationships. I was looking at her drive for success, her tasks, her achievements. I tried to help her with what she had to do more than I had in the previous stage, thc "mothering" stage. I had entered a "fathering" stage with her.

In the first stage, there is nothing you can do to be loved, you are or you are not. In the next stage, you can do something to win love; you are loved if you perform. These two stages do, of course, overlap.

Sandplay, which is largely non-verbal, belongs predominantly to the earlier mothering stage. As John Beebe puts it,

> Since Winnicott, analysts have favored a style of working that depends upon receptive holding of the patient's material. An actively engaged

> interest that does not seek to interfere with the patient's own affective track is now seen as preferable even to interpretation.
>
> (Beebe 1992: 72)

Beebe quotes another similar passage from Jung:

> We must be able to let things happen in the psyche. For us, this is an art of which most people know nothing. Consciousness is forever interfering, helping, correcting, and negating, never leaving the psychic process to grow in peace.
>
> (Jung 1967: 16)

In sandplay, we withhold judgment. We accept the uniqueness of individuals and their ways of coping and dealing with their wounds, their problems, their pathology. We enjoy, without interpreting, the beauty of the sandplayer's process, the beauty of the sandplayer's uniqueness, the beauty of their self-healing. This is what makes the process work.

Chapter 10

Sandplay appreciation

I recently read a dissertation on beauty (Gillmar 1994). The author speaks of "resonance" between observer and object, viewer and painting, listener and music. It occurred to me that this is what happens in sandplay. The therapist is silent, but in that silence there is a resonance with the process in the tray. The therapist empathizes with the sandplayer and resonates with the scene.

Then I wondered, "How is this taught, this resonance? How is it taught in the arts? How do we learn to appreciate the beauty?" I recalled my courses in "Art Appreciation" and "Music Appreciation." Perhaps we should have classes in "Sandplay Appreciation!" We could teach all that we know that is valuable about the background of sandplay: myths, fairy tales, Jungian theory, other psychological theories, alchemy, the I Ching, chakras, symbols, dream analysis. Then therapists have all this background in themselves to use as it is necessary, or as it comes up when they are "appreciating" sandplay and resonating with it.

Gillmar also speaks of "aesthetic arrest." It seems to me that aesthetic arrest is akin to the synchronistic moment in sandplay, when all stops and you and the sandplayer are in tune with something higher than either of you. Something like the all, the whole, the Self. In that moment, each of you is transformed,

Chapter 11

The fourfold base: freedom, protection, empathy, trust

FREE AND PROTECTED SPACE

It is unusual to have both freedom and protection. Wild animals are free but not protected; domestic animals are protected but not free. Children, also, are protected but not free. Adults may have one or the other, depending on the country or the time in history. But to have both is rare. That is one reason why sandplay is so compelling.

What is the freedom? To do what one wants. In verbal therapy one is free to *say* what one wants. In sandplay therapy one is free to *do* what one wants within the frame of the tray. Doing is more the whole person than saying.

What is the protection? From exposure. From being punished or criticized for what one does, or being judged, or even from being evaluated. Also, secrets are kept. It is safe to be oneself. One need not put on a mask. And if one loses oneself and needs to be helped to not harm oneself or the therapist, the therapist protects.

EMPATHY AND TRUST

When we say "Rapport was quickly established," we are referring to the general relationship between therapist and client. But when we talk about transference, we mean something more than that. We are referring to the therapist's empathy for the client and the client's trust in the therapist. And until this positive co-transference exists, I doubt that much therapy can take place.

When I first see a client, I do not usually feel either trust or distrust. I am too busy trying to empathize, to feel with the client. And when clients sense that I am feeling with them, they feel trust in me, trust that I will honor them and their material, trust that they can be any way they need to be with me and I will be accepting of them. They feel safe to be themselves. As therapy progresses, there may be more mutuality of empathy and trust. The therapist develops trust in the patient, and the patient develops empathy for the therapist.

This is what Dora Kalff provided with the free and protected space of her sandplay therapy. She had an almost instant empathy with clients and clients had an almost instant trust in her.

And once this co-transference field has been established, healing and growth can take place.

Chaper 12

Sandplay language

We can speak of a dream language in the sense that a dream is a message from the unconscious of the dreamer to their consciousness. We can similarly speak of a sandplay language. In a sand scene, the experience of the sandplayer is also recorded in a non-verbal, largely unconscious language that we therapists, if we know enough, can pick up on. The extent to which we understand this sandplay language allows us to tune in to or, as Harriet Friedman says, "track" the process. We can read the story of what is happening, what the sandplayer is experiencing. This helps us to empathize. It also keeps us alert and aware.

Nothing we can read, or listen to, or learn from others is as helpful in understanding the sandplay process of other persons as doing our own sandplay process, having our own experience with the same medium of sandtray, miniatures, and the empathy of our therapist. It is akin to what one counselor told a mother, "The best thing you can read to understand your adolescent daughter is your own diary when you were that age."

There is a continuum in sandplay language from the universal or archetypal through the cultural to the personal. The figure of the sun, for example, has several universal meanings. It is a common physical experience for all people in all parts of the globe that when the sun is shining, it is light, and when the sun is not shining, it is dark. When the sun is shining, it is warm, and when the sun is not shining, it is cold. The image of the sun also carries with it a sense of power, of directing, something to do with its being a cosmic object, a higher being, a parent. Our knowing myths and legends and fairy tales in which the sun figures gives us a sense of what this archetypal meaning is. The sandplayer may not know the same myths that we do, but that is not important. There may be many myths all reflecting or expressing the same universal meaning. Each myth is only one representation of the underlying archetype.

The language which comes from our own particular culture is, of course, "closer to home." In most western cultures, for example, the sun is thought of as masculine. Germany is an exception; there the sun is seen as feminine, "*die* Sonne." In Japanese culture the sun is also thought of as feminine, the sun god*dess*, Amaterasu. These cultural differences in gender are reflected in the language of the sandplayer.

In contrast to these more general archetypal and cultural levels of sandplay language, the personal language of the sandplayer is unique. Since we do not usually ask questions of the sandplayers about the objects they use or encourage them to volunteer an explanation during the process itself, we often do not know this personal language until the review done after the sandplay process is completed. Often, however, patients do talk spontaneously about the sand scene, in which case, of course, we do not stop them. It is, after all, their process. Or in the get-acquainted session we may also learn enough to help us "read" the personal elements of the language the sandplayer uses.

My favorite example of an instance when I completely missed the uniquely personal meaning of an object until the review comes from a woman who used a glass bottle-stopper from one of my empty bottles of Guerlain perfume in her tray. Other women had previously used it to represent intuition or as a fanciful glass tree in their scenes. But when this woman used it, neither one of these meanings seemed applicable. I did not know what it meant to her until the review. To my inquiry, she replied, "It's my mother." I was even more puzzled. And then she said, "She used Guerlain perfume, too."

The meaning of the particular item used, regardless of whether it is universal, cultural, or personal, is modified by several other factors: spatial location of the item in the tray; temporal sequence – that is, what preceded the placement of the object and what followed it; what was in the same location in the previous tray(s); and what is happening in the co-transference.

For some sandplay therapists the *location* of an object in the tray is meaningful in and of itself. For some, the top and right sides represent the conscious, the bottom and left sides the unconscious. Dora Kalff, when I initially studied with her, found these locations helpful, but later she abandoned them, saying that the whole tray was from the unconscious.

Joel Ryce-Menuhin has extended this idea by devising diagrams or "maps" for different levels of meaning in the sandtray. On one level he sees archetypes projected onto the left side of the tray and ego projected onto the upper right. On another level, he sees collective unconscious projected onto the upper left, personal unconscious onto the center left, and collective unconscious across the bottom of the tray (Ryce-Menuhin 1992: 91–6).

Ruth Ammann suggests other guidelines for interpreting spatial phenomenon: upper left is inner world; lower left, the instincts; upper right, the collective consciousness and personal father; lower right, earth connectedness, personal mother and body image (Ammann 1991: 47–9). Other therapists see in the upper left the personal father, in the lower left the archetypal mother, in the upper right the archetypal father, and in the lower right the personal mother.

I have not found any of these location maps consistently helpful, even though at times one or another of them does seem to "fit." Perhaps there are too many other variables which preclude consistency in interpreting the meaning of spatial locations.

I do find *sequence* very important. Often the negative, for example, cannot be allowed into the process until the more positive has been given its due. Debbie had been denying any fear connected with her cancer until one day, after making a very pleasant scene, she wanted to do a second tray; it was the only time she did two trays in a session. In that second tray she for the first time could show and experience the fear and anger which, at some level, almost always accompanies a diagnosis of cancer.

Sometimes it works the other way; after showing the negative, one has to revert back to the positive. This can show up when following the *sequence from tray to tray* as well as when following the sequence within a single tray. Sometimes we can follow a transformation occurring from one tray to the next by tracing the changes in objects placed in a particular location. In Ilsa's sandtray series, for example, the location occupied by a threatening figure in one tray was occupied by a protecting figure in the next.

What is going on in the *co-transference* may take precedence over other variables. Positive transference, or simply a positive feeling, is often seen early in the sandplay process. Emmy placed a wise old woman in the initial tray which represented how she perceived me at that time. A later sandplay made the day I was ten minutes late was full of anger. Even in the review it was difficult for her to acknowledge that she had indeed felt angry at me. But she had been able to express her anger in the tray at the time, even though at an unconscious level. This is how the language of sandplay works.

Chapter 13

On interpretation

It has been said that patients of Jungians have Jungian dreams and those of Freudians have Freudian dreams. This means that the patient follows the analyst.

When the patient has a dream, and the therapist interprets it, the orientation of the therapist is out there in front and is picked up by the patient. The patient's subsequent dreams are influenced by each interpretation. The dreams, then, follow the therapist.

Shouldn't it be the other way around? Shouldn't the therapist be following the patient? If patients have a Freudian dream, therapists should use their Freudian knowledge; if patients have a Jungian dream, therapists should use their Jungian knowledge.

There has been so much discussion about the clinical orientation or the symbolic orientation. A therapist has to have both. The patient's material may call for one approach and then for the other at different times in the process. Sandplay therapists are trained as much as possible to relate to the material as it is rather than to impose a fixed theoretical orientation on the material. Sandplay calls for a union of the "opposites" of clinical and symbolic. The figures themselves are conducive to either or both understandings, often in the same tray.

Since sandplay generally proceeds without much therapist intervention by questions or discussion or interpretation, patients can generally follow their own way without the orientation of the therapist getting in their way. This is one advantage of sandplay over dream interpretation. The process is allowed to unfold; the patient's own psyche is the guide rather than the therapist's.

Sandplay really is based on the self-healing of the patient. Given a wound, a free and protected place and an empathic witness, a self-healing process can be initiated. It is the experiencing of the process that heals, not the theoretical interpretation of the process.

About the clinical orientation: the extent to which a sandplay therapist focuses on clinical material or does a classical intake (gathering data on family history, personal history, symptoms, current situation) depends on the circumstances and the therapist. But, as the process continues, more history will emerge. And much of the personal may not be known until the review of the slides with the sandplayer.

And, regardless of orientation, the co-transference is always there. Sandplay therapists remain alert to its manifestation in the objects put into the tray, the effect of where therapists are located while witnessing the making of the tray, the criticism or praise of the objects on the shelves, as well as by what is occurring between themselves and the patient, such as missed appointments or vacations. Therapists can expect that both love and hate toward them will be experienced by the patient at some time during the process. Therapists should be equally aware of their feelings towards the patient. They may also feel both love and hate. One must watch for both. If the feelings of therapists become strong enough to be getting in the way, then therapists should seek counselling for themselves.

About the symbolic orientation: sandplay is a ready medium for symbolic material. Each one of the objects has many symbolic connections. To "read" an object accurately, or with cognitive understanding, one must take cognizance of several levels: the personal, both the historical and the immediate now; the cultural, both where the patient grew up and where they reside now; and the archetypal or collective unconscious.

Our reading about many cultures and familiarity with people from different cultures helps with understanding the cultural level. And our familiarity with the actual biology of animals and other figures, as well as our reading of myths and fairy tales, helps with the archetypal.

It is our own experiences of both wounding and healing that provide us with the grounding, the empathy required to do sandplay therapy. This is a "feeling into," not just sympathy or a "feeling with." This is the reason that doing a process ourselves with a therapist who gives us the experience of freedom, protection and empathy is essential in sandplay training.

Sometimes a therapist comes to another sandplay therapist to "do a process" only because it is required for certification as a member of STA/ISST. This is somewhat like the Freudian idea of the "training analysis." Sometimes this can mean that the analysand or sandplayer does not want to really get into their deep place but only to experience what it means to have their dreams and other material analyzed. But one has to experience what it feels like to go into the deep place in order to appreciate it in one's patients. Often sandplay with a trained sandplay therapist is a sufficiently powerful medium so that a genuine process takes place despite the client's expectation that they can go through it quickly and remain relatively untouched at a deep level.

And sandplay therapists in training also sometimes ask, "Why try to make connections for yourself, why learn the meaning of sandplay objects, why study archetypal symbolism, if you usually don't tell the person you are seeing about your observations?" I think the answer is that it helps us to follow the experience and to participate in the experience that the sandplayer is having. We apply all that we have learned to appreciate what is going on in the tray and to sense what is going on in the person. It is this attentive "listening," done mainly with our eyes rather than our ears, that fosters empathy in sandplay.

So the careful attempt to understand at a cognitive level as well as having had our own experience as a patient with sandplay therapy are both essential for our training. And we continue, even after becoming sandplay therapists, to review cases, both our own and those of others. Every time we go over a process we learn more and become increasingly able to give the necessary empathy. And it is this empathy which is both healing in itself and conducive to the lifting of repressions which allows the patient increased access to the healing powers in their own unconscious.

Chapter 14

Sandplay is meant for healing

AS A SANDPLAY THERAPIST, I REMIND MYSELF EVERY ONCE IN A WHILE THAT

First, sandplay is meant for healing.

Second, what happens in a sandtray may be an expression of distress and pathology, but, more importantly, it shows how the sandplayer is coping with these problems. Even the expression of problems or distress in the tray can be a way of coping with them. Catharsis was one of the earliest forms of therapy. Each sandtray in the process may be seen as part of a series of successive attempts to cope with past and current wounds or as a step in the ongoing journey towards individuation or, almost necessarily, both. The sandplay process is witnessed by a protecting therapist who values, not evaluates.

Third, my role as therapist is to provide freedom, space, protection and empathy so that the twin urges toward health and growth can activate the process of healing and individuation. It is not my conscious that leads the process but the unconscious of the sandplayer. Healing comes from within, not from without. My role is not to educate, direct or even to guide. It is the mutual trust in the inner guide of the sandplayer that makes it work. I need to provide a caring, personal presence and to use my understanding of the process to stay in tune with the sandplayer.

Fourth, I must recognize two levels in the process that may overlap: healing and growth.

Healing: many wounds originate in infancy and childhood. As a therapist, I need to be alert to the possibility of early emotional or sexual abuse or other such trauma and to be empathic and ready to patiently allow a person to move at their own pace. I must wait for a person to recover memories through images and affects without pushing for words. There may be a *silent* sharing of secrets before there is any oral expression. I must appreciate how frightening each stage of this process may be and be prepared to offer protection at critical points.

Growth: I will recognize stages of the development of personality, expansion of consciousness, and individuation in the sandplay that are familiar to depth therapists. These include: reconnecting with one's child self; mother–child and father–child relationships; differentiation of opposites (man–woman, good–bad); union of opposites through the transcendent function; co-transference; making friends with one's instincts; relating to one's contra-sexual gender (animus/anima); searching for one's own spiritual way; confrontation with the shadow; sacrificing old attitudes and building up new attitudes; the night sea journey; death and rebirth; centering; numinous experiencing of the Self; strengthening of the ego–Self axis; experiences of transformation; and a shift of energies from inner preoccupations to outer creativity.

Fifth, it is the sandplayer's experience of the process that heals. It is not my understanding of the process that heals. During the sandplay process, my intellectual understanding is less important than my empathy. My empathy helps to validate the sandplayer's experience and may affirm both feelings and intellect, affect and insight. This may occur at an unconscious level.

Sixth, yet my *understanding* of what is happening in the process is often essential. For example:

1 When I sense I am losing my empathy or not appreciating some aspect of the co-transference or feel discouraged or judgmental. At such times I need to try to understand the process and thoughtfully review it by myself or with a consultant with caring concern for containment and confidentiality.
2 When my role as a protector is called upon. I must try to understand so that I know when and how to offer protection. In cases of physical or sexual abuse or other trauma, my role as protector is crucial. I need to wisely and intellectually grasp what is happening.
3 When I need to make decisions regarding referral, collateral discussion, breaking of confidentiality, termination, and other circumstances that demand thought in addition to feeling.
4 When the sandplayer and I review the process some time after it has been completed. At that time my knowledge and experience are essential. But even then I must not dominate over the sandplayer's input. It is the mutual understanding that makes the experience momentous to both of us.
5 When I teach. It is imperative that I know and understand as much as I can about sandplay so that I am better able to prepare others to appreciate the uniqueness of each process, to be empathic, and to be able to make the critical decisions that often must be made during the course of a sandplay process.

Seventh, my learning about sandplay is never complete. I need to learn as much as I can about symbols, human development, and psychological theories. I need to continue to read, to listen, and to review many sandplay processes alone and in the company of other sandplay therapists.

Finally, with all my learning I must not forget what Jung said: "Learn your theories as well as you can, but put them aside when you touch the miracle of the living soul" (Jung 1928: 361).

Chapter 15

How I do it

Because there are multiple variations in the practice of therapists who use sandplay, no one can recommend a set procedure. But I think the sharing of individual observations and experiences is of value.

Even the positioning of the sandtrays and the objects to be used in them vary with different therapists. My sandtrays – one dry, one damp – are at counter height and stationary, with shelves of objects above the trays and on the sides, within easy reach when standing at the tray. A high stool is available if the client wishes to sit down, but most people stand until the scene is completed.

There is no standard collection of objects for use in the tray. The personal uniqueness of each therapist's collection allows the client to interact with it as an extension of the therapist, and therefore the process remains within the framework of the transference.

Some clients shun plastic miniatures and choose instead those made of wood, stone, metal, or clay. There is often a particular appreciation of shells, dried leaves, fruit pits, driftwood, sea-washed stones, dark lava pieces. The floor and sides of the tray are painted blue so that pools and streams can be easily represented by clearing sand away from the bottom, and sky can be represented by the sides. The water I provide for wetting the damp sandtray is in a squeezable spray bottle. If a larger volume of water is desired, there is a sink with running water in the room. Sandplayers may sometimes not use any objects, preferring to mold the sand with their hands and form furrows and designs with their fingers.

Therapists develop their own ways of introducing people to the sandtray. When I was studying with Dora Kalff, I adopted her invitation to the client to "Look over the shelves until you find something that speaks to you and put it in the tray and then add to it as you wish." I like this, but I do not always use it. I have no fixed set of instructions. They evolve out of the circumstances. At the first appointment I show the client what I call the "non-verbal room," because it has not only the sandplay setup but also paints and clay and colored tissues. I explain that the time may come when he or she will want to come here and work with some of this material.

Later, either the client or I recognize that the time is right and we go to this room. At this point I show them the sandplay material, and say that they may use any objects or miniatures they choose, or, if they prefer, just use the sand. I show them that the floor and sides of the tray are blue, and I may sift some of the sand through my own fingers just to be getting the feel of it myself.

Some clients are initially self-conscious, but the material usually takes over and many people welcome the departure from the more rational verbal therapy. I have found sandplay particularly useful when clients are either blocked in verbal expression or caught up in a stream of over-verbalization.

Occasionally a person comes to me expecting to work in the sandtray and wanting to use it at the first session. In general, I think it is better to wait until a secure *temenos* has been established within the therapeutic relationship.

As the client works in the sandtray, I sit out of view and record the order of placement and the location of objects to help me identify objects later in the pictures that I take. I have developed a system for recording responses that helps me to follow the sequence later and to identify items that are not clear in the photos.

The system is based on the grid system used in maps. I think of the edges of the tray as being divided into equal spaces of about four inches each. The long edge of the tray is divided into seven equal spaces and the short edge of the tray is divided into five equal spaces. I mark these divisions with inconspicuous tapes on the edges of the tray so that the spaces are delineated. I think of the seven spaces along the long side of the tray as being numbered from one through seven and the five spaces along the short side of the tray as being lettered from A through E. Then, when an item is placed in the tray, I can make notes such as: 4C tiger; 7E princess.

Verbal interaction during the sandplay is usually minimal. Since comments about what the client is doing may be disruptive, I usually avoid them. The extent of verbal exchange about the sand scene after it is completed varies. Early on, I found that if I asked a few questions to help me understand what was happening in the initial couple of scenes, the client tended to develop a pattern of completing a scene and then volunteering some explanatory remarks. My commenting on the reappearance of a particular object or theme usually elicited additional remarks from the client. But often there was a mutual recognition that the completed scene was a full expression in itself, and there was an understanding silence. In later years I have found increasing value in a minimum of verbal exchange during the sandplay session and a minimum of discussion about the scene after it is completed. I have learned to just let it work at a non-verbal level.

I think it is important to leave sand scenes intact and to not dismantle them until after the client has left, so that they can more easily carry with them the image of what they have produced. Initially I took both a color slide and an instant print of each sand scene and offered the prints to the client at the time of the review. Later I changed this procedure and took two color slides of the full scene as well as close-up slides where indicated. If the client asks for photos I can always make duplicate slides or prints from my set of slides.

In my early years of using sandplay therapy, after a series of five to ten sand scenes or whenever there was a sense of coming to the end of a phase, we studied the projected slides or prints of the series together. We made connections between the scenes, and then between the scenes and other aspects of the client's psychological development. In later years, I have found it immensely valuable when possible to delay this joint review of the scenes until five years or more after termination of therapy.

I find that clients, like therapists, use the sandplay material in their own individual ways. Children are apt to make a "movie" rather than a single scene, and often want to make more than one scene by using both the damp and dry sandtrays. Adults may change the position of some of the objects, but they seldom act out a drama. A sequence of scenes across several sessions, however, frequently depicts an underlying story. Sometimes the repetition of a scene, with only minor variations, plays a prominent role.

Some people have a story in mind when they start to make a sand scene; it may even be a segment of a dream. For others the scene in the sandtray unfolds without their being aware of what is coming next; this kind of scene often has more unconscious content than a scene that is premeditated. Lowenfeld differentiates between realistic and non-realistic or symbolic features of sand worlds; symbolic elements which come into the scene spontaneously and are not contrived usually indicate engagement of the unconscious (Lowenfeld 1979: 35).

Chapter 16

Some essentials

DO NOT PUSH TO DO SANDPLAY

The first adult I saw for sandplay taught me not to push someone to use the sand. I was so eager to have my first adult "sandplay person," that I did push her. She put a tree into the sand and put a lone monkey in it. When I asked her what it was doing there she said, "Performing." I got the point!

RECORDS

I early discovered the importance of recording both the location of objects and the sequence of their placement in the trays. I consequently developed a system for recording that allows me to keep track of both location and sequence, which I have described on p. 53.

DELAYED REVIEW

At the time of doing my own sandplay process, I did not really realize what was happening. After being an analyst and member of the C.G. Jung Institute of San Francisco for over twenty years, I went to Switzerland for sandplay therapy with Dora Kalff. I went with a specific problem in mind which had to do with my sister. After doing the trays, my relationship with my sister did take an upturn, but I attributed this to other events. I did not realize then that during the sandplay process I had, for the first time, owned my shadow in the relationship. Of course, this recognition of one's shadow is an essential part of working on relationship problems. But it just had not happened to me before.

When Dora and I reviewed my trays ten years later, I clearly saw that I had placed a witch looking at herself in a mirror into one scene. If she had tried previously to call to my attention the meaning of this placement, I am sure I would have defended against it, which might have aborted the whole embryonic development. My specifically seeking out sandplay for this problem may have indicated that I was ready at that time to own my shadow at a non-cognitive level, but not cognitively. Ten years later, I saw the significance of what I had done without having to have it pointed out to me.

Because of this experience as well as my experiences with Kathy of the value of a delayed review, I generally favor waiting about five years before reviewing a sandplayer's process with them. And I do not call it a delayed "interpretation," as if I were the one doing the interpreting. It is a time of mutual understanding of what was going on, a time of mutual insight, of "Aha" experiences. It is a profound time for each of us. It always is.

NOT SEEING OTHER PEOPLE RE THE PATIENT

Part of the sandplay therapist's role, like that of any good therapist, is to instill trust. Often a person starts therapy with the false belief that no one can be trusted. They have to come to feel that the therapist can meet the "transference test" and can be trusted before they will be open in the use of the sandplay material. They have to feel that they will not be criticized or punished and that their work will be held in strict confidence.

For this reason, I believe that the therapist should not see others regarding the sandplayer unless it seems essential for the welfare of the person or, as sometimes happens especially with children, if the sandplayer requests it. And, if possible, the therapist should talk about what the sandplayer wants before the meeting with someone else. A child, for example, may wish to ask the therapist to include or avoid certain things when talking with their parents. And also, whenever possible, the sandplayer should be present at the meeting.

Often my most important role in seeing parents was to support them in the difficult task of parenting. In addition to trying to strengthen the parents' egos, I would encourage them to try to strengthen the child's ego, both by validating their child's good feelings about themselves, and by showing, when they felt it, joy in being with the child. This did not necessarily mean praising the child, which could be interpreted as judgmental, but rather simply validating the child's own good feelings about themselves, e.g., "You must feel good about having done such a nice painting!" or "You must feel good about winning the race!" Or simply, "It's so much fun being with you!"

SANDPLAY AS MYSTERIOUS OR MAGICAL

Sometimes the power of sandplay seems magical or mysterious. But it need not be. Most wounds or problems stem from childhood where there may have been rejection, rigid restrictions, excessive criticism and punishment, and/or failure on the part of the surrounding adults to "understand"

and empathize. It is not so strange, then, that a therapy which accepts, gives freedom, never criticizes or punishes, and empathizes should help to heal and reactivate (or elicit) the normal growth of a person.

Sandplay also permits the reconstruction of past events in the tray. The person can change them so that there is in a sense an undoing. Or the person can concretize the wounding event and with a steadily strengthened ego face the event as it was but look at it with new eyes and a new understanding. Moreover, sandplay can offer a glimpse into the future. Sometimes the making of a mandala gives the patient a sense of what can come: the feeling of wholeness. And that experience enables the sandplayer, regardless of the pain or anxiety involved, to continue in their search for that wholeness.

Chapter 17

Sandplay with children and adults

Play therapy was recognized in the 1930s as a valuable way of doing therapy with children. The concept of therapists actually playing with a child was an innovation at that time. Now it is well accepted. Sandplay with children is an extension of play therapy. And since sandplay with children is done within this context, the therapist can expect to interact much more with a child who is doing sandplay than with an adult.

Because children brought for therapy have typically been hurt in some way or have had too much intellectual analysis applied to their images and fantasies, the therapist may have to actively help the child to play. This can, at times, also be true for the adult. Indeed, since the child is generally closer to the unconscious than the adult, it may be even more essential for the therapist to help the adult engage with the unconscious by some introductory comments about the value of play in our overly mechanized world.

But the interaction between therapist and adult is different from the interaction between therapist and child. With the child, the therapist generally enters into the "play," doing what the child suggests. With the adult, the therapist can quietly and unobtrusively provide the space, the freedom and the protection for the person to do whatever they need to do without intrusion.

Chapter 18

Understanding and interpretation

Granted that the foremost task of the sandplay therapist is to provide freedom, protection and empathy for the sandplayer, their second task is to understand the sandplay – to "read" the scenes, to understand the series as a whole – which may be referred to as interpretation.

I have, in the preceding chapters, generally played down interpretation, preferring to emphasize empathy over evaluation and appreciation over understanding. There are times, however, when the ability to understand with the mind what is going on in a sandplay sequence or even in one tray is essential. Sometimes, for example, the therapist is called on to make crucial decisions about whether or not to refer to another therapist because of difficulties or signs of a greater degree of pathology than the therapist is ready to handle by themselves. Or about whether to call in collaterals such as family members or teachers. These situations must be handled with the greatest of empathy but also with an understanding of what is going on with the sandplayer.

Another time that understanding is necessary is when reviewing the slides with the sandplayer, which occurs, according to my practice, several years after the process is completed. I have found that I want to go over and try to understand the trays in some detail by myself before looking at them with the sandplayer. But my understanding must not interrupt the flow of the client's own insights into the trays and process. It is the mutuality of this review that makes it so powerful.

Understanding is also required when the therapist is going to review a case with a consultant. Or, with the explicit consent of the sandplayer, when the therapist is going to present the case to a professional group or to write it up to submit it to the ISST or for publication. These more public presentations must be handled with great sensitivity. I believe that a case should never be presented until some years after its completion and certainly never while the therapy is still ongoing. Written permission should always be obtained. It is best, whenever possible, to let the sandplayer see exactly what is going to be said or published about them.

Each sandplay therapist has to find their own way of understanding sandplay. What has helped me the most is to watch for levels, stages, sequences and themes, which I shall discuss in Chapter 19. Then Part II will address the question of how to explore the meaning of symbols.

Symbols are the most universal guideposts for sandplay therapists, yet they can never be completely grasped. Symbols are dynamic, not static. What a symbol means depends upon its context. The symbolic significance of a sandplay figure changes when it is placed in a different location surrounded by different figures, just as the color of a chameleon changes when it is put in a different environment. "The symbol always covers a complicated situation which is so far beyond the grasp of language that it cannot be expressed at all in any unambiguous manner" (Jung 1969a: 254). Or again, "symbols always express something we do *not* know" (Jung 1969b: 175).

Chapter 19

Levels, stages, sequences and themes

LEVELS

When I speak of levels, I am referring to the level of consciousness at which the sandplayer is working. This goes from below consciousness or the subconscious level to the more conscious level of immediately preoccupying thoughts. These include the following.

Past events and relationships

Trauma that is still in the unconscious

This refers to traumatic events in the sandplayer's life which may have seriously interfered with their normal development but which are not yet consciously accessible. One such example would be sexual abuse. This may have occurred during a pre-verbal period or for some other reason may not have been verbalized at the time (e.g., threats from the abuser). In sandplay, trauma which is still unavailable to consciousness can be portrayed or re-played without verbalization. When it is shared in this way within the protected *temenos* of the co-transference, the sandplayer can safely begin to get in touch with it. Eventually memories may come more fully into consciousness so that the effects of the trauma do not continue to remain largely outside of conscious control.

Consciously remembered traumatic events

This refers to events that occurred in the past which are not so repressed into the unconscious. We might think here of an illness, the witnessing of painful events, the death of a relative or, sometimes even more painful, the death of a pet. These events that can be consciously remembered and talked about are more accessible to the conscious for verbal re-experiencing and transformation.

Current events and relationships

This refers to ongoing experiences of parents, children, spouses, lovers, friends. Feelings about these current relationships and experiences are often activated in making the sandtray. In fact, the sandplayer may be so preoccupied with a particular active problem that it inevitably enters into the process.

Co-transference

It helps if the therapist keeps alert to indications of both negative and positive transference on the part of the client and of the therapist's own feelings toward the client. This decreases the incidence of blind spots and therefore permits a clearer appreciation of and empathy with the sand-player.

Archetypal experiences

These stem from the collective unconscious and may emerge at any time in ways that are frightening, or ecstatic, or profound. They are nearly always numinous. This level of the unconscious is not the repository of repressed memories, but rather the source of much that is unfathomable. Experiencing the deep unconscious can release creativity.

These levels all interact. Current relationship problems may re-activate memories of past repressed and non-repressed events. Transferential and actual relationship feelings may intermingle with one another. Sandplay can portray the complexities of all these ongoing interactions simultaneously, which the more linear mode of verbalization sometimes cannot do.

And, within each of these levels, the inevitable urges towards individuation are always active.

STAGES

I find it somewhat hazardous to generalize about stages or phases in sandplay process because I know that each process is unique, or one of a kind. Generalizations about them cannot, or perhaps should not, be made. I have, however, noticed certain stages frequently enough so that it seems helpful to list them here.

Beginnings and endings

Initial trays – things to look for or do

1 Respect the sandplayer and their feelings while doing a first tray. It may be somewhat frightening or challenging to them. Try to sense their feeling.

2 How are *you* feeling? This is equally important. It is also important to realize the extent to which their feelings and your feelings may be connected. They are often related.
3 Does the sandplayer bury or hide something in the tray, which may be uncovered or discovered later on?
4 Is there chaos or is it too orderly? Either extreme may lead to more balance in a following tray.
5 What about the transference? Does the sandplayer criticize you or your collection or praise it?
6 Are there signs of nurturing? The appearance of food or feeding in sandplay scenes, for example, may reflect the sandplayer's need to be nurtured, or may suggest that the sandplayer is actually experiencing being nurtured in the tray.
7 Is there use of water? Or, if not water itself, are there buckets or pails or a well which may act as containers for water. A well may suggest a willingness to bring up contents from the unconscious.
8 Is there any indication of the mother–child unity?
9 If a problem is presented, how is the sandplayer coping with the problem? Initial trays often depict both the problematic situation and a possible solution.
10 If the scene makes you feel anxious, consider seeking consultation with a trusted consultant. No matter how experienced we are, we all can profit from a consultation.

Final trays

We might wonder what constitutes a "final" tray. How do you know when a process is completed? These two questions are not synonymous. Sometimes processes are interrupted because of circumstances unrelated to the sandplay series. At other times, the sand scene itself clearly shows that the sandplay has come to an end. In Ursula's final scene, for example, a figure representing herself riding a horse was galloping right out of the tray!

There are no final answers to the question of what constitutes a completed process. There probably are as many kinds of completed processes as there are sandplayers. But, since one of the requirements for becoming a member of the ISST and STA and other sandplay organizations is the preparation of a case report of a "completed process," the question of just what constitutes such a process is frequently asked. I think the answer which Estelle Weinrib came up with is the most helpful one I have heard. She said,

> No one's maturational life process is ever complete. Hopefully, we continue evolving all of our lives, going through many stages of

> psychological development; completing (relatively speaking) one stage and moving on to the next. Therefore, it follows that one can "complete" a particular phase with [one] therapist and go on to the next . . . and both are valuable. In any case, when a particular phase has been adequately completed, both the patient/client and the therapist usually recognize it.
>
> (Weinrib responding to questions at the 1989 STA Conference)

Stages in between

In adults, some of us have found that, after an initial tray, there may be a gradual or a sudden "going down" or regression into the collective unconscious. Trays from this period are frequently characterized by a watery area with water-related objects, such as shells and fish, and the absence of land animals or humans. Often, after this stage, come trays that we colloquially call "back to the marketplace." In these scenes there is a return to the use of people, buildings, and other objects representing collective consciousness and daily life. This return may be accompanied by creativity. The person may build something in the tray, or make something with modeling clay (which I always keep in the sandplay room) or with any of the other materials offered by therapists on their shelves.

This going down and returning may recur several times. And, of course, these different stages are not always clearly delineated. Again, I find myself reiterating, "Each process is unique." It is probably better if the therapist does not expect this to happen but is merely aware of it as a possibility and therefore alert to its appearance.

Other stages which may be experienced during the sandplay process include the period of mother–child unity. Often this will appear first on an archetypal or animal level before human mother-and-child figures are used. Another frequently observed period is a time of differentiation between the masculine and the feminine followed by an integration of the two, sometimes in a classical *coniunctio*.

Intermixed with or following these developments may be scenes that eventually lead to what is called a "Self" tray, when a "psychic situation of repose-within-oneself is generated, which often effects a numinous experience and establishes contact with the spiritual" (Kalff 1991: 12).

Again the question comes up, "What is a Self tray?" Dora Kalff replied to this question in her presentation at the ISST conference in Japan in 1987: "I think there are as many ways to portray the Self in the tray as there are people, but what is common is the depth and the silence of the numinous quality." Dora Kalff often emphasized the numinosity that accompanies a Self tray. I think of Ursula's statement, "It's cosmic." And of the comment of Ilsa's analyst when she saw Ilsa's Self tray, "It sends goose bumps up and down my spine."

There is a tendency to use the terms self-constellation and self-manifestation interchangeably. There was a time when I tried to make a distinction between them based on the theories of Neumann and Kalff regarding stages of development. I was dissuaded from this attempt by Fordham's writings on the Self (Fordham 1969:98–103). Regardless of which theoretical lens one may be wearing, the appearance of a Self tray is a momentous experience for both sandplayer and therapist. It releases energy and is often followed by a strengthening of the ego which can be seen in the subsequent scenes, as in Ursula's series of sandtrays.

The appearance of a mandala frequently represents the constellation or the manifestation of the Self but, unfortunately, there has been a tendency to equate mandalas with Self trays. A mandala in its simplest form is a squared circle or circled square. It was originally a Buddhist image used to promote meditation. Centering is also often associated with Self trays but, again, they are not synonymous. A Self tray can take a variety of forms and a mandala can occur at a variety of times. Sometimes they do occur together; sometimes they do not.

SEQUENCES

I find that knowing the order in which objects were placed into a scene can be tremendously helpful when I am reviewing a sandplay process in depth in preparation for a review with the sandplayer or for a presentation. The client may place a negative mother symbol followed by a positive mother symbol, for example, or portray being deprived followed by being nourished, or use figures that represent denial of fear followed by figures that express the fear. Keeping track of these sequences helps me understand what is going on in the sandplayer as they play out the scene.

The therapist usually has to record the order of placements while observing the making of the scene in order to do this sequence analysis. Some therapists find this recording disruptive to their connection with the sandplayer, a too rational or too intellectual approach. The grid system that I use has become more or less automatic for me so that I can make the recordings without being distracted (see p. 53).

The therapist may also, of course, follow sequences from scene to scene. Because some objects are hidden or difficult to make out in the photo, this requires careful recording of the identity of objects. Some of the same principles can be observed in following sequences between trays. But it is following the sequence within a tray that I particularly value.

THEMES

I have found it useful to keep a few key themes in mind when reviewing or interpreting trays. These are listed below, together with references by name to the case studies in the section on individual cases which illustrate how the sandplayer (or the sandplayer's psyche) goes about working in this area.

Place of incubation

Sandplayers often include an enclosure of some sort in their trays, the shelter that they need for their growth and transformation to occur. Kathy used a greenhouse. She closed the door of the greenhouse early on, but opened it in her final trays. Towards the end the greenhouse no longer appeared. It had done its work.

Ida used a "sacred pool" with minor variations in twenty-one trays. At one point she made an exit from the pool going to the outer world. But her psyche recognized that this was premature; in the following tray she made another sacred pool, without an exit. Eventually she, too, was able to leave the pool behind.

Providing energy for the journey

Energy may be shown in many forms, including: water or food; mechanical energy (cars, gas stations or gas pumps); animals (primitive animals suggest aggressive energy and domestic animals more controllable energy); sailboats and gliders (natural wind/spirit energy).

The leopard Ilsa used in her initial tray represented the more wild animal energy that she needed. An additional "plus" was that the leopard was coming out of an oven, a feminine container; the aggressive energy of the feminine was coming forth. In the next tray she experienced energy in the form of the water she provided for the fawn who was continuing on the journey that had started in the first tray.

Ursula put a figure representing herself whom she described as "very nearly hopeless" sitting in a garden. She did, however, have some energy available to her, the dynamic masculine energy of the cars outside the garden, which she was able to use for herself later on.

Blocking of energy

In one of Kathy's trays, she put a plane up in a tree. When I asked her what the plane was doing up there, she answered, "It's stuck there." She was feeling stuck in her process; after she portrayed this stuck feeling in the sand she was able to proceed forward again.

Ilsa made a blocked stream in her initial tray; her referring analyst said that Ilsa seemed stuck in her analysis and Ilsa said that she felt stuck in her life. In her final tray, Ilsa put in a little bear on a raft floating on a water passageway that gave her access to every place in the tray. She had become unstuck.

On the journey

There are many ways that sandplayers represent their journey: boats on water; paths; cars; planes about to take off. The first woman described in Chapter 23 on the torii had such a long line of animals and people going with her on her journey that she had to use two trays.

Rhoda placed five steps in her second tray leading into a circle of figures; this seemed to be a path that led into the process of her five sandplay scenes.

Being controlled by vs. confronting authority

Ilsa started out with a domineering, threatening, stepfather figure, which she also thought represented authority in general. Then she added a tiny bear cub who was confronting him. Later she was able to face and depotentiate a masculine "devil" who, she said, was just bluffing.

Handling anger

When Kathy displayed anger in the tray, towards me, or in talking about her family, she invariably followed this with a tray in which animals were fenced in. Kathy was afraid of her anger, which had built up over the years. One of her tasks was to find out that she could control it and therefore did not have to be so afraid of it. Fencing in animals helped her experience this kind of control.

When I was late for one of my appointments with Emmy, she clearly expressed anger in the tray she made that day. But even in our much later review it was difficult for her to remember feeling anger. But letting the anger into the tray unconsciously still did its work. Shortly thereafter, in the same tray, she found the treasure. Similarly, in Amy's trays, she first experienced anger in one tray which then led to her experiencing strength in the following tray.

Debbie started out denying both anger and fear at having cancer. She was eventually able to experience these emotions together in her third tray; this experience released more of her energy for the work of getting ready to die.

Development of the masculine and feminine

In a series of trays there may come a time when the sandplayer experiences the need to become more deeply grounded in their own gender identity or to more clearly differentiate their contra-sexual side.

Ursula made a tray which was almost all shells, a classical feminine symbol. Jim put a powerful male gorilla on top of a mountain who was undaunted by having to face the many animals coming up to threaten him. Debbie differentiated masculine and feminine by grouping masculine items on one side of the tray and feminine on the other.

Union of opposites

The sandtray provides many opportunities for connecting two sides or two parts of a scene which are in opposition to one another. Later, the sandplayer may be able to unite the opposites, bringing the transcendent function into the process.

Kathy focused on bad versus good, and associated bad with masculinity and good with femininity. She placed what she called all bad boys in one classroom and all good girls in another classroom in an early tray. In later trays, she intermingled girls and boys who were both bad and good. Finally she placed a bridge in the middle of a tray where many opposites appeared, and said that this was a "city for everyone."

Rhoda, in her second tray, identified the dark whale as her all bad father and the light whale as her all good mother. This dichotomy had been a problem for her into her adulthood. In a later tray she combined or united these opposites in one object, the black-and-white penguin.

Debbie initially believed that the feminine was inferior to the masculine and, of course, she resented the "superiority" of the male. One of her tasks in preparing for death was to come to terms with this and to transform it. In one of her later trays a boy baby and a girl baby were represented as equals side by side, with the sun rising up over them out of the unconscious.

Attaining the treasure

Rhoda's treasure was her long neglected sense of spirituality. In her first tray the way to the treasure was blocked, but there was a possible route around the blockade. In her final tray, she gained access to the spiritual treasures that had been out of reach before.

Ilsa scattered bits of colored glass like jewels in her initial tray, anticipating the possibility of finding treasures in the unconscious. In her fourth tray, she found the treasure, a heap of gold coins. After Emmy had experienced her anger, a treasure chest holding coins and a crystal appeared.

These are a few examples to give a sense of how to focus on possible themes and key areas in a case. I do not necessarily look for these, but when they do occur in the trays I feel reassured that a process is indeed underway.

Part II

Symbol studies

Chapter 20

Introduction to symbol studies

Both in the evolution of our species and in individual biological development IMAGE comes before WORD. Later, spoken words were developed for communication across distances. And finally, written words were added, allowing communication across time as well as across space. The non-verbal technique of sandplay relies primarily on images rather than words. It takes the client back in both evolutionary and biological time, back to the time when visual imaging predominated over verbal conceptualization.

There are numerous books on the meanings of these visual images which can be purchased or borrowed from a library, but I think the best way to go about understanding them is to prepare one's own "book." Dora Kalff used to urge therapists to become aware of the symbolic meanings of all the items in their collection. In response to her admonition, I made up my own list of symbols from books, seminar notes, and discussions with colleagues. This list expanded as I saw how different sandplayers used the items over the years. And this, in turn, led to my studying several symbols in some depth.

As examples of how I have gone about studying symbols, I am including a talk on the turtle and three articles on other frequently used sandplay figures: the bridge, the torii and the sun and moon. And I am including two articles on more general symbolic concepts which can help us understand the significance of a sandtray series, one on Hestia and Athena and another on Neumann and Kalff's stages of child development.

I have presented the material on turtles many times to both Jungian and sandplay audiences. It has become so familiarly associated with me that I have become the happy recipient of many turtle objects and newspaper clippings over the years. I never seem to be able to go over this material without adding something to it. I have substituted verbal descriptions for the illustrations used in the talk on the biology and mythology of the turtle for this written presentation, but have retained the all-important illustrations of the sandplay scenes.

The bridge and the torii chapters grew out of my noticing that both these objects were frequently used in sandplay. I became curious as to whether knowing more about them might help me to better understand how they were used. And my brief commentary on the sun and moon was stimulated by Dr. Hayao Kawai's study on the sun goddess with notes on the moon (Kawai 1992).

The chapter on Hestia and Athena is not about a particular sandtray object but rather is about two sides of the feminine which I first became aware of in my analytic work. After studying these two aspects of women in a group of "home" and "career" women in my practice, I realized that the same opposites were often depicted in sandplay scenes done by women.

And Chapter 26 demonstrates how to use Eric Neumann's and Dora Kalff's theories to elucidate the meaning of the initial and subsequent trays of children at several different ages and stages of development.

Chapter 21

Turtles and transitional objects

In 1987, I announced to all my clients that I would be retiring from my analytical practice in one year. During that year each person coped with my impending retirement, or we might say impending abandonment, in their own way. One woman asked me, "How can you retire? What will happen?" I replied, "I don't know. I've never retired before. We'll just have to wait and see." One woman left therapy nine months before the date of my retirement; she told me that she wanted to leave me rather than to have me leave her. And I realized in myself that I, also, was having to cope with losses. I felt sad about separating from and closing off the kinds of relationships that are so special in analytic work.

In thinking of all this, I realized that we all experience periods of being abandoned from the time we are left in our cribs as infants up through childhood and into and through adulthood. These experiences tend to be cumulative; each new experience reactivates feelings left over from previous ones. When our therapist takes a vacation, or is sick, or retires, we of course feel abandoned, no matter how much we intellectualize about it.

But these experiences of abandonment constellate other feelings within us as well, feelings of increasing strength. Over time we also accumulate the ways we have of coping; we become stronger. I could recognize some of these ways of coping in the people I was seeing: repression; denial; compensation; expression of anger; activation of a support system; and looking inward to one's inner support, finding one's inner guide.

And I wondered why the turtle kept appearing in so many sandtrays near the time of my retirement. A number of women who were doing sandplay with me put turtles, especially masses of turtles or birthing turtles, in their scenes done at the end of the year just before I actually did retire. Were turtles related in some way to my leaving, and their coping with the loss? It was in an attempt to understand what had happened that I started out on my turtle quest.

THE SCENES

These final sand scenes were made by six women in their late 30s to 50s. All had been in therapy with me for a year or more. None of the women suffered from severe pathology. Most had already made at least twenty sand scenes before these last trays.

The first tray (see Plate 1: "Turtle rings of safety") was done by a woman who had made many sand scenes with me but had never used turtles before. She did this scene about half-way into the year after I had announced my retirement. A ceramic turtle and a mother turtle with three baby turtles are in the center of the scene. There are many other turtles grouped in a semi-circle around them, sixteen turtles in all. Outside the semi-circle of turtles is another semi-circle of eight horses. And above them all is the snake goddess, looking over the whole scene.

In addition to the mother turtle with her babies, several other images in the scene refer to birthing: birds in a nest in the upper right, a pregnant woman in the upper left and a hen hatching chicks on the lower left.

The woman called this scene the "rings of safety." She said, "I was worried for a minute, but now we have the rings of safety." She used turtles in five of her six subsequent trays.

The next woman's final tray (see Plate 2: "Celebration of a divine turtle birth") was a celebration of birth. A baby turtle hatching from an egg is in the center. Two woman musicians accompany the birth of the little hatchling. Behind the central scene there are two trees in flower, another birthing in the realm of plant life. And a group of turtles is intently watching this event from the lower right.

There is also the feminine watching. In the upper right a group of archetypal feminine figures are looking on: an Etruscan goddess, Lisa de Goia; a Greek snake goddess; the oriental goddess of compassion, Kwan Yin; and the "wise old woman." Below these divinities two peasant women are turned facing the birth. A giraffe, a pig, a hare and a skunk in the center right, and even the three birds in the lower left and the swan in the curving stream, all appear to be witnessing and celebrating this event. The overall scene gives the impression of a holy birth with the goddesses, the women and the animals in attendance.

There is a little boy wearing a blindfold near the hatching baby turtle. Perhaps the woman who made this tray has a youthful animus who is willing to accept "not seeing" it all. He does not have to stare consciously at such sacred mysteries happening so nearby; he can look within himself to know them.

Another woman in her final scene (see Plate 3: "Turtles circling towards a goddess") made two circles of turtles in the tray, one on each side. In the middle of each circle of turtles is an egg. Inside the right circle is the same baby turtle hatching from an egg that was used by the previous woman. Surrounding these circles again are flowering trees in each of the four corners and another tree in bloom at the top.

The circling turtles are all going towards the goddess as though they are coming to a sacred place to honor her. The goddess is Lisa de Goia, an Etruscan goddess or priestess, also the same one used in the previous woman's tray. She is said to represent a priestess who heralds the birth of something new.

The next scene (see Plate 4: "Turtles climbing to a god") is another circling and honoring with a group of turtles climbing up towards a divinity. This time the god in the center is Fukurokuju, one of the seven Japanese gods of good fortune. He is a philosopher, a performer of good deeds for humankind, who is known for his wisdom and very much honored in Japan.

This tray was made ten years before my retirement. So, when I remembered it, I thought that this must be an instance where a group of turtles appear in the sandtray without any connection to impending separation or loss. But when I looked back in my notes to see what was happening at the time the woman made this scene, I found that this *was* a kind of "final" tray. She made it just before she stopped coming in once a week and went to once a month sessions.

Again the focus in the next tray (see Plate 5: "Hatching turtle on the way to the black Madonna") is on the baby turtle who is hatching on a beach near a pond or lake. There are broken pieces of eggshell lying beside the turtle, emphasizing the breaking out of the egg that occurs during birth. The turtle is headed towards a path, led by a black baby. The path passes by a dragon and goes up to a house in the woods. A black Madonna stands on the roof of the house; she holds the Christ child in her arms.

The last tray (see Plate 6: "Turtles journeying towards the jewels") is the final sandplay scene made by a woman who had done many trays during the time we had been seeing each other. The ceramic turtle followed by a brass turtle and two baby turtles are on a path centered around a mountain surrounded by water. In the top of the mountain is a depression, which is like a nest. But it is not filled with eggs; it is filled with jewels.

In reviewing the turtle trays of these six women, we note several overlapping themes:

groups of turtles:	Plates 1, 2, 3, 4 and 6
birthing:	Plates 1, 2, 3 and 5
journey towards the sacred:	Plates 3, 4, 5 and 6
numinous quality:	all six scenes

And all of them include figure(s) representing the sacred or the Self:

Plate 1:	The snake goddess overlooking the tray
Plate 2:	A grouping of goddesses witnessing the divine birth

Plate 3: A single Etruscan goddess in the center
Plate 4: An oriental male god elevated on a hill
Plate 5: The black Madonna and child
Plate 6: The jewels of the Self

The same ceramic turtle appeared in the first and the last sandtrays in this group. There is a story about this turtle object. Years before, a ceramicist whom I was seeing made this turtle in her studio and gave it to me. Thirteen years later, at the time of my retirement, I reviewed her trays with her and again thanked her for giving me the figure. She then told me about how she became interested in turtles. In 1975, she had come across a newspaper account about a woman who had been saved by a turtle. Of course I was interested and I asked her if by any chance she might still have the newspaper article. She found it in the journal that she had kept at the time:

> Shipwreck victim Candelaria Villanueva, 52, was the beneficiary of the good offices of a heroic sea turtle. According to a Navy report, she rode on the back of a huge sea turtle for two days after the sinking of an inter-island ship. After she was pulled from the water, according to the report, the turtle swam around the rescue ship twice to make sure all was well.

Then in Minneapolis, when I was presenting this study to a group, someone asked if I had seen the *Minneapolis Star-Tribune*. Synchronistically, that very morning there had been an account of several people who had been saved by a turtle in the Philippines. The 21 May 1989 *Star Tribune* article reads:

> Manilla, Philippines. A giant sea turtle towed five weak and weary survivors to safety after their boat sank during the height of a tropical storm. The Inquirer quoted one of the survivors as saying the five stayed afloat for three days on a makeshift raft before they spotted the sea turtle. They tied the raft to one of the turtle's legs and the turtle towed the craft for two hours before they were spotted by fishermen and rescued.

So, my first finding about the turtle was that the turtle rescues. The turtle saves people who are threatened by drowning. And, I thought, my patients – who may have felt a little lost at sea themselves at the time of my departure from practice – had found in the turtle an appropriate image to help carry them to shore.

THE TURTLE IN BIOLOGY

When I started on this quest, I really knew very little about turtles. I knew that the turtle was an androgynous symbol, a symbol of the union of opposites. Dora Kalff pointed this out many times. The turtle combines the sky – the dome-shaped top shell – with the earth – the square base; it combines the masculine – the projecting head – with the feminine – the round container. And I recalled that Jung had written about turtles as an image of the Self in dreams.

I also knew of their longevity. Many live to be over a hundred years old. I had read that in China they believed turtles lived much longer, more than 2,000 or even 3,000 years. And I knew that turtles had been on the earth for a very long time, but I did not know for how long until I found a chart in one of Joseph Campbell's books (Campbell 1983: 18–19). This chart shows that the turtle dates back 220 million years. The turtle was on earth for nearly 100 million years before the dinosaurs appeared. So it must be very adaptable as a genus. Think of all the catastrophes it has survived: glaciers, droughts, floods, movement of continents, appearance and disappearance of whole bodies of land. So, I thought, perhaps my patients used turtles in their trays in part to reaffirm their ability to adapt. They, too, could cope with and survive change.

According to biologists, turtles have undergone very little morphological change during the millennia they have been on earth. They have remained remarkably similar in appearance throughout their long history. Perhaps this partially explains the numinous atmosphere of the final turtle trays. The turtle naturally brings with it an archetypal quality, for the archetypes, like the turtle, are ancient and relatively unchanging throughout the ages.

And what is the secret of the turtles' survival? Biologists marvel at the efficacy of their unique shell, calling it the "most remarkable armor ever assumed by a land animal" (Bustard 1973: 14). In times of danger, turtles can simply withdraw into their shells and be protected. It is good to have such an effective defense system available when we experience fear. I do not think that we as therapists should challenge the personal defenses of our patients when they feel they are in a crisis. The key is to remove the danger, either the actual danger or the sense of danger.

As I continued to study, I learned more about the life cycle of the turtle. I discovered that they never even see their mothers. Mother turtles abandon their babies before they are born. They never see their fathers either. According to Jack Rudloe's book on the life cycle of the sea turtle, scientists were not sure for a long time that there even was a male turtle. They did not know how fertilization took place because male sea turtles were never seen on land. Finally they discovered that there is indeed a male turtle, who mounts the female turtle in the water, sometimes far out to sea (Rudloe 1979).

After copulation, the female returns to the beach where she herself was hatched. Or, more specifically, she returns to the place where the egg she hatched from was first dropped, regardless of where it later hatched.

Scientists discovered this when they tried to protect endangered turtles by removing their eggs from nests on beaches that were near big cities and taking them elsewhere to hatch. But the females returned to the beach where the eggs had originally been laid, not to the beach where the scientists had taken them for safe hatching. It was as though the location of the initial nest was somehow imprinted in them; in some way they were directed back to the place where they began. How they do this remains one of the many mysteries about turtles (Rudloe 1979: 222–3).

After fertilization, the female turtle comes to the shore, digs a deep hole above the reach of the high tide, drops the eggs into the hole, pats the sand over them, and smoothes the surface as if to erase all visible signs of a nest. She may come back two or three times in the next several days or weeks and lay as many as 400 eggs from the one fertilization. Finally she departs, not to return for several years (Rudloe 1979: 72ff).

I began to recognize some similarities between the life cycle of the turtle and the situation my clients found themselves in when I retired. My patients, too, had been held for a time in the "nest" of the *temenos*, the therapeutic container. And then I, like the turtle mother, went off into the unknown sea of retirement, leaving them to hatch on their own and get on with their lives without further assistance from me.

In about eight weeks, depending on the species, the turtles begin to hatch. But the first ones to crack an egg will not continue hatching until the others are ready. One naturalist placed a glass down the side of a turtle nest and observed the actual hatching (Carr 1967: 78). He saw that the first turtles to hatch lay still until the other nestmates were also free of the egg. Then the turtles on the top layer scratched down the ceiling, those on the sides undercut the walls, and those on the bottom compacted the sand that filtered down from above and stirred up activity during spells of lassitude so that the other hatchlings were stimulated to keep on working. There was no parental care and no teaching or guarding. As Carr describes it, "The little survival band is not trained or prompted by any coach. . . . It's just a lot of baby turtles getting restless, [but whose working together] takes them steadily up to the surface of the ground" (Carr 1967: 79).

The nest is placed high on the beach so the tidal waters do not come up and destroy it, but now the baby turtles have to make their way, sometimes a very long way, down to the water. Scientists have discovered that they instinctively go towards light. In one experiment, hatchlings were attracted to a glowing lamp held near them by a scientist at night "like moths to a flame" (Watson 1992: 24). In nature, they are apparently guided at night on their way to the sea by the light of the moon reflected on the water. It is best if there is a full moon to maximize the brightness of the light.

I realized, when I thought more about this discovery, that the moon gives light because the sun shines on it. So the baby turtles, abandoned

Plate 1

Plate 2

Plate 3

Plate 4

Plate 5

Plate 6

Plate 7

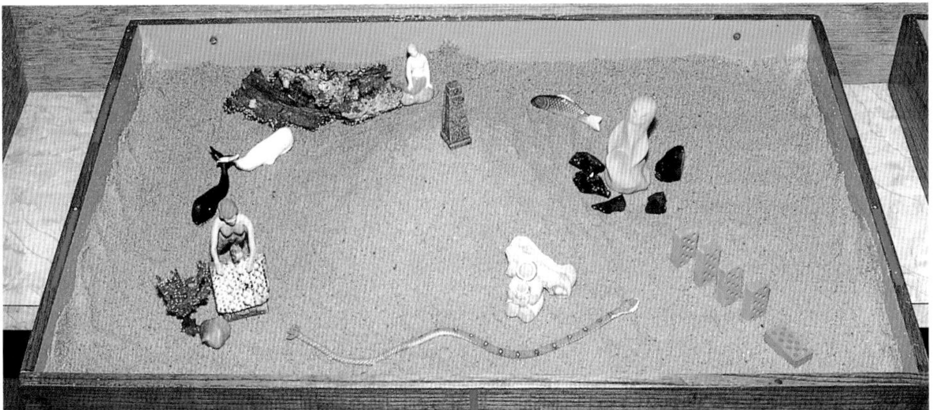
Plate 8

Plate 9

Plate 10

Plate 11

Plate 12

Plate 13

Plate 14

Plate 15

Plate 16

Plate 17

Plate 18

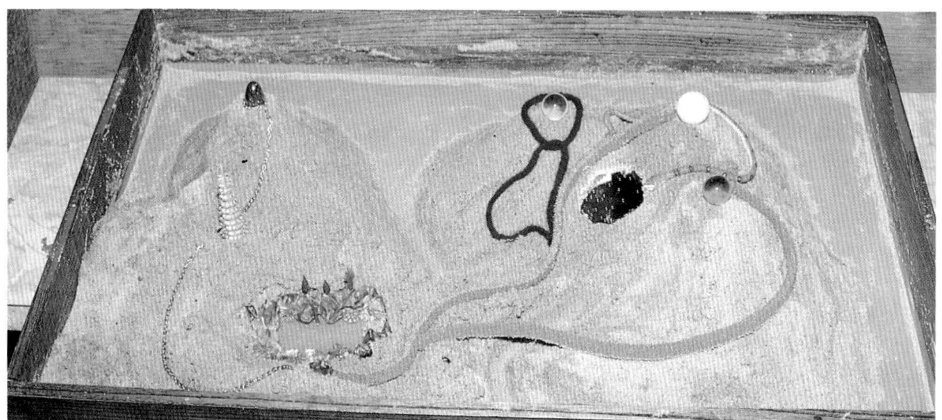
Plate 19

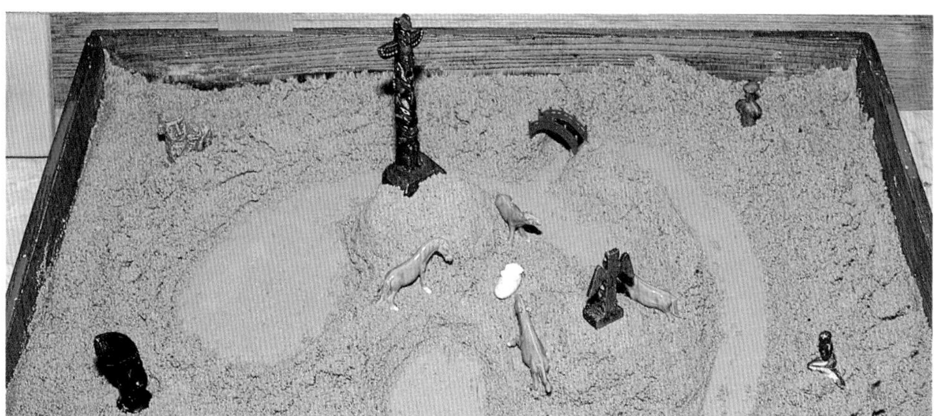
Plate 20

Plate 21

Plate 22

Plate 23

Plate 24

by both turtle parents, use the light of both sky parents – the sun and the moon – to direct them. My clients, too, in their final sandtray scenes, may have found access to these archetypal parents, these gods and goddesses, who are ever-present and can guide us all on our way.

What happens after the turtle hatchlings get safely to the sea is still one of the baffling mysteries of science (Carr 1967: 94). It is sometimes called the lost year. No one knows where the baby sea turtles go. They just are not seen again until the time comes when they are mature enough to fertilize and be fertilized, and the females return to the same beach and the cycle starts all over again. The journey between nestings may take them thousands of miles. Carr reports on a turtle that was tagged in August 1964 and re-caught 1,400 miles from the original spot in October 1965 (Carr 1967: 36). And Rudloe writes of a turtle fitted with a satellite transmitter in Costa Rica who swam 2,700 miles before her signal faded out (Rudloe 1994: 118).

So, in nature, it is only at the time of birthing that large groups of turtles come together. Masses of fertilized female turtles come to specific beaches to lay their eggs and then leave them behind. Masses of hatchlings make their way down the beach to the sea after emerging from the eggs. Until the fertilized females return to the shore to lay their eggs again two or three years later, there are no communities of turtles to be found. They travel in relative isolation. In nature, then, as in my patients' final sand scenes, there is an inevitable connection between gatherings of turtles, abandonment and birth.

THE TURTLE IN MYTHOLOGY

As I studied more about how the turtle is understood by various cultures as well as by biologists, I found that one of the earliest cultural uses of the turtle was in foretelling the future. In China, the turtle was used for divination as early as the Shang Dynasty, about the twelfth century BC (Allan 1991: 112–23). Diviners heated the turtle shell with fire and then poured water on it until it cracked. They then interpreted the pattern of cracks and marked the shell with messages for the gods. Perhaps my clients, too, found themselves using turtles in their last sandtray scenes partly for this purpose; they were wondering about, and wanting to find out about, what would be happening to them next.

The archeological and mythological material is also rich with images of the turtle as a support. Many cultures depict the turtle carrying a variety of creatures on its back. Sculptures from Buddhist China, for example, portray turtles with serpents, frogs, dragons, and even buildings riding on their shells.

> It is said that the wooden columns of the Temple of Heaven at Peking were originally set on live tortoises, under the belief that as these

> animals are supposed to live for more than 3,000 years without food and air, they are gifted with miraculous power to preserve wood from decay.
>
> (Williams 1976: 405)

Some cultures believe that the turtle is holding up the entire earth. According to the Hindu religion in India, for example, the earth rests on four elephants who are all, in turn, standing on the back of a turtle (Kenton 1928: 41–2). Another story from the Seri Indians in Baja, California, tells how a turtle came up from the depths of the sea with soil on its back and then brought up plants and then animals and finally went to the depths and brought up the Seri Indians. So the turtle is sacred to them. For certain festivals they capture a turtle and leave it on the beach before they ritually kill it. It is said that the women of the tribe come to it and tell it their secrets and their problems and feel they are helped by it (Rudloe 1979: 201).

In a similar Iroquois creation myth, a woman was pushed through a hole in the sky heaven by her angry husband. The water creatures below saw the woman falling and quickly gathered together some earth from the bottom of the sea. A turtle swam up to the surface of the water and the birds placed the soil on the turtle's back. The shell of the turtle then grew enormously and became solid ground and the woman was carried safely to it by the birds (von Franz 1972: 31).

Other mythologies speak of the turtle who supports the divinities while they are creating the earth. In one Indian myth, the gods and demons churn the milk ocean into butter to make the earth. The churning stick they use, the axis mundi, rests on a turtle at the bottom. On top of the turtle is the world axis with Vishnu on the top (O'Flaherty 1975: 273–80).

The turtle carries other gods on its broad back. In one image from the Aztec religion, a goddess is squatting down giving birth on the back of a turtle. Or the turtle itself can give birth directly to the sacred. The Hindu god Vishnu is sometimes represented as emerging, or being born, from the mouth of the turtle (Cavendish 1983: 1921). Here again, I thought, there is a connection between the turtle and birth.

Sometimes the turtle supports the entire cosmos. The earliest example I have found is a Babylonian boundary stone, Kudurru, from the twelfth century BC. At the top levels of the stone are the solar gods, then the Babylonian gods, the guardians of the four world quarters, and unidentified war gods. Below the ground are goddesses. Finally, in the abysmal sea, there are symbols of the four elements and a small swimming turtle who supports the entire cosmic mountain (Campbell 1974: 88–9).

Finally, in one of Jung's books on alchemy there is a picture of the Trimurti, the sacred Hindi contemplative symbol (Jung 1953: 147). Once again, a turtle is at the bottom, supporting all that is above. Jung interprets this turtle as the primordial chaos, the alchemical *massa confusa*. On the back of the turtle is a skull which has fire coming out of its eyes, the *vas* of transformation. Out of the flaming-eyed skull grows the sacred flower of the east, the Lotus, which also represents the Self.

So, in reviewing these cultural artifacts, I realized that the women who were using turtles in the sand were contacting an image that linked their experience of abandonment with a source of inner support that was related to the creation of new life. My leaving them was not just the end of something, but also a kind of birth, a new beginning. As Jung wrote, "It is . . . only in the state of complete abandonment and loneliness that we experience the helpful powers of our own natures" (Jung 1969a: 342).

And, indeed, when I saw each of these women some years later to jointly review their slides, I found that all of them had made significant progress in their lives. One had obtained her PhD. Others had published articles. One was writing a book. It seemed that in some ways my retirement had stimulated their own powers so they could go ahead fruitfully on their own. It reminded me of the times before my retirement when I had taken long vacations from my practice. When I came back, my clients would be eager to tell me of all the successes they had had while I was gone.

Perhaps we are talking here about something that is akin to what Winnicott calls the "transitional object." If the infant has had the experience of a good enough mother, it learns to cope with her absence by finding a comforting object that it can hold onto when needed whether the mother herself is actually present or not. Eventually the baby internalizes the object, making the physical presence of the outer object unnecessary. And it is not just the object itself that gives the baby support and comfort, or perhaps not at all the actual object, but rather what the baby experiences within itself in the presence and possession of the object that sustains it (Winnicott 1977).

I started this study in 1989, but it was not until five years later that I remembered an important turtle in my own life. I recalled a turtle pillow that I had had on my bed when I moved away from my family home and went to live in the East. The turtle had a red top and a yellow bottom. Then I remembered that my mother had sent it to me the first Christmas that I was living on my own. So I, like my analysands, had the image of a turtle as a transitional object to take with me when I left home!

One of the mysteries about sea turtles that is most baffling to scientists is the question of how they navigate during their deep ocean journeys. How do they find their way home to their original beaches after having travelled thousands of miles at depths of 800 feet or more? Among many theories, scientists have speculated that they use the magnetic fields of the earth to guide them.

But the older native peoples in such places as Costa Rica and Nicaragua have another theory. There is a turtle spirit. There is a turtle mother rock who guides them. When Rudloe was in Costa Rica in the late 1960s or early 1970s, he found older natives who swore that they had seen the turtle mother stone up on top of the volcanic mountain at Turtle Beach. And they said that the rock turns 180 degrees into the land when it is time for the turtles to come in to the beach, and rotates another 180 degrees to face out to sea when it is time for them all to go out again (Rudloe 1979: 255–65).

No one had seen the rock rotate but they were entirely convinced that it did. In Nicaragua, the rock could no longer be seen because it had gotten so annoyed at all the people climbing on it that it had moved itself to Costa Rica. In Costa Rica, it was no longer visible because it had gone into a cave to avoid the people coming up to look. So Rudloe never actually saw the turtle mother rock, but when he questioned the native people they all insisted that it was still there guiding the turtles. They said, "Witness the turtles coming in by the droves at certain times and then all going out once again at other times. What other answer is there?" And of course Jack Rudloe had to answer that he did not know.

In 1975 another scientist was studying the remains of a 3,000-year-old Indian ceremonial site in Guatemala. All of a sudden the needle on his compass jumped. It was pointing to a rock which was shaped like the head of a turtle. On closer investigation, he found that all of the lines of magnetic force were directed toward the turtle's snout. Later he found out that this snout was made of loadstone, a magnetic rock (Rudloe 1979: 263).

In the epilogue of his book, Rudloe says that the year the scientist came across this rock was the year of the lowest populations on the turtle breeding beaches in recorded history. Biologists around the world were predicting that the turtle populations could never recover. Yet, the following year, there were turtles everywhere. Almost 2,500 turtles crawled up on the five-mile stretch of beach at the foot of the volcanic mountain where the turtle mother rock is said to be looking out to sea, and turning to guide her turtles in to shore (Rudloe 1979: 268).

Rudloe's long-anticipated book, *Search for the Great Turtle Mother*, ends with "I turned to go home. . . maybe believing in Turtle Mother for the first time (Rudloe 1995: 271).

So the analysands who used turtles in their last sand scenes with me were calling on an image that is a source of strength. It is the solid base within us that can support any burden, no matter how heavy; and it is the inner guiding spirit that goes with us on our journeys, no matter how far and no matter how deep, and eventually brings us home.

Chapter 22

Bridges and the transcendent function

Jung's concept of the transcendent function clarifies the process of transformation in sandplay therapy and throws light on the significance of the use of the bridge, a special and important miniature, in sandplay scenes. In his major article on the transcendent function, Jung describes how the psyche struggles with and sometimes transcends its own deep divisions, which so often involve the claims of apparently irreconcilable opposites such as instinct and spirit, love and fear, dependence and independence. The transcendent function mediates between these warring opposites and unites them with a reconciling symbol. This is experienced consciously as a new attitude which transcends the original divided state of the self. After this change in attitude it is then possible to effectively change our behavior in a natural and stable way (Jung 1969b: 67–91).

Jung notes that the word "transcendent" does not denote a metaphysical quality but merely indicates that this function facilitates the *transition* from one attitude to another. Later Jung would say that conflicts are not so much solved as outgrown. The new attitude goes beyond the conflicts implicit in the old, although the new attitude may well lead to a fresh opposition between conscious and unconscious to be overcome once again by further activity of the transcendent function.

According to Jung, what is required to bring the transcendent function into play is first and foremost an active unconscious, along with an ego capable of receiving the activity of the unconscious. He refers to the value of drawing or painting or working with plastic materials and emphasizes that it is not important for the product to be technically correct or aesthetically satisfying, but merely for the fantasy to have free rein so that a product is created which is influenced by both conscious and unconscious. This then embodies, he says "The striving of the unconscious for the light and the striving of the conscious for substance" (Jung 1969b: 83).

Sandplay like these other plastic media avoids cognitive solutions. Instead of using words, clients use their hands to bring a fantasy production into being. As Jung says later in the same essay, "Often the hands

Figure 22.1

know how to solve a riddle with which the intellect has wrestled in vain" (Jung 1969b: 86).

Sandplay is a special opportunity for the transcendent function to appear naturally and spontaneously. The therapist's role is to recognize this phenomenon and to honor it.

Sandplay encourages the activation of the transcendent function in three ways:

1 A sandplay scene is a collaborative product of both the unconscious and the conscious.
2 Sandplay is conducive to the "synchronistic moment."
3 Sandplay provides for the presentation of, confrontation between, and uniting of the opposites.

COLLABORATION OF CONSCIOUS AND UNCONSCIOUS

A comparison of two consecutive sand scenes made by a man whom I shall call Sam demonstrates that sandplay is indeed a result of collaboration between the unconscious and the conscious. Sam put a dinosaur in his first sandtray (Figure 22.1), which he saw as the bad or evil part of himself. The priest (Sam is Catholic) represented the judging part of himself and the cannon aimed at the dinosaur was the part of himself that was trying to destroy the evil.

In Sam's second sandtray (Figure 22.2) another dinosaur appears in approximately the same location. The priest at the top has become a king, suggesting that the Self has now been constellated. The cannon has been replaced by an owl. Sam commented, "I guess the owl is the wise part of

Figure 22.2

me wanting to deal with evil (dinosaur)." The mermaid is a new figure. Sam added, "I am attracted to the Siren mermaid."

Sam had terminated analysis a few months after making the initial sandtray and had functioned satisfactorily until he became enchanted with a woman in the office where he worked. He re-entered analysis and, soon after resuming, made the second sand scene. The mermaid, the tempting pixie, the anima, is in the center of things, suggesting her central role in his psychological life at this time.

But the most remarkable feature about these two sand scenes is that the second was made ten years after the first! Sam had no conscious memory of having made the previous sand scene. I, too, had completely forgotten about the first scene and discovered it only when I filed my notes and picture of the second one. So the sandplay image of the dinosaur and its surroundings was preserved in the unconscious without the help of any conscious memory in either Sam or me, and formed the pattern for the subsequent sandtray, thus demonstrating that sandplay is indeed a product of the unconscious as well as of the conscious.

SYNCHRONISTIC MOMENT

Kalff defined the "synchronistic moment" in a public lecture in San Francisco in 1975 as follows:

> The presentation of the unconscious by the patient in the sandtray and the simultaneous recognition of it as such by the therapist provides the link between the unconscious of one and the conscious of the other and is the synchronistic moment that is healing to the patient.

At such a moment of deep sharing of an emergent attitude, the therapist does not need to make any verbal comments. In Kalff's book on sandplay, she describes a session in which she simply puts her arm around her little client Marina to show that she understands. At another point in her sandplay therapy with Marina, Kalff asks her what a man in the tray is doing in the woods. Marina replies, "He has to bring the light into the dark forest." Kalff then adds, "I knew that her psyche had started on the healing path, and I was greatly touched by this" (Kalff 1980: 130). Kalff was not only knowing with her mind but also appreciating with her heart. This coming together of mind and heart is an essential feature of the synchronistic moment in sandplay therapy.

CONFRONTATION BETWEEN AND UNITING OF OPPOSITES

Sandplay provides a physical space in which the opposites can both be presented and perhaps be united. The left and right sides of the tray, the far and near halves of the tray (top and bottom in pictures), and the two diagonals provide opposing sites where objects or sets of objects which represent conflicting polarities can be placed.

What is placed between these opposites sometimes brings them together. We can then speak of bridging the opposites. This important event may be represented by a literal bridge, or by other less literal images such as a path, a river, or even a figure looking from one section towards an object in the opposite section, anything that dynamically connects the two sides with one another.

The bridge, when it is used to unite the opposites in a sandplay scene, is a physical manifestation of the transcendent function as defined by Jung. A bridge in the sandtray does not just suggest that it might be possible for the patient's psyche to make a connection between the two sides. It actually does bring the opposites together in that moment.

Pairs of consecutive scenes made by three different men demonstrate this process. In the first scene in each case there is a bridge which unites two opposite sides of the tray. In each following scene a clear-cut centering appears.

In Hal's first sandtray (Figure 22.3), the opposite corners of the tray are divided by a stream which extends from a tree with two huge worms on it at top center to three lily pads at bottom left. On the left side of the dividing stream are two arms coming out of the sand. Hal said, "I see the hands as the feminine buried in my unconscious – ominous." On the right side of the stream there is a blue horse and a male gorilla. Hal used a ladder to make a bridge across the stream. He then added, "I need something small to be inching its way across," and put a nude boy on the "bridge."

Figure 22.3

Figure 22.4

In this tray, the young boy crawling across the ladder/bridge is making a connection between Hal's buried feminine anima on the left and his masculine spirit (blue horse) and physical energy (gorilla) on the right. The worms on the tree might be threatening to new growth. Or they may be larvae which will develop into butterflies or moths, thus symbolizing transformative energy. How it will turn out remains to be seen.

Figure 22.5

Hal's second tray (Figure 22.4) centers around a circular pool of water in the middle of the tray. He dropped paint into the water to color it blue. Below the pool is a clay pot, a feminine symbol, also holding water and two pieces of turquoise. It is balanced on the other side of the ladder that Hal used in his first tray by a fanciful animal head. Above and to the left of the pool is a gorilla holding onto a scorpion. Hal said, "The gorilla represents known overt aggression; the scorpion represents unknowable hidden power."

The multiple representations of water in this tray – pool, pot of water, Zodiacal water sign (Scorpio) – suggest that Hal now has greater access to the unconscious. And the several unburdened trees in the upper right side of the pool indicate new growth. This second tray demonstrates the centering that occurs after the initial bridging of the opposites in the first tray – particularly in the lovely peaceful arrangement of the pieces around the pool.

A dividing stream also cuts through the two halves of the tray in Carl's initial sandtray (Figure 22.5). A black priest in robes on the upper left side of the stream is surrounded by a semi-circle consisting of figures suggestive of spiritual or religious energy: a fruit tree, two bonfires, a stalk of roses, and a boy playing a flute. Men and women working on a farm on the right side of the stream represent the contrasting work-a-day world.

A bridge crosses the stream at left center. A woman carrying a baby is about to cross the bridge and another woman carrying a water jug is coming off the bridge. Baby- and water-carrying are traditional feminine activities. In retrospect, I see the two women crossing the bridge as the

Figure 22.6

feminine making a connection between the spiritual sphere on the left and temporal sphere on the right. The red carriage drawn by four white horses at bottom left suggests a journey, but it is separated from both the sacred and the everyday areas by water which has no bridge across it.

Among the last items Carl put in the tray was an Eskimo with a gun in the lower left which he positioned in many ways. I asked if the gun was aimed at anyone. "It's aimed across the bridge." And then as if to counteract this destructive impulse, he put a shepherd, a protector of animals, and a house, a protector of people, on the far right of the tray. Finally he placed a skull on top of the carriage, but almost immediately removed it. Perhaps he had an indecisive sense that something had to die in order to foster forward movement.

Carl's second sandtray (Figure 22.6), like Hal's second tray, is focused around a centered pool. And in this pool, as in Sam's second tray, a mermaid appears. Here again the anima is in the center of things. A huge shell at bottom center emphasizes the presence of the feminine. The working world, suggested this time by athletic performers, has been displaced to the far right, and the spiritual world is represented at the top by temples and a Greek goddess. The flute player, who is often connected with feeling, reappears in left center. Carl remarked, "I identify with him the most."

A bridge again appears in this tray, but the area to the left of the bridge contains only a single object, a female torso. An Eskimo is pointing a spear at it. Although there is still some ambivalence towards the feminine here, the bridging between the spiritual and secular worlds which Carl experienced in his first tray has led to a profound centering around the feminine represented by the mermaid in the pool and the shell.

Figure 22.7

Figure 22.8

The opposites in Jim's first sandtray (Figure 22.7) are less well defined. The bridge spans a dry trough. The figures on the left of the bridge include: a walrus, a dried tree, pieces of wood, stones and coral. To the right of the bridge there are: two wells, a house with a dog in front of it, a green tree and a cow drinking from a trough. So the bridge joins a water area on the left that has dried plant life in it (dried tree, wood) and a land area on the right that has implied connections with water below the ground (wells, miniature garden pool, trough). Each side represents a mixture of both dry and wet, both aridity and life-giving moisture. The leafless dry plant bespeaks the lack of rain or sky (father) water. The sources of water on the right indicate the presence of earth (mother) water. His father had died a few weeks before; his mother was still alive.

Jim's second sandtray (Figure 22.8) is, like the second trays of the other two men, a centering, this time around a central mound rather than a central pool. On the top of the mound is a powerful masculine gorilla. Many animals "are coming up to challenge this guy." Water is depicted below the mound at the right. Water birds, which are able to live and move in all three realms of sky, earth and water, are coming to drink. Here masculine values (physical strength and aggression) and feminine values (provision of nourishment) are differentiated, but are closely juxtaposed to one another.

At the next appointment a week later, Jim told me that he had been able to have sexual intercourse for the first time, with a woman he had been dating for the past few months. Within a few months Jim's long time dependency on me had decreased significantly and he was able to successfully transfer to a male analyst.

All three men first made a tray in which a bridge uniting opposites appeared in the sand, and then made a second tray in which there was evidence of the centering activity of the transcendent function. And at this time each man experienced in himself as well the activation of a new source of energy, a new wholeness.

Chapter 23

Toriis and transformation

The torii or Japanese sacred gate was one of the first items I purchased for my sandplay collection when I went to Japan years ago. Twenty years later when I was in Kyoto again, I planned to purchase some more of them. At first, I didn't have much luck finding them.

None of the shopkeepers seemed to understand my pronunciation of the word "torii." Finally, one shopkeeper seemed delighted – I had come to the right place! He waved his hand in a circle around the walls to show me how many he had. But all I saw were little bird objects. I protested, shaking my head, that this was not what I wanted and tried to draw a torii. But this was no better, until my artist husband drew a real likeness. Then the shop owner understood, and directed me to another shop where indeed they had the toriis I wanted.

In this way I discovered that the Japanese word for "bird" is "tor*i*" with a single "i," and the word for "sacred gate" is "tor*ii*" with a double "i," and that only careful pronunciation differentiates between the two words. Later, I learned that the suffix "i" in Japanese means "perch," so the word "torii" literally means "bird perch."

In the book *We Japanese* (Miyanoshita 1964), there is a story about the mythological origin of the name "torii." The sun goddess Amaterasu had a very rude and obnoxious brother, who finally disgusted her so much that she hid herself in a cave behind a rock door. And because she was the sun goddess, the world was thrown into utter darkness. In consternation, the 8 million gods met to talk about what strategies they could use to get her to come out of the cave. Finally, they hit upon the plan of having the rooster crow at the entrance of the cave. They constructed a perch for him out of two upright posts and a crossbeam. When the cock crowed as at dawn, the curious goddess peeped out. Prince Mighty-Power seized her and pulled her out of the cave. So again there was sunshine in the world (Miyanoshita 1964: 200).

Because of this miraculous happening, the structure of two posts with a crossbeam that the cock stood on when it crowed was preserved, and this bird perch or torii later evolved into the sacred gate. Passing through it was seen as passing from darkness into light, as at dawn.

Figure 23.1

Historical accounts report that roosters were ritually sacrificed in the early Shinto religion and the dead birds were ceremoniously hung on top of a crossbeam resting on two vertical posts (Cram 1966: 94–5). Later, after ritual sacrifices were abandoned, the structure that had been used to hold the sacrificed cocks was preserved and became a symbol of the sacred. In Japan, it is usually found at the entrance to a holy place such as a shrine or temple.

This torii, when it is used in sandtrays, is often associated with recurring themes or imagery connected with transformation. The placement of the torii may refer to:

1 the readiness or preparation one must make before going on a journey
2 the objects or obstacles blocking the way
3 the boundary between the conscious and unconscious; movement may be in either direction, from conscious to unconscious or from unconscious to conscious
4 the experience of passage, which may be extended by a bridge appearing in association with the torii
5 the release of energy for life which occurs after the experience of passing through the gate.

The woman who did this first scene (Figure 23.1) wanted to make a long parade, so long that she had to use two trays; the principal action was in the left hand tray shown here. She explained that the Arab cavalry man heading the parade wants to explore a new land across the river and make some part of it his own. The only way to this land is across the bridge and through the torii. But, she pointed out, the bridge is so narrow that

Figure 23.2

most in the procession will find it hard to cross and some must be left behind. And the torii is so low that many will have to lighten their loads to enter the new land. It was as if this woman sensed at some level that to explore the unknown, the unconscious, she would have to sacrifice something, let go of some of her previously held ideas or attitudes.

After many months of analysis and several intervening trays, this woman made a final tray in which the bridge and torii again appeared together (Figure 23.2). She said that the tribal warriors in the upper left, where the new land had been in the first tray, represented for her the primitive; while the right and center were the more conventional. The dragon in the lower right would prevent the warriors from escaping once they had gone through the gate to the center. Perhaps she has found some more primitive parts of herself while exploring the unconscious, the unknown land, and is now ready to let them be integrated into her more conventional side.

In the trays of two men who used the torii, this same dragon appears. The entering complaint of both men was their difficulty in relating to women and these men both used the torii as part of their getting in touch with the feminine.

The man who made the next scene (Figure 23.3) had had a negative relationship with his mother. The problems with his mother had continued to influence his feelings in adulthood towards all women and had interfered with his finding a wife. He felt that he just could not trust women.

In this tray the focus is on the right side where there is a torii at the edge of the tray. A trail starts at the torii and leads to the top. To follow the path, it is necessary to go past the dragon. The trail beyond the dragon goes

Figure 23.3

into an enclosed area at the top. The man said this represented the place where a black woman had taken care of him for a period when he was a child, when he had felt protected and contained. He even lifted off the roof of the cabin and placed an apple inside it to represent the nourishment he remembered and placed the goddess of compassion next to it. So the torii here initially functioned as the starting point for a path leading back to a place of maternal security that he recalled from his personal childhood.

After he re-experienced this sense of security and containment, he said, he could risk going back to look at his origins, the black totem behind the torii. So the torii also functioned as a gateway back to his ancestral origins, connecting him with the collective, or universal, unconscious.

The two black tribesmen dancing were celebrating a marriage. And, indeed there was a marriage in the future for him. He found the right woman not long afterwards and they were married and had two children.

The first items the second man placed in the tray were the torii and the dragon in the center (Figure 23.4). He identified the dragon as himself. The dragon has started out on a journey from a source of wisdom at the top left and has made it across the bridge. Now he has to go through the gate and past the frightening figure to the girl. It looks as if this man must deal with negative parts of himself, represented by the fearsome figure, before he can contact the feminine, the girl in red. He felt that the king, the small figure with its back toward us, was there to help him. We might see the helpful king as the central part of his psyche, the overseeing Self.

The next two trays were the initial and final trays made by a woman who was at a crossroads in her life. She did not know which way to choose. For a couple of years she had been in analysis with another analyst who did not do sandplay, so she came to me specifically for sandplay therapy.

Figure 23.4

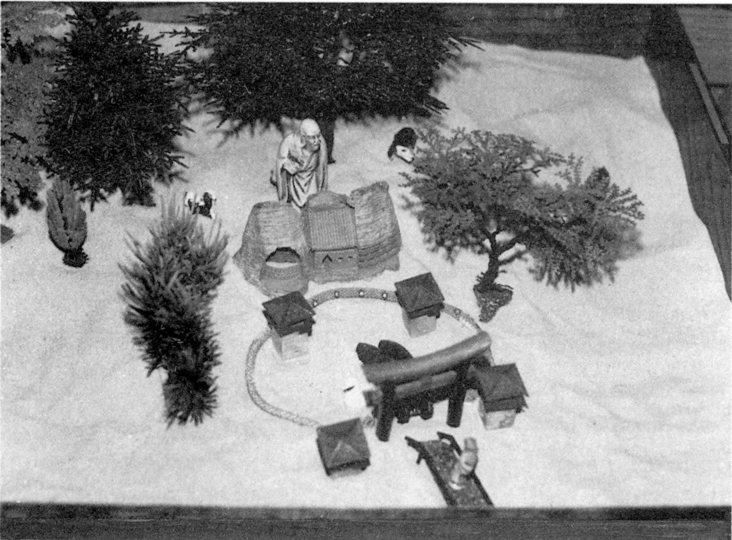

Figure 23.5

While making her initial tray (Figure 23.5), she volunteered that the small figure on the near bridge is a supplicant who is fearful and trembling. She is approaching an enclosed sanctuary guarded by a snake and four watchtowers. The woman seemed to identify with the trembling supplicant who is attempting to gain access to the inner sanctuary. There are two bridges to cross and the sacred gate to go through. A large figure looming up in the background is in control. This scene may portray in

Figure 23.6

part her initiation into the new therapy with another analyst whom she sees as being in control.

The next scene is her final tray (Figure 23.6). She said that the girl behind the torii was herself. She is about to go through the gate to view what is below. She said that each of the ridges below the torii represented a different possibility in her life: hedonistic, spiritual, domestic, and professional.

In this sandtray sequence the ego figure has been transformed; she has changed from feeling apprehensive to being competent. In the initial scene she was going to go through the torii to submissively enter the sandplay process and was giving control completely over to the therapist, the large figure presiding over the tray. In this final tray, in going through the torii she is taking the authority into herself to consider the options in her life. By differentiating between them as she has done here on the four ridges, she will be better prepared to make the necessary choices.

Ursula, as I call the woman who did the next scene (Figure 23.7: "Being judged"), was never able to say anything good about herself and could not accept anyone else's saying anything good about her either. There was a judgmental part of herself that she seemed unable to cope with. In the sandtray this judgmental part is represented by the Aztec god who blocks the entrance to the torii. She herself is represented by the tiny figure in the left center with its arms folded across its chest as if in submission. She is being judged by the Aztec god along with an array of other figures. Only the woman goddess to her right is supportive of her.

In Ursula's next tray (Figure 23.8: "Release") the way to the torii is no longer blocked. The tiny figure in the center that she saw as herself

Figure 23.7

Figure 23.8

is positioned to go through the gate. Two guardians protect her on her way. Beyond the torii is the temple that is now available to her. The readiness to go through lies within her.

The last scene in this torii series (see Plate 12) was made by a woman toward the end of her sandplay process. There is a rose petal path going to and through the torii. The path follows an archway which forms a bridge. In the water under the bridge is a duck-like bird. And at the top of the bridge is a goddess. Here it is not the raging sun goddess Amaterasu who appears, but rather Kannon, the oriental goddess of compassion.

Chapter 24

Sun and moon

Of all the symbols represented by the objects on our sandplay shelves, the sun and moon are the most universally experienced by all people. From the beginning of time and in all areas of the planet, the sun and its reflected light coming from the moon have remained constant outer stimuli for all living beings. But our inner perception of these figures and what they mean varies across cultures. Professor Kawai notes some of these variations in his article, "The sun and moon in Japanese mythology" (Kawai 1992). There Kawai refers to Jung's view of the sun as corresponding to the conscious in men and to the unconscious in women "due to the contrasexual archetype in the unconscious: anima in a man, animus in a woman" (Jung 1963: 135).

In my own experience in the sandplay room, persons in general used the sun more often than they used the moon. Women used both together more often than men did. The moon was never used alone without the sun by anyone doing sandplay. According to Kawai's article, the reverse is true in Japanese poetry; there the sun is never spoken of in the absence of the moon.

When women used both sun and moon the two were always in some relationship to each other. Sometimes they appeared on opposite sides of the tray, as if in opposition to one another, perhaps concretizing an experience of the tension between, or the differentiation of, the opposites. Sometimes they were in close proximity to each other, perhaps representing the union of the opposites of conscious/unconscious, male/female, light/dark, day/night, hot/cold.

As I was studying photos of sandplay scenes in which the sun or the moon were included, I noticed that the scenes using the sun often also included images of new life, especially babies and eggs. In checking further, I found that of the fifty-five women who started sandplay with me after I acquired images of the sun and moon, fifteen placed a sun in one or more scenes and thirteen of these fifteen women also included babies and/or eggs in at least one of these trays along with the sun. Out of a total of twenty-eight trays in which the sun appeared, eighteen or nearly two-thirds included babies or eggs.

But, I thought, perhaps this is not a larger proportion of babies or eggs than is usual in sandplay scenes, or perhaps this particular group of women included more babies or eggs than is usual in all their trays. To check, I looked at a random sample of another twenty-eight trays by the same group of women. Only one-third included babies or eggs. The use of the sun in the trays doubled the proportion of images of new life that also appeared. In thinking about this finding, I realized that perhaps it is not so surprising. The sun is ultimately the source of all life.

One woman, who had included three babies in her first sun sandtray and two babies in a later sun scene, came in one day and said, "I think I'm pregnant." She then took down a sun and put it in her tray, but added no babies. I later learned that she had indeed become pregnant. I wondered whether carrying her own baby within herself obviated the need to add an outer baby to this third sun scene.

Another person in the group of women who used the sun was Debbie, a woman with terminal lung cancer who came to do sandplay on her journey toward death. She also used babies in her two sun trays. On reflection, this seems consistent with a perception of death as not an end, but as a transition into a new beginning.

These comments are based on relatively few persons, but they indicate my interest in what sandplay can teach us about psychology and about the development of the psyche. I have brought up more questions here than I have answered. Answers must come from focusing on processes of individuals as well as on group comparisons. But perhaps the curiosity of other therapists will be stimulated and they will add to these observations and comments. I feel that as we accumulate more experience in the study of sandplay we will be able to contribute to a deeper understanding of the human psyche.

Chapter 25

Hestia and Athena

Over a hundred years ago, Nora in Ibsen's play *A Doll's House* made an appeal for all women. When her husband admonished, "Before all else you are a wife and mother," Nora replied, "That I no longer believe. I believe that before all else I am a human being, just as much as you are."

The psychology of women as human beings in their own right has always held a deep interest for me. I appreciated Jung for having helped to raise women out of the inferior position they had been put in and I wanted to learn more about women within the framework of Jungian psychology by drawing upon the experiencing of actual women, both my own experiencing of myself, and the experiencing of my colleagues and my analysands. So I began to study a group of the women patients that I was seeing at the time.

Also around this time, two other women analysts and I voiced our need to get together to talk about ourselves. These mutual exchanges were enormously important to all three of us. It was a time when we could shed professional and family responsibilities and focus on sharing inner experiences. We did not try to be secretive about our meetings, but we did feel kind of "found out" when the program chairman for the Public Lecture Series at the San Francisco Jung Institute asked us if we would present something together on the psychology of women. The idea was entirely contrary to our mood in meeting with each other. We had been inner-centered rather than outer-directed. Preparing something to say to others would require a change in mental set. We would have to organize our thinking, consider the expectations of an audience, respect professional responsibilities, produce. And we had been trying to get away from such demands. Despite our initial reluctance, however, the request sparked a response in each of us; it activated the part in us that did want to conceptualize our experience. And so we appeared on a panel together later that year.

In subsequent contemplation, I realized that the self-disclosing we did in those small meetings had called upon a more relating, or eros, side of myself, while being on the lecture panel had called on a more achieving, or logos, side. The relating side is often thought of as the feminine, the side that cares for people, for all life. It enjoys creating in a non-competitive way. For many women it is associated with needing some time for space and solitude, for "just being." But, at times, the relating side can feel uncomfortably dependent. I remembered one young woman who described it as her "puppy-dog feeling."

The achieving side relishes meeting a challenge and completing a difficult task. It wants to slay a dragon or two, to accomplish heroic feats, to "count," not only in the family but also out in the world. In its negative aspect, this achieving side can interfere with relatedness. Its single-minded driving quality may push others away. We might identify this side as the animus or the masculine. Unfortunately, "animus" has come to have a mostly negative connotation for many women. It has become identified with the pushiness that sometimes accompanies the desire to achieve.

As women come to value their achieving side more positively, some experience it as a part of themselves that thinks, feels, acts or envisions in an excitingly creative way, arousing a sense of elation. This achieving or logos side seems to be becoming more differentiated in women. New aspects are emerging which reflect "woman strength," something which is neither identical with nor opposite from "man strength."

THE WOMEN ANALYSANDS

I came to realize that most of the women seeking analysis with me around this time also seemed to have arrived at a point in their lives where they had been getting along okay, but they were discontent. Something was wrong. There was a neglected side of themselves that was not being heard from or lived.

There were the women who had looked forward to getting married and having children, to being homemakers. But, having fulfilled their primary desire, they found they were not as happy as they had expected. They wondered, "Is this all?" And then there were the women who had made it in their careers, but felt stuck. These professional women often did not have the time, energy, or inclination to really experience being in relationship. Studying for an advanced degree is not exactly conducive to developing one's nest-building instincts.

Out of thirty-one women that I saw during a five-year period, all but one fell into one of these two contrasting groups. One group consisted of eighteen married women. Sixteen of them had children, all had at least one year of college and only one had a job outside the home. The other group consisted of twelve unmarried women who had graduate degrees in nursing, social work, psychology or medicine and were actively engaged in their professions.

The women in both groups were between 20 and 55 years of age (that is, principally in the first half of life) and well educated. The women in the "home" group were predominantly Introverted Feeling Intuitive in type; the "career" group were predominantly Extraverted Thinking Intuitive according to the Gray-Wheelwright Jungian Type Survey (Wheelwright *et al.* 1964). The "home" group were more likely to be first-born children, more likely to carry on the family traditions (Stewart 1992); the "career" group more likely to be last-born, not so bound by traditional stereotyping.

THE UNDERLYING ARCHETYPAL IMAGES

Initially, I used the names "hearth tender" and "warrior" women to refer to these two groups in a more psychologically descriptive way than "home" and "career" women. But when I came across Elined Kotschnig's (1968–9) article, "Womanhood in myth and in life", it struck me that the Greek goddesses Hestia and Athena might better personify these two sides of women (see also Bolen 1984: 75–155). Kotschnig points out that both Hestia and Athena were virgin goddesses, women who were complete in themselves, not merely counterparts of male consorts. They developed wholeness through the integration of parts within themselves, unlike many women who first experience those parts primarily in projection onto others and only later withdraw the projections back into themselves (Kotschnig 1968–9).

The Greek word "hestia" means hearth. When a member of a family in ancient Greece departed to found a new family, a parcel of fire, the hestia, was taken with them from the parents' hearth, thus symbolizing the family continuity. The hestia very early took on a sacred character and was later personified by a deity. The goddess Hestia was known for not taking part in wars or disputes and was a protectress of supplicants who fled to her. She invented the art of building houses. She represented personal security and the sacred duty of hospitality.

In the Roman pantheon, Hestia became Vesta, a symbol of idealized maternity. The Vestal temple in Rome represented the hearth or home of the Roman people where the eternal flame was tended. Yearly festivals were celebrated in honor of the mothers of families who were allowed to enter the sanctuary. They performed a simple ceremony using pure water and fire; there were no blood sacrifices.

Athena was connected not with fire but with moisture. Originally, Athena was the goddess of storm and lightning. Her attribute was the "aegis," a shield made of magical goatskin, and her epithet was "goddess of the brilliant eyes." Athena was later venerated as a warrior goddess as well as a storm goddess. She personified warfare that was purposeful, as opposed to bloodthirsty. She was a champion of justice, a protectress of brave and valorous heroes. She was also known as a goddess of the arts of peace. She was the patroness of architects and sculptors, spinners and weavers. She invented the potter's wheel and was given the title of "Hygiea" because of her miraculous healing powers. Because of her wisdom, she became the goddess of the Assembly. Her emblem was the owl.

According to legend, Athena sprang fully armed from the head of Zeus. Robert Graves suggests that this story reflects "a dogmatic insistence on wisdom as a male prerogative" (Graves 1957: 46). Some of today's women might recognize a parallel to this story when they hear that their keen intellectual accomplishments must have sprung from their animus, their masculine side, not from their own feminine self.

Although the goddesses Hestia and Athena in many ways represented opposite archetypes, they both were protective and inventive. Hestia invented a place of refuge, the house. Athena invented an object used for actively making something, the potter's wheel. Hestia received and protected those who came to her; Athena protected those who went out into the world on dangerous expeditions.

THE COLLECTIVE CONTEXT

One of the reasons the women in both groups came into analysis at this time was because of conflicts involving this question of family vs. career, or doubts about their abilities to relate to others or to achieve. When we consider the enormous change in what has been expected of women in the last few decades, this is not surprising.

In my own case, for example, I was married during the depression of the 1930s with its record low birth rate. I obtained my PhD during World War II in the early 1940s, when many women were being employed to replace men. By the end of the 1940s, I was juggling five part-time jobs. Then the 1950s came, with their record baby boom. Women were told that their place was in the home, where I was not spending much time. Coping with all this was what sent me initially into analysis. In the 1960s, the women's liberation movement got under way and women were told that they must reject their role as housewife and their financial dependence upon men. And in the 1970s up to the present, the message has been that women must make it both as a wife/mother in the home and as a working woman in the world.

Most of the women in the two study groups were born or grew up in the 1930s and 1940s and came into analysis in the late 1960s or early 1970s. They, too, had been subjected to this series of changes in what was expected of women. The home or Hestia women came into analysis expressing a desire to do something more with their lives than "just" keep house. And the women in the career or Athena group often wanted a husband and children. So each wanted what the other had, not to replace what they already had, but to add to it.

An almost universal complaint common to both groups was that they did not want to be like their mothers, whom they saw as inadequate, critical of themselves and of others and unable to give. In hearing their description of their mothers, I got the impression that the mothers were not really so terrible, but that they, like their daughters, had had to struggle for self-esteem.

At least since the rise of patriarchal cultures, women have generally felt inferior to men and, until recently, have tended to accept their secondary position. The current awakening among women, however, helps each successive generation of women proceed a little further up the ladder of self-esteem. Daughters must become unlike their mothers to carry their generation to the next higher rung on the ladder.

Esther Menaker sees the rebellion of many young women against identifying with their mothers as a healthy testimony to the strength of their ego in its drive to achieve autonomy. She believes there is also a deep and more unconscious rebellion going on which is struggling against the incorporation of the mother's devalued self-image, her self-hate. The struggle for self-esteem and ego autonomy requires a psychological separation from the mother who unconsciously denigrates both herself and her female child (Menaker 1974).

Neumann observes that daughters are more influenced by their mother's negative self-evaluation than sons are. He believes this is because of their necessarily closer identification with the same sex. So women's sense of inferiority is passed on (Neumann 1959). Women now live at a significant time in history when this chain of socially inherited feelings of inferiority is being broken.

In spite of their differences, women in both study groups had in common this sense of low self-esteem and a felt lack of an inner core. Women in the Hestia group expressed guilt for not making more of themselves; women in the Athena group expressed guilt for not being married and having children. And women in both groups recognized a pervasive self-neglect. They had learned their early girlhood lesson well: be nurturing to others. Women with families tended to forget about themselves and make sacrifices for their husbands and children; women with careers put professional responsibilities above the care of their own bodies and psyches. Both had to learn to give to themselves and had to find ways of preserving blessed islands of release from outer demands.

THEIR ANALYSIS

Many of these women started out their analysis with feelings of emptiness or hollowness. A Hestia woman modelled a clay figure as she talked; it turned out to have a huge hole in its stomach. An Athena woman spoke of a deep, empty cavern inside. Several reported episodes of compulsive eating associated with a greedy devouring need to fill the inner nothingness. These feelings of emptiness seem related to what Spencer has called the "phenomenon of invisibility," which she found only in women, not in men (Spencer 1977). As a young woman in the Athena group expressed it, "I get to feeling depressed and empty and then like I'm nothing and that no one can see me."

The women in both groups hoped that analysis would help them find an inner value, an inner sense of self-esteem. One woman said, "I want to find my inner core." Another woman referred to "an inner flowing." Another said, "The core of a person is a different quality from the rest. It's like the nucleus of a one-celled animal. It contains the essence, and when that becomes vitalized, you can sense it and growth can start."

I was first struck by the symbolic significance of the tree for all these women when I was practicing in an office which had a linden tree in a planter in the bay window. Many of the women I was seeing showed special concern about its condition: "Was it getting enough water?" "Enough sun?" "Too much sun?" I recall one woman who, when she came into the office, always carefully inspected the tree before telling me how she herself was feeling. One day when she had been going through a particularly difficult period, she brought plant food to feed the tree.

One woman from each group made drawings of trees. The Hestia woman's first drawing was a starkly barren trunk; the second, made two years later, was a group of trees covered densely with foliage. The first drawing by the Athena woman was a four-branched tree with an unstable base; the last, made in the same evening, was multi-branched, with lots of greenery and a solid base.

Another woman in the Hestia group had a recurring dream of a garden that she was not tending. She felt guilty for neglecting the garden. Later, she dreamed of a garden full of green trees which had green figs hanging in their tops. She wondered whether they were too high for her to reach. But she was delighted that they had survived on their own.

One of these women wrote a story about a giant redwood tree. Its unwavering aim was to grow up, up, into the life-giving light, while its roots groped blindly downward for the water and nutrients in the soil, just as we reach up for the light of consciousness and down for nourishment from the unconscious.

All the women spoke in their analysis of a need for "just being," and they found different ways to experience this. Some women in both groups worked on becoming more aware of their bodies. They took classes in dance, Yoga or Tai Chi. Others had regular appointments for massage. Some took the time to just sit in the garden or the home. I have always appreciated Jane Wheelwright's comment that a woman needs some time in her home all by herself, so that she can just "rattle around." And I recall one woman who liked the feeling of being pregnant because something was being created by her without her having to do anything but just be. And so the sense of imbalance and discontent that was initially present in both these groups of women was gradually replaced by an awareness of a quietly growing center within them.

DIFFERENCES IN THE SANDPLAY SCENES

My impression in studying the sandtrays done by women in both groups was that they were all striving to get in touch with and develop a neglected part of themselves. The Hestia women generally had a good connection with their femininity, but needed to develop their more assertive side, or to make friends with their animus. The Athena women already had a strong animus working for them, and sometimes against them, and needed to get better related to their softer more feminine side.

The initial sandtray scenes of the Hestia women generally showed a notable lack of either ego assertiveness or animus aggression. They pictured domination by others and acceptance of a passive position for themselves. In Ida's first scene for example (see Figure 30.1, p. 138), a woman is diving through an arch away from the conflict shown on the other side between masculine authority (policemen) and instinctual life (animals). Another "home" woman used no humans or animals in her initial tray; she put a cage within a cage into the tray and said that she felt trapped inside it. Several figures carrying burdens appeared in the initial scene done by a third Hestia woman I call Ursula (see Figure 34.1, p. 173); we saw these as the many burdens of the devoted wife and mother. One woman moved the sand around a bit and then poured water onto it, making a large lake that almost filled the tray. She let nature work without trying to assert herself to change it. Another woman's first scene portrayed a boy fishing, creating an overall impression of reflective passivity.

The initial scenes of the Athena women, by contrast, dealt predominantly with assertive and aggressive energies. Two career women, for example, depicted a horseman jumping over a hurdle in their first trays. One added a man on a racing bike. She said that a man had already been killed in the competition. A third Athena woman put men wielding swords on both sides of her first tray.

In the final sand scenes symbols of greater wholeness predominated in both groups. Circles and circling around a center was the most recurrent motif in the last trays done by the Hestia women. One woman made an off-center circular mound with a road winding up it in her final tray. Two other women made circles in the sand around a central object – a piece of driftwood and a god.

The final scenes of the Athena women were more balanced and less preoccupied with aggression than their initial trays had been. One woman depicted a royal couple watching a play about fighting. Aggression now takes place on stage; it no longer has the immediacy of an actual event. And another career woman made a peaceful nature scene in her final tray, much like the initial tray of one of the Hestia women. And, like the Hestia women, many of the final scenes of the Athena women showed evidence of centering. Irene put a witch in the center of a circus ring in the middle of her last tray (see Figure 32.2, p. 161). Another woman made a centered mound in her last tray and then placed a tower on the top of the peak.

OUTCOMES

And what happened to these women after their analysis? The last time I was in touch with them, about one-fourth of the women were no longer solely focused on their families or their careers. Several in the Hestia group had developed their Athena side by taking academic courses or working in a job. Most of them also reported improved relationships with husbands and/or children; thus they had maintained their original values as well as developing those of Athena.

Several of the Athena group had expanded their capacities to relate through marriage or through stable partnerships. Three had had children. Most of them had also maintained their achieving side, acquiring licenses in their specialty or promotions at work.

The women in both the Hestia and Athena groups had in common the quality of protecting or giving to others, be it family or patients or clients, which had sent them outside themselves. And they went through a similar process, regardless of whether eros or logos had been their initially dominant value. The resolution in both groups came from relating to their inner core rather than from identifying with either side. This then freed them to develop the opposite archetype. Yet the functioning of the initially dominant side was not jeopardized; it was typically enhanced.

I do not believe we really know what happens in analysis that brings about this process of centering. We can show after the fact the sequence of what has happened, but we cannot claim to really understand. Part of women's rebellion against patriarchal tradition has been not only against the inequality of opportunities for outer achievement, but also against being "understood" by men, explained in their terms, from the point of view of masculine values.

Jung warns against the analyst's "understanding" the analysand. In one of his letters, Jung states:

> Understanding is a fearfully binding power, at times a veritable murder of the soul as soon as it flattens out vitally important differences. The core of the individual is a mystery of life, which is snuffed out when it is "grasped."
>
> (Jung 1973: 31)

Chapter 26

Developmental stages in the sandplay of children

When I look at a child's sandplay series, I find it helpful to relate the scenes to the stages of ego development that were initially described by Neumann (1973) and Kalff (1971 and 1980). Neumann distinguishes five stages. In the first two of these, the ego is primarily in *participation mystique* with the mother archetype. He describes the initial "phallic–chthonian" period, for example, as follows: "Its vegetative and animal form is still in high degree passive. . . . It has not yet freed itself from the dominance of the matriarchal power of nature and the unconscious." Although in the next "phallic–magic" stage the ego begins to have "considerable activity of its own," it is only when the child enters the third or "magic–warlike" stage that the ego

> first overcomes its dependence on the matriarchate, so much so that it effects the transition to the patriarchate with which the ensuing "solar ego" is correlated. In the solar–warlike phase, the ego identifies itself with the father archetype. It is followed by the solar–rational stage of the adult patriarchal ego, whose independence culminates in relative freedom of the will, and by the likewise relatively free cognitive ego.
> (Neumann 1973: 139)

Kalff's experience corroborated Neumann's theory and led her to propose three similar stages of ego development: "animal–vegetative," corresponding to Neumann's first two "phallic" stages; "fighting," similar to Neumann's two "warlike" stages; and "adaptation to the collective," which

Table 26.1 Comparison of developmental stages

Neumann	*Kalff*
Phallic–chthonian	Animal–vegetative
Phallic–magic	
Magic–warlike	Fighting
Solar–warlike	
Solar–rational	Adaptation to the collective

Figure 26.1

can be equated with Neumann's "solar–rational" stage (Kalff 1980: 32). A comparison of Neumann's and Kalff's stages of child development is shown in Table 26.1.

I have found that Kalff's three successive stages are often represented in the initial sandtrays of children at different ages, e.g., 6-, 9- and 12-year-olds. The children may then go on to elaborate on the same stage in their subsequent trays, or they may make the transition into the next stage or stages.

ANIMAL–VEGETATIVE STAGE: A 6-YEAR-OLD

The first sandtray by a 6-year-old boy, for example (Figure 26.1), is made up exclusively of the animal and plant life which is typical of the animal–vegetative stage. All of the animals are prehistoric; there is a procession of dinosaurs going from right to left across the front of the tray. Children in general use prehistoric animals more frequently than adults do, which seems consistent with the chthonic character of this stage. The dark areas in the middle left and upper right of the tray are water holes which he made by scraping the sand away from the blue floor of the tray. Many children provide water and also food for the animals they put in the sandtray. This is often their first step in learning how to actively obtain nourishment for themselves, rather than to just passively receive nourishment from others, and is thus a step towards a higher level of ego autonomy.

Although the addition of trees and plants to sand scenes is typical of the vegetative stage, it may appear at any age or developmental level.

Figure 26.2

The presence of plant life can suggest activation of the inner forces of psychological growth, in contrast to sand scenes devoid of vegetation which may connote feelings of lifelessness.

There is a large mound just left of the center in this boy's scene and there are four smaller less visible mounds in other parts of the tray. He said these mounds were volcanoes and made craters in the center of each one. They suggest pent-up, possibly explosive feelings. As these feelings emerge they can propel the boy further out of the more passive matriarchial stage into the more active fighting stage, the beginning of the patriarchal sequence of stages.

As might be anticipated, the next two scenes made by this boy were fighting scenes, first a war between the soldiers of two different countries and then a sea battle. Then came a scene portraying a king protected by many guards, representing the first emergence of the archetypal masculine. (Similarly, for a girl, the use of a queen may coincide with the emergence of the archetypal feminine.) This boy seems well into the transition to the patriarchate. The appearance of the king may reflect the beginning of his identification with the father archetype, which is characteristic of Neumann's solar–warlike phase.

FIGHTING STAGE: A 9-YEAR-OLD

A 9-year-old boy in his first scene (Figure 26.2) skips the animal–vegetative stage and starts right out with the fighting stage of ego development. Two armies are lined up facing each other in readiness for battle, complete with cannon, cavalry and infantry soldiers. He made more battle scenes in his next two trays. While he was making this fighting series he also directed critical comments at me and "shot" a cannon in my direction.

Children at this stage often engage the therapist as an opponent in the drama depicted, or demand their adversarial involvement through testing limits by, for example, "letting" sand spill over the sides of the tray onto the floor. Later, they may initiate some kind of joint creation with the therapist. Children often alternate with some regularity between negative and positive approaches towards the therapist as they develop.

The boy called his third fighting scene a "war over a baby." He may be experiencing conflict or ambivalence about something new growing in himself. He put a well in one corner of the tray; he is obtaining energy from below the earth, from the unconscious, to aid in the resolution of this conflict. His next tray continued this theme; animals are drinking from a water hole.

Sources of energy, including wells, food, or gasoline pumps, often appear during periods of transition. It is as if the ego needs an additional supply of energy in order to cope with the struggle between inner and outer forces.

After "shooting" the therapist, fighting over the appearance of a baby and providing himself with water, this boy made a tray in which, for the first time, he used fences. He may be beginning to recognize the need for more restrictions or controls.

A child's use of fences usually coincides with their emerging ability to "battle with external influences and . . . come to grips with them," as Kalff describes the stage of adaptation to the collective (Kalff 1980: 33). Other indications of this stage in the sandtray can be: school scenes; contests or sporting events; interactions – especially conflictual – with authority figures (parents, teachers, police); and contrasts between good and bad.

The period of transition from the fighting stage to the stage of adaptation, which may last for several weeks or months, is often marked by battle scenes alternating with scenes of animals fenced in. Frequently one can accurately predict that a scene in which aggression appears will be followed by a scene in which animals are enclosed.

ADAPTATION TO THE COLLECTIVE STAGE: A 12-YEAR-OLD

The first scene done by a 12-year-old girl (Figure 26.3) skips both the animal–vegetative and the fighting stages. She begins with Kalff's third stage, adaptation to the collective. In her initial scene, she places fences around farmyard animals. She is not attempting to restrict the potentially destructive aggression seen in the boys' fighting scenes. She is not fencing in tigers and lions. Rather, she seems to be experiencing the need for further restriction of her already somewhat domesticated animal instincts.

Figure 26.3

One of the farm girls is scattering grain for the animals; she is actively nourishing her animal self, another step towards ego independence. The two boys made water holes in the sand where the animals could come to drink; the girl chooses figures who provide food directly to the animals. This more direct activity may be related to the higher level of development of the 12-year-old. Or there may be a link between feeding animals and nurturing as a generally feminine value.

A second girl is milking a cow. Here the human is obtaining nourishment from the animal. The sandplayer does not have to identify with an animal being fed in order to obtain nourishment for herself; instead she can identify with a human girl figure very much like herself.

In this scene, the negative aspects of the instincts, implied by the need to restrict them, are balanced by their positive aspects, implied by nourishing and being nourished by them. So, there is a full circle: she gives nourishment to her instinctual side and she obtains nourishment from it.

The availability of energy from a deeper level is again suggested by the presence of a well in the lower right corner. But in this scene, unlike the scene made by the 6-year-old boy, the well is not just sitting there. A male figure near the well is carrying buckets balanced on a pole across his shoulders, apparently on his way to get some water. Here the masculine is again more actively working to obtain the nourishment.

At the left top of the scene a man and woman are standing by a house – usually thought of as a feminine symbol – with a car – usually thought of as a masculine symbol – on the road in front of it. On the lower left side a man on a horse is riding towards a bridge. Both the car and the horse are forms of transportation energy although one is mechanical and the other is alive. Both bring the dynamic masculine into the scene.

The bridge indicates that she is making connections between opposing parts of herself. The parts to be related are not decisively delineated in

Figure 26.4

this tray, although the several representations of masculinity and femininity as well as the contrast between locomotion and nourishment in this tray provide clues. Sometimes, as in this scene, it is not even clear how the bridge serves to connect. But its symbolic value as a connector is still valid. And this recognition of and tolerance for opposites can lead to a transformation in the psyche.

The 12-year-old's next two scenes showed a girl diving into the water, again a more active way of gaining access to the unconscious. Both scenes also included gasoline stations, which supply energy for locomotion.

Her fourth and final scene (Figure 26.4: taken from lower right corner) further develops the theme of adaptation to the collective. Two sections are devoted to sporting contests: "Olympic gymnastics" in the left section and racing bicyclists in front. A schoolroom is depicted in the large section on the right. Children are sitting at their desks; one is interacting with the teacher and the principal. In the upper middle area the diving girl is again poised to jump into a pool of water. In retrospect, I might interpret this continuing appearance of the diving girl as a readiness in this client to continue on with more in-depth psychotherapy, but circumstances did not allow further sessions with her at the time.

Although there is a relation between chronological age and the appearance of the successive developmental stages in children, the relationship is, of course, not a perfect one. Nor is the progression from one stage to the next a rigidly fixed sequence. These examples are not meant to suggest an invariable course, but rather to aid in identifying the stages of ego development proposed by Neumann and Kalff and to illustrate their helpfulness in understanding the sandplay scenes of children.

This kind of understanding is not usually communicated to the child in words. In fact, as with adults, I avoid making interpretations to the child during the ongoing process of sandplay in favor of spontaneous, often non-verbal, communication. An appreciation for what the sand scenes are depicting, an empathy for the struggles which the child encounters, and a rejoicing in their achievements are generally enough to provide the *temenos* within which development will occur. After the sandplay series has been completed, a joint viewing with the child of the projected slides of the trays provides the opportunity to exchange more verbal observations on what has happened. At that time cognition can beneficially join the feeling experience.

Part III

Individual cases

Chapter 27

Introduction to individual cases

This third part consists of ten cases that illustrate various points made throughout this book. Kathy demonstrates self-healing in the sandplay of a child. Kathy was the first client who did sandplay with me over a period of time. Her process introduced me to the use of fences to control anger, the inclusion of a container for incubation, the inter-weaving of the co-transference with the trays, and the development of the masculine without sacrificing the feminine.

Jim's initial two trays were included in Chapter 22 on bridges (Figures 22.7 and 22.8, p. 90). His complete sandplay process is presented here. I saw Jim in analysis for more than twenty years, but the sandplay series was done over just a few months. His work in the tray enabled him to realize his erotic masculinity in his life for the first time at the age of 51 years.

Ida is the only sandplayer I have seen who had a diagnosible psychosis. She was referred to me after her initial psychotic break. She suffered a second, less severe, break during the course of the sandplay.

Ilsa's process illustrates the way in which the psyche can respond when there is a limited time in which to do sandplay. She had only five visits, and yet during that time she did complete a process.

Irene was one of the career women included in the study of Hestia and Athena. Her sand scenes started out with the broken segments of a ring and ended up with an intact circle.

Rhoda also had only a limited time for her sandplay series. Her initial tray anticipated a search for the spiritual which was continued and came to fruition in the following four trays.

Some of Ursula's trays were mentioned briefly in the symbol papers on turtles and toriis and in Hestia and Athena. Her whole process is included here because of the remarkable fact that she made just ten trays over a period of fifteen years of analysis. Some scenes were separated by as much as three years. And yet the ten trays hold together as a cohesive, completed process.

Amy's trays first alerted me to the analysis of sequence. Even in her initial tray there were several examples of the sequence of compensatory placements and growth.

Emmy, like Ilsa, continued to see her analyst regularly while she was making trays with me. And it was during her sandplay therapy that I became increasingly aware of the importance of being alert to transference–countertransference issues, which I came to identify as co-transference.

And the last client is Debbie, a woman who came to me to do sandplay in order to help her prepare for her death from cancer. The way she used sandplay to deal with her unfinished tasks is a tribute both to sandplay and to her.

Chapter 28

Kathy: self-healing in the sandtray

Kathy's sandplay series demonstrates the process of self-healing. I am always in awe when I am privileged to observe this psychological healing, just as I am in awe when I observe the healing of a bodily wound such as a burn or cut. The skin cells go about mending themselves with no help from the outside, except protection from infection or further injury.

Many psychological wounds can also heal themselves. The healing of psychological wounds, like body wounds, requires a space where the healing can take place and safety or protection. The "free and protected space" of sandplay work provides both these conditions, since the person can make or do anything they wish in the tray while the therapist remains close by, offering protection.

Kathy was approaching her tenth birthday when she was brought to me for therapy. Because of increasing difficulties at school, she had had an extensive psychological work-up. The final diagnostic evaluation read in part:

> Serious emotional problems related to low self-esteem and inability to assert herself in interpersonal relationships. At least average intelligence, but poor written language and poor visual motor coordination, supporting a diagnosis of dyslexia. Extremely sensitive to failure.

Kathy's father had a history of over-achieving. He demanded perfection in himself and in those around him. He suffered from obsessions and depressions and had been in analysis with a Jungian analyst. He died from a brain hemorrhage four months before I started seeing Kathy.

Kathy's mother was in general more lenient than her husband. She, too, was in Jungian analysis. Kathy had a younger brother who was 8 and a sister who was 7.

When I talked with the father's analyst, he told me that Kathy's father had never talked about either Kathy or her sister during his analysis. He had been interested only in his son. He was disappointed in Kathy and thought she could do better in school if only she would try. But Kathy continued to fail in school and became increasingly reticent and self-deprecating. So we have school failure, paternal condemnation, low self-esteem, inability to assert or express herself – all reinforcing each other in a vicious circle from which she was unable to escape. Her father's death had not released her.

I saw Kathy for about a one-and-a-half years, in a total of forty-three sessions. Kathy's overall task during her work was to become more self-assertive. Her sub-tasks were:

1 To overcome her fear of authority and consequent fear of failure.
2 To learn that she could control her expression of aggression (so that she did not have to suppress or repress it).
3 To correct her polarized impression that mother or the feminine is *good* and father or the masculine is *bad*.

Kathy was a naturally outgoing youngster, but yet her verbal expression had become associated with failure and pain. Initially, she often talked little during the hour and instead made multiple sand pictures during a single session. She had a readiness, a hunger, for a technique which gave her a means of non-verbal expression. She even used the sandplay figures non-verbally to practice her visual-motor skills. When she discovered the flower plots, for example, she spent several sessions carefully putting the flowers into the holes provided for them, showing immense pleasure with her increasing success.

Her early display of inhibition and rigid self-discipline in the sandtray was followed by a gradual relaxing of controls. Until late in the therapy, however, whenever she showed any aggression in the tray or in her relationship with me or even in talking about others, she typically placed fences around animals in the subsequent sandtray – either in the same session or at the next session. I saw in this her need to reaffirm her ability to control her feelings and instincts.

In her interaction with me, Kathy very quickly overcame her earlier reticent compliance and began to test the limits that I tried to set on the use of water, the spilling of sand onto the floor and the opening of boxes storing reserve items in the closet. I had been given permission to use the sandplay room at the San Francisco Jung Institute, and I did not want that permission rescinded.

So I set rules and Kathy questioned them. Sometimes I became anxious and annoyed. Often I could admit that she was right. Frequently I just became more lenient. As this happened, she became more self-confident and less in need of being either submissively compliant or aggressively defiant. She learned how to negotiate. Finally, she even wrote her own rules. On the back of the grass plots she wrote "No sand." This was a message to the other children who used the sandtray that putting the grass plots into the sand was forbidden.

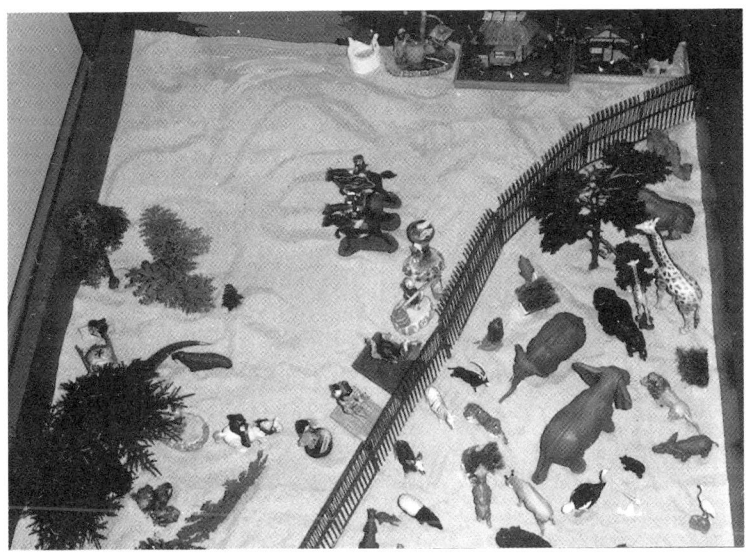

Figure 28.1

She also experienced becoming the authority in her relationship with me. She asked me to put some items together and, when I had difficulty, she derided me. When I finally succeeded, she said, somewhat mockingly, "I told you you could do it!" I thought to myself how often she had probably been in the opposite role with her father, who had derided and mocked *her*. Kathy sometimes had us do battle in the sandtray, shooting tiny cannons at each other. Her aggressiveness towards me was intermingled with acts of caring; sometimes she would bring cookies and soft drinks for us to share after she had finished the scenes.

The development of masculine achievement and assertiveness without sacrificing the development of feminine caring and receptivity is a universal task for most young girls and women, and, indeed, for men also. After Kathy experienced her masculine or assertive side in one tray, she often returned to and reaffirmed her feminine identification in the next, using mothers, gardens, shells, houses, and other familiar feminine symbols.

In addition to these more or less conscious uses of the sandplay material, there were times when Kathy's unconscious came into play, often at a deep, or archetypal, level. The unconscious is, of course, operating at all times. But there are times when the unconscious makes itself particularly visible. In Kathy's sandplay there were four instances of centering where she seemed to touch the Self.

Kathy's initial sand scene (Figure 28.1: "Zoo animals fenced in") reflects her fear of aggression. She has to hold aggression under control,

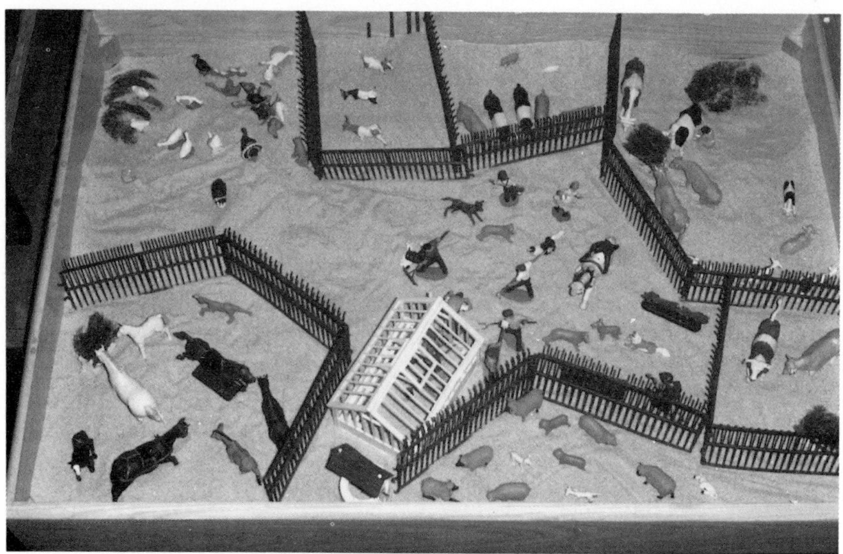

Figure 28.2

to fence in the wild animals. Her fear has two roots: a fear of failure; and a fear that the anger that has been pent-up during years of frustration will overwhelm her if she allows herself to express it. The horses, however, are not fenced in; people are riding around on them. Some animal or instinctual energy is available to her for her analytic journey.

A crocodile is hidden behind trees on the left; the devouring aspect of the negative mother is partly conscious and partly unconscious. The houses bring in the sheltering aspect of the more positive mother.

The well at the top is also a positive sign. Bringing water up from below the earth is akin to bringing up contents from the unconscious. The Japanese figures with the pails are preparing to get the water. Kathy seems ready for the analytical process.

In Kathy's second scene (Figure 28.2: "Animals being fed") the animals are still fenced in, but the ducks are outside of the fence. She is ready to give more freedom to her feelings and instincts. And these animals are domestic rather than wild; they are "safer." There is even food for the animals; she is willing to nourish her instincts. The well is still present. And greenery, growth, is represented. Kathy also introduces a greenhouse, or hothouse, into this scene. It figures as an important symbol for her in many of her subsequent trays. The greenhouse, like the therapeutic *temenos*, is a place where natural growth is protected and fostered.

The circus ring in the center of the next scene (Figure 28.3: "The circus") suggests the beginning of a centering or totality in herself. The animals here are no longer fenced in; they are performing under the

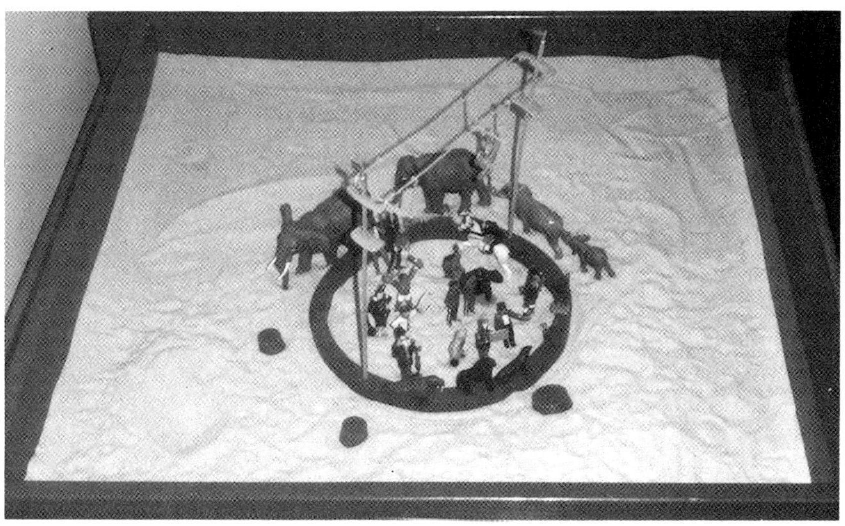

Figure 28.3

guidance of human intelligence. This is a different kind of control, requiring skill and judgment. A family of four elephants is circling outside the ring. The elephant is apparently of special significance to Kathy.

During this session Kathy told me that she was going to be on a jury at a pet show. So she was going to be the judge rather than the one judged. She also commented on a scratch on her arm. She said that her cat did it, but that he did not mean to. She added, "He does it when he is purring. It's a purr scratch." Loving and hurting may be combined in the same act.

At the next session Kathy made four sand scenes. The first three included: motorcycle and horse races, again referring to developing skills and to being judged; a woman about to dive into a pool, into the unconscious; and a prince who wins a duel and will wed the princess – a royal marriage, a union between Kathy's internal masculine and feminine is underway.

For her final scene in this session, Kathy placed a baby in a crib in the center (Figure 28.4: "Nativity scene"). She then added the Virgin Mary, Joseph, and the wise men around the baby. She built up a whole forest around the crèche and finally she added her familiar greenhouse.

The emphasis on plant life and growth (the trees and hothouse) and the newborn baby in this tray speak of new developments that are going on within her. The baby is the Christ child. This may just be because she did this tray in December near Christmas, but it may also be that there is process taking place on an archetypal level, the birth of the divine child.

Figure 28.4

Figure 28.5

In the following session she made an almost identical scene (Figure 28.5: "Second nativity scene"). The first nativity scene must have been so important that it was imprinted into her unconscious. She could not have consciously remembered it so exactly. This time, however, she added a bride, recalling the earlier sand scene where a prince and princess were to be married.

Kathy said her next sandplay scene was a celebration of the queen's birthday. Again the image refers to a royal birth, this time the emergence of the archetypal feminine.

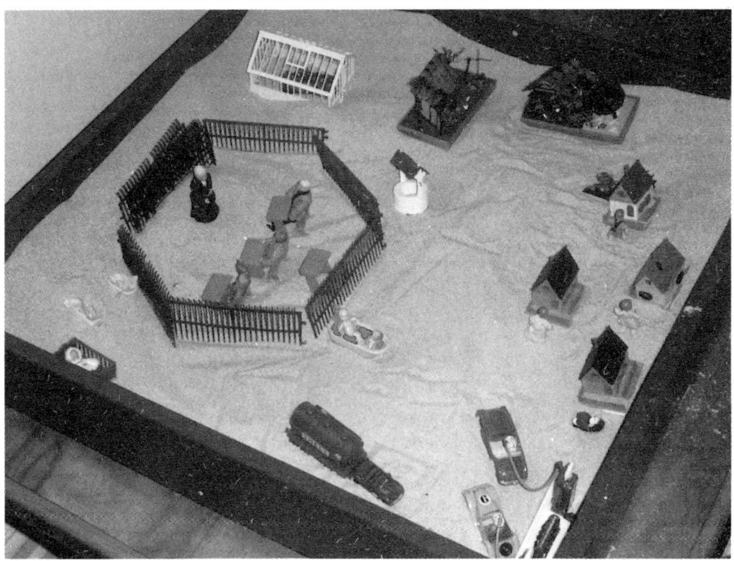

Figure 28.6

In her next scene (Figure 28.6: "Parents attending school") adults are sitting in a classroom on the left and children are in front of the four houses on the right. This is a real switch; the parents have to go to school and the children get to stay home!

There is lots of new life in this tray, babies in cribs and babies in tubs, nine babies in all. Two autos are getting gas and the gas truck carries an additional supply of energy. The cars and the houses suggest the activation of both the masculine and the feminine. Kathy must learn both to perform in school and to relate to or care about others.

The next six sand scenes alternated between nurturing (mothers with babies, woman milking cow, animals eating or drinking); uncontrolled aggression (Indians shooting indiscriminately); controlled aggression (animals inside and fenced in); and gradual lessening of these controls (animals inside *and* outside of fences).

And then we come to another centering (Figure 28.7: "Black knight riding a black horse"). This time Kathy put a knight dressed in black on a black horse into the sand. She moved the horse and rider around and around in a circle which eventually spiralled into the center. At the very end she put in an elephant coming into the scene from the left. The elephant may represent contents emerging from the unconscious and approaching her dark heroic masculine, but not threateningly.

During the next series of sessions, Kathy made many scenes of daily life, sorting out girls vs. boys, good vs. bad, gardens vs. schools, compliance vs. rebellion. In one she made a school for boys, who were "all bad,"

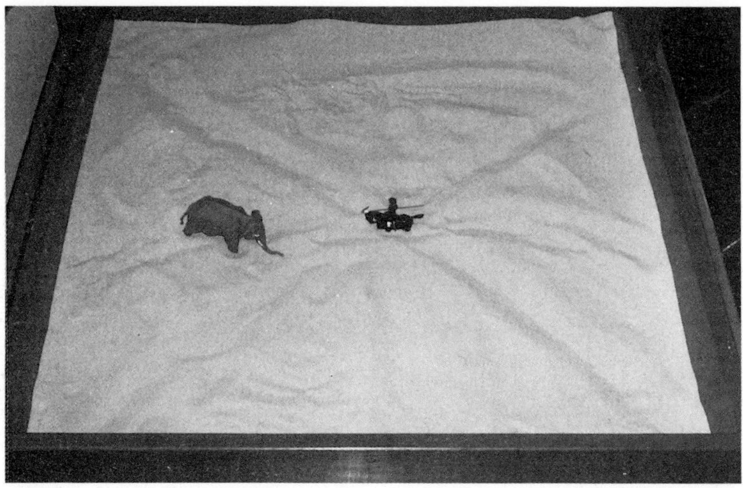

Figure 28.7

she said. There were many containers in this scene as well (thatched houses, bungalows, ships, cribs with babies). So she was providing herself with multiple experiences of containment in the sandtray.

In this same session she wanted permission to use the reserve items stored in the cabinet. I attempted to contain her, firmly prohibiting their use. She said that she could not complete the scene without the extra items. At the next session, we negotiated, and I withdrew my too confining prohibition. This was one of many transference–countertransference interactions that paralleled the making of the sand scenes.

In another scene, she separated the school, which connotes achievement or performance and the masculine, from the garden, nature, which connotes the feminine. And she said that both "bad boys and bad girls stay in school." So now not all boys are bad, and not all girls are good.

Later Kathy combined the achievement-oriented school with the naturally growing garden. And during this same session Kathy devotedly practiced her visual-motor skills by putting flowers into garden plots, again combining masculine performance with feminine nature. Kathy admired what she had done. Her feeling good about herself further strengthened her ego, which in turn increased her good feelings about herself. The reinforcing vicious circle had been replaced by a reinforcing self-healing circle.

In the final scene of this series (Figure 28.8: "A city for everyone") there are boys and girls; children and grownups; a black girl with black doll; American Indians and Japanese. There is a river through the center with a bridge over it connecting the two sides. But here the two sides do not seem to represent differentiated sets of opposites. Perhaps in this scene the bridge signifies a more generalized connecting or bringing

Figure 28.8

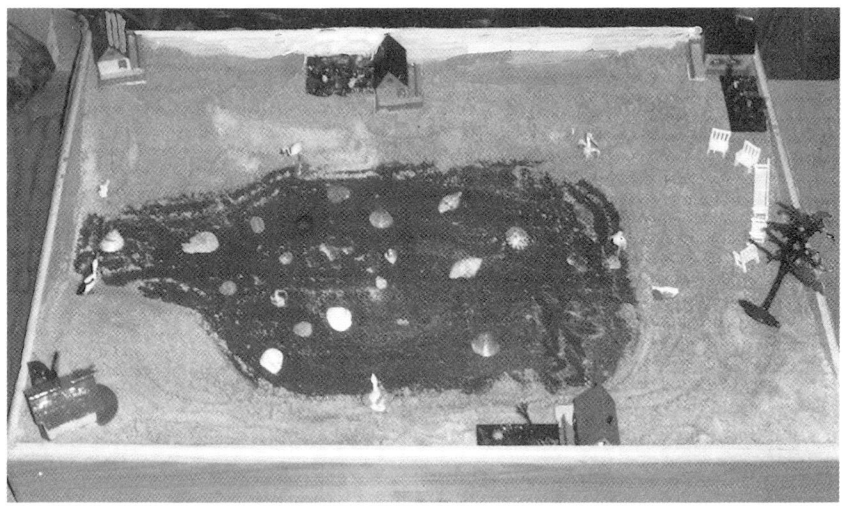

Figure 28.9

together. Kathy called this tray "A city for everyone," indicating an integration of many facets of herself.

Kathy told me that the water in the stream was holy water but there were germs in it that went from the lower right to the upper left; therefore people had to drink out of it at the lower right. She put a green stone in the stream and said that people try to dive in to get it, but they can not get it because it is too deep. Perhaps there is some "treasure" in the unconscious that is too deep for her to obtain at this time.

In the next scene (Figure 28.9: "Water scene with shells and birds") there is water shaped like a bottle or perhaps a womb. There are other feminine symbols in this scene along with the water itself, shells, and houses. The positive feminine is being reaffirmed or strengthened.

After this tray Kathy made a contrasting scene which represented an experience of the negative, hostile feminine. In it she portrayed a mother bawling out her daughter. And at the bottom there is a cannon ready to shoot.

The next sessions alternated between fighting (she had us shoot at each other and talked about fights with her brother and her mother) and fencing (elephant family fenced in). Then came a session which was marked by more testing and general negativism than any other. She dropped wet globs of sand on the floor. A couple of times she started to make something and then destroyed it. She made "rules" for her benefit and then rescinded them. Finally she had us play in the sand shooting at each other with the miniature cannons.

At the following session she wanted to talk. She talked about teachers and children, and grownups and children, and baby sitters. It was a good session of sharing.

In her next scene, there were oriental figures crossing a bridge. She said that everyone was afraid of the salamander and snake. A person with a lantern at the upper right was watching to see that the water flowed down to the stream. Kathy said, "They drink it and wash their hands and face in it." As a symbol, the lantern represents consciousness, which here insures that the water can be used for purification.

In the next three sessions Kathy made gardens outside of the tray, on the table, using the hothouse each time. In all three sessions, the door to the hothouse was left open. Kathy did not use the greenhouse again after this. It was as if it had served its purpose; it had provided her with a protected place where she could grow and flourish.

At the next session, we did some shooting over a sand wall she had made in the tray. At the following session, which was the last for a period of four months of vacations (hers and mine), she brought me a pencil holder, a gift related to school performance, and drew "love" on the blackboard. Her anger had been shown at one session and her caring at the next. She did not need to enclose animals in fences.

She sent me a postcard from Italy with the statue of Moses on it. Moses must truly epitomize the law-giving masculine authority of the father. She was sending me a picture of one of the main themes in her life and her therapy.

The first three trays Kathy made after our separation repeated some of the motifs she had focused on earlier (animals in fences, schools and

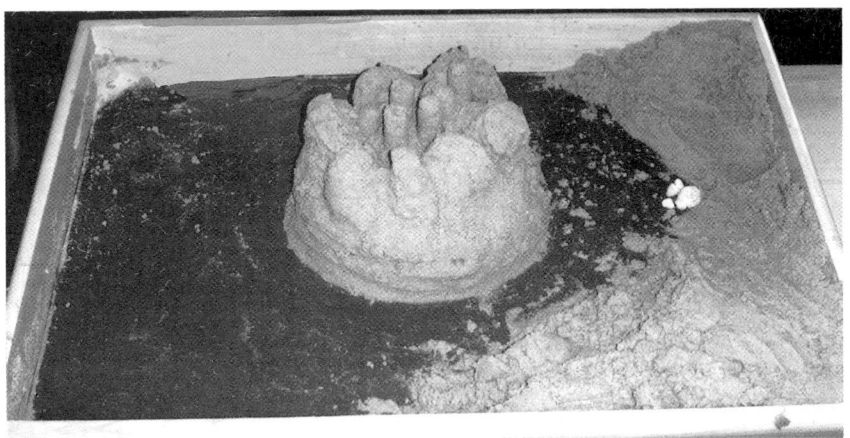

Figure 28.10

gardens, children and grownups). This commonly happens after a vacation; it is a kind of review of the course of therapy prior to the interruption. She talked about school and, for the first time, asked me many questions about myself, such as "Did you like pretty new clothes as a little girl?" She was now identifying with the therapist, the authority whom she had previously either opposed or loved.

Her last sandtray scene (Figure 28.10: "Castle") was again a centering. She made a central mound of sand and then had us make towers together. We put wet sand into test tubes, and then carefully turned the molded sand out onto the mound, forming a castle. At the right center, where the greenhouse had most frequently appeared, she placed three shells, bringing together the feminine symbol of the shell with the masculine number "three."

She said that a princess lived in the castle and explained, "Her father keeps her there." I asked if he was mean to her and she said, "No, he protects her."

We did some more shooting at each other with the miniature cannons from one side of the tray to the other. She said that the princess went to the bottom of the castle during our battle. So she was able to hide and protect herself when fighting was going on. Then, while looking for a lost bullet, Kathy destroyed the whole thing. I think this may have marked the freeing of herself from her negative father complex.

At the next session she talked about school and did not use the sandtray. Then she set up another garden scene on the table with a bridge over a stream and explained, "The water goes under this bridge and comes out and it is pure." The holy water which was previously contaminated with germs now flows clear.

In our final session in the sandplay room, Kathy drew a boy and girl going to a party on the blackboard. The union between masculine and feminine had appeared in archetypal form as the wedding of the prince and princess in her earlier trays. Now the inner unity between them comes in the form of a relationship between an ordinary boy and girl of about her own age. After this, I saw Kathy once a month in my office for the next six months until we mutually decided to terminate the therapy.

Two years later her mother sent me Kathy's report card showing all good grades. And she wrote, "What pleases me especially is that she is being a 13-year-old to the hilt at home with me!" Three years after that her mother called me and said that Kathy was doing very well in high school. She was well launched on her journey.

Chapter 29

Jim: the development of the masculine

Jim first came to see me in his late 20s because of phobias. He was primarily afraid of heights, and also of closed and open spaces, crossing bridges, losing his parents, being on a sphere in space, and the unknown. He asked, "Where did we come from, why are we here and where are we going?", the same questions that we all ask when we are growing up, and many times afterwards. He also had a fear of having sexual relationships because he had grown up being made to feel that sex was bad and dirty. He later said, at the age of 47, "It all still remains a mystery to me."

Jim saw his father as a strict, cold and unloving man who was more interested in his manufacturing company than in his family. His father once wrote, "Let us always maintain a strong sales force that eats, sleeps, lives, and dreams our products."

Jim loved his mother but complained that she "smothered" him to death. He resented this, saying, "You can't develop yourself when you're dominated by your mother." Jim was the youngest of four children. He had one older sister, and two older married brothers. When Jim first came for therapy, he stayed for nearly ten years. By the end of that period, he had joined his father's company, had achieved considerable control over most of his phobias, and felt more at ease with a few women.

Ten years later, when his father died, Jim returned to therapy. He was now in his late 40s. His phobias were again bothering him. He bought a tape recorder and talked into it while he took an elevator up as high as he thought he could go and then brought the tapes to my office and played them so we could listen to them together. He also spent many hours lambasting himself because of his inertia. He felt worthless and yet wanted to succeed. He had apparently internalized his father's demands.

During this time I had acquired a sandtray, and one day Jim said that he would like to make a sand picture. He made four trays in four successive weeks, and then two more, each after intervals of several months.

Jim described his first scene (see Figure 22.7, p. 90) as a vacation cabin at the beach. But he made no attempt to move the sand away so that the blue base of the tray could represent water. Jim also used a bridge in this first tray, but the opposites on either side of the bridge were not well defined. There is a dry land area on the right that has implied connections with water below the ground (garden pool, two wells, trees). And there is a water area on the left that has dried plant life scattered around in it. Each side is an unclear mixture of wet and dry. Even the stream under the bridge was not made until after the whole scene was completed, as if it were a kind of afterthought.

I asked him about the fence after he had completed the tray and he explained, "It is the edge of the property. It's between where you are living and the outside world." He added, "Maybe I need a cow," and put in a bull drinking out of a trough. A cow is certainly a mother figure, but he chose a bull instead of a cow. This seems like another reversal or mix-up, he confuses the masculine and feminine as he does the dry and moist. Or perhaps he unconsciously detected a bull-like animus behind his mother's overly solicitous attentions.

He initially put a large egg in the tray, but shortly afterwards removed it, saying that it appealed to him but that it belonged in the mountains, not at the beach.

In his second scene (see Figure 22.8, p. 90), he scraped sand off the bottom of the tray to make water and pushed sand with both hands into the middle of the tray to make a mountain. Land and water are here clearly differentiated, and a centering process seems to be going on around the strong masculine mountain. He said, "Maybe they're all coming up to challenge this guy at the top (of the mountain), and these guys (shellfish etc.) don't give a damn. And this guy (crocodile) is half way between. He would care if the gorilla came down to the water." The gorilla on top of the mountain seems to be unafraid of heights. And his male animal strength can intimidate the crocodile below, which may represent the devouring side of the negative mother.

At the next session, Jim told me that he had had sexual intercourse during the week, for the first time in his life at the age of 51 years. He was elated! He asked, "Do you think it was the sandtray I did last time that let me do that?"

Jim's next scenes depicted this release of new vitality in different forms. In his third scene, he pushed the sand aside to make a creek, so there was immediately the sense of movement, of a new flowing. He added a frog carrying a baby on its back, and then a large upright egg almost in the center of the tray, which he later removed. In addition to the frog and the egg, there were many other signs of the new, of transformation, in this tray, including snakes and flying white doves. And there were baby frogs and geese with their parents, indicating an acceptance of the dependence of the young.

Jim put a canoe in the stream and said the figure in the canoe was himself. He added, "I don't know whether I'm going up or down the river." But he has begun a journey.

His next scene was all dry land, in contrast to the previous scene. But Jim made a road in the sand with his fingers, again signifying a journey. He included a gas station which provided him with energy for his trip; the "Shell" sign on the gas station brings in an allusion to the feminine.

A man with a basket of flowers, emblems of feeling, was the "station keeper." Phallic guard towers overlook and protect the journey. There is more differentiation within the masculine in this tray. Not only can men now run a business, like his father, but they can also carry feelings and be protective.

He placed a fence in front of a house with a dog coming through the open gate. In his first scene, the fence isolated him from the rest of life. Now there is a gate in the fence and the dog, his instinctual feeling, can go through the gate and connect the house with the world outside. The last figures he put in the tray were a boy and girl, each carrying a pail. Male and female can be together, and both can be nurturing.

And, at the very last, he put a woman with her hand outstretched in an upper corner of this tray. Two months later he reported a dream: "I am walking with a woman (the one with whom he had had sex) along the edge of a grape arbor way up high. I jumped down and then I helped her down. She was helping me and I was helping her." His fear of heights had started in college after he had gone to the edge of a cliff at the instigation of a woman. Now, in a dream, he and the feminine work together, helping each other down from the heights.

His fifth scene again included a house, fence, and open gate. A man (replacing the young boy) was working, accompanied by a cat. A woman (replacing the young girl) stood in a patio with a dog by her side. Masculine and feminine are more grown up and comfortable together.

Jim tried to place an owl on top of the house, but it kept sliding off so he put it into a tree. The owl, like the gorilla, does not seem to mind being up high. Jim described him as a "wise old owl that has his eye on everything." The owl seems here to be the Wise Old Man type of Self symbol, the masculine Self. Looking at the whole scene, Jim said, "It's like an oasis away from it all. Tranquility and peace."

In his final scene (Figure 29.1), Jim differentiated clearly between land and sea. After building up the upper right of the tray with driftwood, he added dried foliage and said, "It's something that's died." He then put in black and yellow rubber figures, which he saw as a woman and a man. He identified the black figure as his woman friend and the yellow figure as himself, and noted that each had one foot in the water. Immediately afterwards he put in an egg. So there is first death, then a coming together of the abstract masculine and feminine, and then a birth. And this time

Figure 29.1

he placed the egg horizontally, saying that it should be that way. And he is right; that is the way eggs are in nature. And in this final tray he left the egg.

Jim terminated analysis soon after this sandtray. Four years later, he called me to come in again. We met for two appointments, and then decided together that he might profit from seeing a man for more therapy. I referred him to one of my male colleagues. I learned from both of them, after a few months, that a good relationship had been established. At the time I retired nine years later, Jim was still seeing his new analyst.

In my last contact with Jim's analyst, he told me that Jim had left his father's business and had become a consultant. Most of his phobias had abated, except for fear of travelling by plane. He was still dating the same woman, but it had become a platonic relationship. It had been sexual for only a brief period after his breakthrough in the sandplay series.

Jim's need for continued therapy throughout much of his adult life suggests the presence of a deep pathology. Yet, according to his analyst, Jim often refers to his sandplay experience with me and values it. Although sandplay did not bring him a complete healing, it did help him to experience a breakthrough in his masculine development.

Chapter 30

Ida: a woman's individuation through sandplay

A question sometimes asked about sandplay is whether it only reflects the place a person has already reached in their individuation, or whether it actually brings about that individuation. I think it both reflects and effects. The creative process is always therapeutic, and the creative product may also picture the stage of one's development.

To illustrate how the individuation process can take place in sandplay, I am going to present the sandplay series of a 40-year-old woman whom I shall call Ida.

Ida was the kind of woman who wanted to understand with her intellect. She was a bright, introverted, intuitive person whose feeling function was naturally superior to her thinking function. But she had lived under the domination of rationality for so long that she had grown to believe that masculine logic was superior to feminine eros. She had to use her intellect to "hold things together."

She started to do sandplay nearly two years after beginning therapy with me. During the next two years Ida made seventy-one sand scenes in ninety sessions with me. Typically, for the first forty-four sandplay sessions, she made a scene in the first half of the session and we talked about the scene in the last half. But the forty-fifth scene marked a change in the course of her therapy. After that we made almost no references to her subsequent twenty-six trays. And it is this last sequence of twenty-six scenes that shows, in its minute changes, the actual process of her individuation.

Ida's initial sandplay scene (Figure 30.1) depicts her primary conflict and anticipates a possible resolution. The mostly female animals in the left upper corner (elephant, cow, mare, and colt) represent her instinctual or natural feminine side. The policeman standing with his hand raised and the policeman on a motorcycle on the lower left side represent patriarchal authority. Ida commented, "Law stops growth; I like the instinctual."

Ida identified herself as the diving girl right of center and indicated that she was going to go through the tunnel in the mound of sand to the

Figure 30.1

lower right. The woman on the horse and the man on the bicycle are also headed towards the tunnel; the feminine and masculine are accompanying her on her journey. It is as if Ida is turning her back on the conflict represented by the animals and the policemen on the left side of the tray and is ready to submit to another direction, to take a different course.

Ida made no reference to the American Indians in the top right corner: a teepee, a chief, a squaw with a baby, a totem pole. Yet she is heading towards this side. In retrospect, I realized that a dual respect for both authority and instinct is deeply ingrained in Native American culture. So the upper right portrays a possible solution, an integration of these opposites which would resolve the conflict. She did not say anything about the Indian grouping, which suggests that the possibility of this resolution was not yet in her consciousness.

Ida's twenty-eight sand scenes over the next eleven months were dominated by a conscious struggle to extricate herself from her bondage to patriarchal authority which was linked to her idealization of her father, her husband, and her minister. In several trays, for example, she deliberately portrayed other feelings, both hostility and vulnerability, in relation to her husband.

She also translated her reading in Jungian psychology into sand scenes. During this phase of her work, there were no haphazard arrangements of figures. All of the items she placed in the tray played a part in a unified, often geometrical, whole. And, after completing each sand scene, Ida usually volunteered a description of what was going on and what each scene meant.

In one tray from this period, for example, she built up the sand into four successively higher terraces. She said that the lowest level on the right was the collective unconscious, the next was her own personal unconscious, the next was practical everyday outer life, and the highest on the left, populated by priests, kings, and Indian chiefs, was the spiritual level.

Figure 30.2

The last thing she placed was a stone close to the center of the sandtray which she said was herself.

At another session, she consciously set out to make a scene which represented her current understanding of the four psychological functions. At the top center of the tray she grouped together several figures representing "Sensation" including a girl diving into water. On the lower end of this same vertical axis she placed a cluster of figures representing "Intuition" such as the witch who could make magic. On the horizontal axis she portrayed "Feeling" on the left with, among others images, an impulsive child. And on the right she used several objects to depict "Thinking," including a man teacher. She said that the figure in the center, this time an oriental girl, unified all of the functions in herself.

In her outer life during this time, Ida was trying to cope with an unhappy marriage, the critical illnesses of both her mother and her father and her guilt feelings about all three. Ida's level of anxiety fluctuated, but was always intensified when she had any gynecological symptoms requiring medical attention. In the past, she had had a psychotic break after undergoing a D&C (dilation and curetage). At the time I began seeing Ida, her gynecologist was trying to postpone further surgery. She hoped that Ida's anxiety could be diminished and her inner resources could be sufficiently strengthened so that she could withstand future gynecological procedures without feeling that she was being robbed of her femininity.

Ida was working hard in therapy. She made a clay torso figure at home to use in the sandtray to represent herself; she brought in dreams, drawings, poems, her diary; she took correspondence courses in psychology and writing so that she could write her own story; she took a class in sculpting. Each creative activity revealed her innate talents. She was highly commended for her essays and stories in her writing course and won a prize for one of her first pieces of sculpture. She read avidly in her eagerness to understand psychology and tried to apply what she was learning

Figure 30.3

to break through the net of confusion in which she lived. In many sessions she bombarded me with questions, both general and personal – about ideals and reality, masculine and feminine, sex and religion – trying to sort out all of these areas.

Despite all of her dedication to her task, Ida's sand scenes mirrored an increasing disturbance. In one scene (Figure 30.2), Ida portrayed her homicidal and suicidal fantasies in the sand; she buried both her husband and herself. Two sessions later she came in with intensified anxiety, expressed her distress at having "done such a thing," and hastened to un-bury the figures. Since the earlier sand scene had been dismantled, she first had to re-bury the figures representing her husband and herself before she could go through the process of un-burying them and bringing them back to life. The shadows behind the two figures at right center are from the indentations left after Ida raised the figures up out of the sand. She could portray these fantasies in the sandtray, and experience them more tangibly than she could by visualizing them or describing them in words, and yet avoid the risk of acting out in a real way in the world.

Ida also reported to me that her gynecologist had advised her that she might need further surgery in the near future. In the following session, Ida placed figures representing herself and me alone together in the sand-tray. And shortly thereafter she suffered a second psychotic episode. But gains had been made. This episode was brought under control by medication and more frequent therapy sessions; hospitalization was not required.

In subsequent trays, Ida used the king and queen figures for the first time. She placed them in the center of the tray for three consecutive sessions. Looking back, I now feel that she was attempting to regain her stability and control by repeatedly representing the royal *coniunctio*. She was trying desperately to hold onto something and to think herself out of the dreaded place of psychotic disturbance.

Figure 30.4

Then one day Ida came in and put a single figure who represented herself in the center of the tray, all alone (Figure 30.3). This did not appear to be a gesture of feeling abandoned or of giving up, but rather a representation of strength. She had the strength to confront the fact of aloneness. In the earlier scene, she and I had been alone together in the sandtray. But, this time, she was all alone. This forty-fifth session marked the turning point in her sandplay work and in the course of her illness. At the next session she came in saying she felt better, and she was better. The psychotic episode was over.

It would be difficult to over-emphasize the contrast between the sand scenes preceding and following this scene of herself alone. She left the intellectual stance; she stopped trying to make everything have a rational meaning. She let the psyche take over, and an inner centering process was activated.

In her next scene (Figure 30.4), Ida made the first of many centered pools. There is a stream coming into the pool from the bottom left corner. Two American Indians are canoeing in the pool. A tree and the tepee and Indian squaw with baby that had appeared in her initial sand scene are in the upper left. Contrary to her practice after making all of her sand scenes prior to the one of herself alone, Ida volunteered no comments on this tray, and I asked for none.

Sometimes the left and lower parts of the sand scene represent the unconscious, and the right and upper parts represent the conscious. While not invariably true, this can at times be a helpful guideline, and may be true here. So the water coming from the lower left seems to represent energy from the unconscious coming into an inner centered place.

The area in Ida's initial tray that had hinted at a solution to her problem had been peopled by Indians; this scene, which ushers in a new phase of her individuation process, is also peopled by Indians. There were no

Indians in any of the intervening forty-five scenes. Thus, there appears to be a link between the initial scene and this one made fifteen months later.

The following scene was remarkably similar to this tray; again there were Indians in a canoe in a stream that connected the lower left with a central pool. But there were small, significant changes; this time Ida added a piece of driftwood that looked like a huge rock. The same piece of driftwood appeared in the next twenty sand scenes. In retrospect, I think that it provided a kind of solidity for her.

In the next scene only animals appeared; for the first time, there were no humans. This represents what Kalff calls the animal–vegetative stage or earliest stage of ego development (Kalff 1980: 32). This apparent regression to an earlier developmental stage coincides with Ida's release from trying to reason things out. She is now able to let something happen without consciously having to will it.

In subsequent scenes, Ida returned to using human figures. In addition to the familiar Indians in a canoe, she re-used the diving girl. She had appeared in the initial tray but only rarely since then; now she would continue to appear in most of Ida's remaining trays. She also used a girl lying on her stomach and a boy sitting near the girl, who were to reappear in the next twenty sand scenes. She usually placed them on top of the driftwood "rock". They may have represented youthful feminine and masculine parts of herself observing from a solidly secure place. At one point she said, "It's like they are looking at a myth." Feminine and masculine companions had also been present in her initial sand scene. Again there is a link between this final sequence of sand scenes and her first tray. It is as if Ida, or the part of herself represented by the diving girl, had gone through the tunnel into another space.

In one of these scenes, Ida used a bridge for the first time. The bridge was placed over a channel which itself connected two bodies of water, so connections were made between water masses as well as between land masses. Connectors such as bridges and channels can represent the joining of parts of one's self. Perhaps, for Ida, the bridges between land masses brought together more conscious parts of herself, and the channels between water masses joined more unconscious parts.

The following scene had a large mound of sand, rather than a pool, in its center. This mound was surrounded by water, a mountain island, like a Self symbol rising up from the unconscious. An oriental ship replaced the Indian canoe. The man–woman couple that Ida had un-buried in Figure 30.2 was included here, perhaps as a reference to her married self as compared with the more individual self represented by the diving girl.

She also placed several trees in the scene. One or more trees, a symbol of vegetative growth, of life, appeared in each of the twenty-five scenes following the scene of herself alone. This was again in marked contrast to the earlier scenes; she had used trees only rarely in her first series. In

Figure 30.5

fact, in those earlier trays so dominated by the intellect, she rarely used any symbolic images. And when she did use them, it was in a studied and conscious manner.

In her next scene, Ida again made a central pool. A pool would form the center of all her subsequent sandtrays until the final three. She also brought in some glue from home to mend the oriental ship, having noticed that it was broken. The act of mending the ship seemed to coincide with the mending of her psyche. Or, perhaps, it signified the repairing of the vehicle she needed for her journey. A couple of sessions later she drove to my office by herself. It was the first time she had been able to come alone in many weeks.

An important new addition – treasures – appeared in her next trays. In the first of these, Ida placed pieces of turquoise and three small colored spheres next to stones and a tree in the left center of the tray. She said that the turquoise was a treasure and the diving girl on the right side was going to get it. In the following scene, the turquoise and glass spheres were placed around the diving girl, who was now on the left side.

In the next tray (Figure 30.5), the treasures again returned close to the diving girl. And a new object appeared, a red raft in the center of the pool. The water vehicle for her journey has changed from an Indian canoe to an oriental ship to a red raft. The raft has a double symbolic value. It keeps her above the water, so she can avoid the risk of being lost in the unconscious like the diving girl. Yet, on a raft she is near the water, almost a part of it, not enclosed and away from it as she would be in a ship. And the redness of the raft represents and helps her hold onto her ever stronger feeling function.

A cow, a bull, and a calf stand together on the right side beside a tree. This is the first time that a complete animal family with both parents and

Figure 30.6

a child has been shown, again a manifestation of a more secure feeling function.

In the following scene the animal mother and child changed from cow and calf to mare and colt. Perhaps this represented a transition from a more complacent to a more spirited form of mothering. The man–woman couple was separated for the first time. The woman was joined in the upper right of the tray by a bride, a milkmaid, and a witch. The man was joined on the lower right by a knight on horseback. After the feeling function is secure and the feminine becomes more diversified, a strong animus can appear.

A Japanese geisha, whom Ida called "feminine mystery," appeared in the next tray on the right side, and continued to appear there, rising from bottom to center to top, until the last scene. The red raft was now beached on the shore. It had done its work and was not seen again. For the first time Ida used shells, often a symbol of the feminine principle, along with a well, which provides nourishing access to the unconscious. A cottage with a car in front of it indicated another juxtaposition of feminine and masculine.

Several of the next scenes nearly duplicated this tray. After completing one of these trays, Ida made one of her now rare comments: "The left seems inner, real, stable. The right, or outer, is changing." She seemed to have *observed* this trend in her scenes rather than to have consciously tried to *make* them this way. Something important was taking place that did not require her conscious judgment or decision. She just had to let it happen.

In one of these trays, Ida added a dog and a cat on a stone jutting out over the pool. The addition of domestic animals to the trays reflected further participation of the instinctual and feeling sides of herself. These same animals continued to appear for the next four sand scenes.

Figure 30.7

In the next scene (Figure 30.6), Ida made a stream running out of the pool towards the right to the man–woman couple. She put the canoe with Indians in this stream exiting from the pond; previously (see Figure 30.4) they had been entering the pond. At the next session, Ida said that she had not liked what she had done the previous time when she made a stream that ran off to the right; it was as if she had become fearful that she might be prematurely letting something leave the sacred inner place and enter outer reality. But the fact that she could make the exiting stream at all manifests a growing strength to deal with the outer.

She returned to the central pool in the following scene (Figure 30.7) and added sheep and lambs heading down an incline to the pool – the replenishing of the instinctual life after a too precarious exit. She added a knight on horseback on the left. He had originally appeared in an earlier scene on the right, which is sometimes seen as the more conscious side of the tray. Perhaps she had previously been projecting her animus out into the world. And, in moving him to the left, to what may be the more unconscious side, she was beginning to introject him. Perhaps she was no longer so dependent on the outer men in her life.

Ida's gynecologist, meanwhile, had recommended another D&C in the hope of forestalling the need for a hysterectomy. And now Ida was able to uneventfully undergo the same surgical procedure that precipitated her psychotic episode five years before. When I went to the hospital to see her the evening after the operation, she showed no adverse reactions.

At her next visit, the sandtray Ida made (Figure 30.8) was remarkably similar to the one she had made five days before her surgery (Figure 30.7). But there is an important addition to the post-surgery sand scene: her three children are there along with her husband and herself. After the surgery, which she may have experienced as a threat to her child-producing organ,

Figure 30.8

Figure 30.9

she brings the children she has actually given birth to into the sand scene, demonstrating an appreciation of her own womanness.

The centered pool had served its purpose in stabilizing her inner being. After this first post-surgery tray, she made no more pools. And she had no unfavorable effects from the surgery. She had developed a secure inner feminine.

The following two scenes were almost identical. In both, the central pool is again replaced by a large mound. In the first (Figure 30.9), a treasure is on the top of the mountain and a new figure representing Ida stands at the bottom; the diving girl is gone. A girl with a trowel squats beside two workmen to the upper left of the mound. Ida, her husband

Figure 30.10

Figure 30.11

and her children are again present on the right side behind the trees. The sitting boy and recumbent girl are at the bottom of the mountain in the lower left.

In the second version of this scene (Figure 30.10), two pieces of turquoise have been uncovered on the left at the bottom of the mountain. One piece is beside the girl with the trowel, and one piece is by the girl and boy. The young developing parts of herself have secured treasures close at hand. They did not have to scale the mountain to get them.

The similarity of these last two scenes is an example of a scene's being "imprinted" into the sandplayer's unconscious. The similarity is too close to have resulted from conscious memory. A similar imprinting occurred in Kathy's two nativity scenes (Figures 28.4 and 28.5, p. 126); and in Sam's two scenes made ten years apart (Figures 22.1, p. 84 and 22.2, p. 85). Ida's many sacred pool scenes showed this same phenomenon. The ones she made before and after her surgery (Figures 30.7, p. 145 and 30.8, p. 146), were nearly identical except for the addition of her children. And her two mountain trays were also nearly identical, with the only significant change being the addition of the treasure at the bottom of the mountain. I think this phenomenon is a remarkable indicator of the ability of sandplay to engage the unconscious and effect an ongoing relationship with it.

In Ida's final tray (Figure 30.11) she used almost all the human figures that had appeared in her previous seventy scenes. The torso at top center is the piece she made at home to represent herself; the figure opposite it is a witch. Going clockwise from the torso at the top, the figures are: nun, diving girl, policeman, boy on bicycle, three Japanese women, the Geisha, armed warrior, witch, Robinson Crusoe, Indian chief, squaw with baby, priest, young girl, milkmaid, girl squatting, girl lying on stomach, boy sitting, girl, woman, man, torso. It was as if she was bringing all these inner parts of herself, both masculine and feminine, as well as significant people in her outer environment, together into a whole. There are pairs of animals in three of the corners; in the fourth upper left corner there is a family of lambs under a tree. So the final form was a squared circle, a mandala, a symbol of wholeness. Ida had come to the end of her sandplay journey.

Ida was to be challenged by one more critical test of her emotional as well as her physical stamina. One month after this final sandtray, she began to hemorrhage massively, and had to have an emergency hysterectomy in the middle of the night. When I saw her the next morning she looked up at me and said, "I'm all right."

After I had made a second hospital visit two days later, Ida and I did not see each other for five weeks. In preparation for my vacation, I had arranged for Ida to work with another therapist while I was gone. After my return, Ida spent our first session mostly in telling me how well she had gotten along. The fact that she could successfully withstand the hysterectomy and almost immediately undergo an extended separation from me had demonstrated to Ida the solidity of her new emotional strength.

Ida continued her analytic sessions for several months after this, consolidating her gains. Some sessions were spent reviewing pictures of her sand scenes, bringing the two levels of therapy, verbal and non-verbal, together. And, after over five years of therapy, she completed her work with me.

I have been in touch with Ida several times since she stopped, and she has not only maintained her gains but also made further advancements. After the break-up of a mutually unsatisfying marriage, she established herself in another state and took courses in a field which allowed her to get a well-paid job. She continued to have a close relationship with all three children. The last time I heard from her, she had completed her autobiography, changed jobs, and obtained an advanced degree.

What happened in the twenty-six sessions after the herself-all-alone tray? I believe they demonstrate that sand scenes are not merely portraits of developmental stages that are occurring, that sandplay is in itself a form of therapy. The very act of moving the sand and adding water, of repetitively forming identical backgrounds and adding identical figures, of using symbols of the feminine more and more frequently, of changing the location of significant figures, of "un-burying" the murdered figures, of "un-doing" the exiting channel, all of these experiences in the sand contributed to Ida's healing process. She made so many nearly identical scenes that it seemed as if something like a numinous imprinting was going on in her unconscious psyche.

While this second series of sand scenes was being created, our verbal interchange following the sandplay was not about the sandtray Ida had just made, and was seldom about her dreams. Our talk was about day-to-day coping with outer things: her husband; the children's activities; visits to her ill parents; misunderstandings with her sisters; the drudgery of keeping house; sexual fantasies and reality; religion; her feelings about me. Often we discussed what she had been reading and sometimes what she had been writing; our relationship at first supported, and then strengthened, her ego. A different level of analytic work took place in the sandtray. Both were going on side by side, without making any direct verbal connection between the two.

Dora Kalff wrote in a letter to me her thoughts about the two series of trays that Ida made, the first forty-four with comment, and the last twenty-seven without comment:

> I thought it was very interesting that the first forty-four pictures did not show so much the process as the later ones where hardly any explanations were made. This proves what I say that a silent understanding constellates the synchronistic moment from where the next step evolves. However, as this patient started by the verbal analysis she probably experienced the explained "scenes" as an intermediate state between the verbal and the non-verbal analysis.

The symbolic value of the centered pool was primary in Ida's progress. The pool served as a womb throughout the series, representing not only her own physical uterus but also her inner psychic center, the holding container of the analysis, and a place of access to the unconscious. Its sexual implications may be important: the initial pool with the entering channel could suggest impregnation, and the later pool with the exiting channel could represent a birth which Ida experienced as premature.

The central pool was above all for her a deep inner core, a sacred place where the incubation of her self could take place. She was silent about it, compared with her volubility about her earlier series of scenes, and she put treasures in and beside it. Ida, like most of the women in my Hestia and Athena study, needed to withdraw from being over-extended outside herself and to relate to her inner self; as the inner achieved validation, she could eventually go forth again. I think that Ida's final twenty-six sand trays demonstrate this process, or, rather, *are* themselves the process.

The sandtray Ida made after her D&C (Figure 30.8) was nearly identical to the one she had made just prior to it (Figure 30.7). This continuity in the trays speaks to the continuity and security she had discovered in the inner place regardless of what happened on the outside.

After that, she could give up making the pool and produce an opposite form, the mountain. And, after both going down into the water and coming up into the sky, Ida was ready to make her final scene (Figure 30.11). In this tray there is a staying on the surface of the earth. The centered and squared circle is a symbol of the wholeness she had achieved. And then she was able to take her place in the outer world without jeopardizing the inner sacred place that she had found.

ADDENDUM: A LETTER FROM IDA

Dear Dr. Bradway,

I received your manuscript on Friday, and I have read it several times. I want to write right away to let you know how much I like it. Also, I hope you don't mind, but I made a copy of it for myself.

You have written the truth. I agree with everything. Several points which we never talked about were clarified for me. One place was where you refer to the psychotic episode. *No* one would ever put it into words for me, and I guess I'm glad they didn't. I was better off not knowing. But now I am glad to know it because it explains the irrationality of those times. Also, it is nice to have the whole thing put in a nutshell, so to speak. It seems so simple now.

I am truly pleased and honored to have this study done of my sand worlds. I have learned so much from it – both the general picture as you saw it, and the symbolism of the various characters and creations manifested.

The point of your article is that sandplay *is* therapy. And I agree with you. I feel that it definitely contributes to the healing process. It makes the inner world visible and more readily available for observation, comment, self-knowledge and eventual change. At the time of my forty-fifth sandtray when I was all alone, I was fully aware of the fact that I was getting nowhere. All the scenes were repeating the same thing, and I knew that it wasn't what I was looking for. So I gave up trying. I had worked for so long, and I was tired. And I had no place else to go. I really feel that the opportunity of seeing the same pattern being expressed week after week made me realize that it was futile. I was not aware that my thinking was too rational, but I was aware of the futility of it all. The sandtrays *showed* me that I was presenting theory after theory. And it was done in a comparatively short time. I can't imagine how I could have come to the same conclusion without the aid of the sandplay.

Chapter 31

Ilsa: a journey in five trays

Two circumstances sometimes complicate sandplay work which might have a questionable effect on the process. First, a client has two therapists. This situation usually arises when the patient continues with one therapist for verbal therapy while doing a sandplay process with another. What are the problems in such a dual therapy for the patient and for each of the therapists? What are the advantages, if any?

Second, there is an explicit limit to the number of sandplay sessions that can be arranged. Is it detrimental to the process to have a limited number of sessions? What is possible, what can happen in just a few sessions?

Ilsa was one of the first patients I saw for sandplay therapy under these conditions. She was referred to me by a Jungian colleague who does not do sandtray work, in response to her request for a supplementary process at another level. When I talked briefly with this analyst, she said that their analytic hours in the preceding months had been taken up with the kind of everyday problem solving which tends to limit work with the unconscious. The analyst hoped that a non-verbal method such as sandplay might encourage a going beneath the surface. We agreed that: Ilsa would continue with her regular analysis; there would be no interchange between her analyst and me during her work with me; she and her analyst would refrain from discussing her sandplay process until she had completed it; and that six months after completing the process the three of us would meet to go over the slides of the sand scenes together.

Ilsa and I knew at the outset that we could have only a limited number of sessions together. This time the limit was five. I had previously found that the psyche can somehow "rise to the occasion" and make use of whatever time is available if the client is highly motivated, as Ilsa was. She had made a few sand scenes a couple of years before when working with another therapist and had had a good feeling about it. And, although she had great confidence in her current analyst, she was feeling stuck in her life and wanted to try sandplay to see if it would help her.

Figure 31.1

Ilsa and I met for one session to get acquainted and to schedule our sessions for sandplay. I believe that sandplay should not be started until a comfortable co-transference has been established, which may take more than one session, so that the client can fully trust in the safety of the "free and protected space" which is so essential to a successful sandplay process. Perhaps because we were both in a warm trusting connection with the referring analyst, rapport between Ilsa and me was quickly established.

After a brief interchange at the second session, Ilsa made her first sand scene with me (Figure 31.1). She added water to the wet tray, the only tray she used throughout her process. She then formed a stream down the right side of the tray and blocked it with a pile of sand in the center front. The ending of the stream made her feel sad. She said, "It just stops." At our review meeting with her analyst several months later, all three of us realized that the abrupt disappearance of this stream paralleled the disappearance of her own energy for life that she had been experiencing.

The figure in a monk's habit with a white-haired skull head and claw dominates the tray. Ilsa said he seemed threatening. In my mind, I thought of him as an image of how she saw her emotionally cruel stepfather. As is my usual practice, however, I did not tell her my thoughts at that time. When we went over the completed process later, she thought that the "wild monk" might represent more than her stepfather; possibly it also represented her sometimes stormy relationship with her woman partner, or even her frustrated spiritual feelings.

She placed a piece of black obsidian and another stone of the same size made of an amalgam of gray and white behind the threatening monk. She later said that she thought of the obsidian as her stone; as an Aries, she was drawn to the fire of a volcanic rock. She said that it perhaps symbolized her need to be active rather than passive in her struggles with the wild man.

She put an African hut and some palm trees in the lower right corner diagonally opposite the "mad monk." This corner was, for her, a still, serene and sacred place. There was a warm, maternal, holding quality about it. Later, she placed a bridge on the same diagonal, attempting to connect or transcend the opposites represented by these two corners.

Ilsa then set a clay oven in almost the exact center of the tray and added a leopard coming out of it. She saw the oven as "real" and "vital," and the leopard as "not threatening." The leopard represented animal energy coming out of a feminine container, the aggressive side of the feminine coming forth.

She added an autumn tree in the top center; she saw this as a passing away of something, a making room for something. She was then drawn to a crystal shaped like a pyramid. She elevated it, placing it on a mound of sand. It was, she said, "Almost like a watch tower – not protective, but sensing." She associated the pyramid shape with the healing influence of intuition. Perhaps this was an early anticipation of a manifestation of the Self.

After trying out the universal egg entwined by the winged snake in several different places, Ilsa settled on the lower left corner. When we reviewed her slides, I told her the myth of the cosmic egg. Euronome, goddess of fertility, divided the sea from the sky and danced on the waves until the great serpent Ophion raped her. She then assumed the form of a dove and laid the Universal Egg. Ophion, the serpent, encircled the egg seven times and split it open. Out of the broken egg came the whole world.

I see her use of this cosmic or world egg as an attempt to touch down into deeper layers of the unconscious. She also added a silvered tree, which she said was like mercury, an underground element, reinforcing my impression that she was trying to go beneath the surface. And she put many colored glass pellets into the tray which she called "jewels," treasures to be found in the unconscious.

The last figure Ilsa added was a little bear cub. It faces the threatening monk, but its head is turned to look back toward the opposite corner where the maternal or sacred African hut waits. When we looked at the scene later, it seemed as if all that went in the tray before was done in preparation for this confrontation. The successive experiences of threatening monk, sacred hut, aggressive leopard, crystal tower and cosmic egg, all led to this moment when the little bear could challenge the dominating, dangerous man.

On the left side of the second scene (Figure 31.2), two transformations have occurred. The bear cub has become a fawn drinking water from a

Figure 31.2

pond. And the threatening monk has been replaced by Jizo, a Japanese god who is the protector of children. Her stone, the black obsidian, remains in the top left corner. The diagonally opposite corner is now occupied by the world egg encircled by the winged snake. Here it possibly stands for a bringing together of sky (wings), earth (snake) and water (goddess who danced on the waves). The obsidian brings in the element of fire, so that all the four elements are represented on the diagonal.

The pool at the upper right reminded Ilsa of the sign for infinity: ∞. She placed several figures around the pool: a turtle, another symbol of longevity or relative limitlessness; two self-sacrificing pelicans (according to myth, the pelican mother pecks its own breast to obtain blood to feed its young); and a Central American god.

Ilsa described the Russian lady off center right as "strong" and "contemplative." She appears to be circling a mound. Under the mound is a black-and-white stone, which is often used as a symbol of integration. Since the stone is buried here, integration is represented as potential, not yet achieved.

But there has been considerable movement in this tray. The most significant items in the scene are connected with the spiritual or the divine: Jizo, the protective male god who replaces the threatening monk; the baby deer quenching its thirst who replaces the courageous, but all alone, bear cub; and the Central American god positioned in the upper right where it can oversee the whole scene.

Ilsa's next scene (Figure 31.3) brings an image of the mother–child unity into the process, the Eskimo mother holding her baby on the bank of the pond. It also brings in an image of masculine–feminine unity, or perhaps father–mother unity, the pair of wolves barely visible in the lower left corner. Wolves mate for life and make very good parents, something

Figure 31.3

that Ilsa had missed out on. Ilsa placed seed pods, the beginnings of new life, next to each of these images.

Ilsa said that the devil in the lower right, unlike the mad monk, was not threatening. He is "a mock threat, supposed to be scary, but he is not." The baby is being securely held by its mother and Jizo is again close by in the upper right; he also "is not threatened by the devil; he can see through him."

The pond is shaped this time like a seed or a kidney, referring again to the potential for new life (seed) or to the living organ that makes water (kidney). Ilsa felt that the beaded snake slithering into the pond in the lower right represented something spiritual. Ilsa later saw the pool as a centering place and the movement of the snake into its waters as the unblocking of the stream which had come to such a sudden end in the first tray.

A ladder used as a bridge crosses over a depression in the sand. Ilsa said this place felt like a "pit." It is filled with pieces of white shells and black obsidian, a mixture of two sets of opposites: white and black; and water and fire. In the review, she went on to explain that the place of potential treasures in her first sandtray (Figure 31.1) had here become an open wound. The pit needed to be "unlayered" for the true treasure to be found. The ladder over the dry stream bed forms the shape of a cross. Perhaps this represents the painful cross she has had to carry, the cross of positive and negative feelings which could have no resolution until she had experienced the mother–child unity and the coming together of masculine and feminine.

A white horse is headed towards the ladder. Ilsa had initially placed the horse in the upper left corner, where the bear cub had been located in her first tray (Figure 31.1). After putting all of the remaining items in

Figure 31.4

the sand, Ilsa moved the horse to its final placement at the head of the dry stream bed, where the fawn in the second scene had been located (Figure 31.2). All three animals seem to be representations of herself on her "hero's journey." First she was the cub willing to stand up to the threatening man, then the protected fawn getting sustenance for itself, and now the horse facing the final challenge, the deep wound of the pit.

The figure of the white horse unites the instinctual with the divine. The realization of the spiritual or divine must come from the instincts and not from the head. The ladder that seems to block the way is also a bridge that connects, and in connecting, crosses over.

In Ilsa's fourth scene (Figure 31.4) the Self is manifested. In the center of the tray a pine tree is coming out of a round shell, the natural Self is growing out of a feminine source. Jizo and the white horse are looking at this central tree of life. Jizo is standing on a base made of the piece of black obsidian that Ilsa thought of as her stone. To the right of Jizo, where the black-and-white rock was hidden in her second scene (Figure 31.2), treasures have been uncovered, the golden coins.

When Ilsa shaped the sand at the beginning of making the tray, she said it looked like a big butterfly. So the background of the whole scene is the butterfly, a symbol of the psyche, of the soul, of transformation. It seems a most appropriate background for this manifestation of the Self.

When this scene was projected onto the screen at our joint reviewing of the slides, we were all silent for a few moments. Then Ilsa's analyst said, "It sends goose bumps up and down my spine."

This last scene (Figure 31.5) completes Ilsa's series. After experiencing the numinous power of the manifestation of the Self, Ilsa returns to some of the more familiar items that she had used in previous trays. This is as

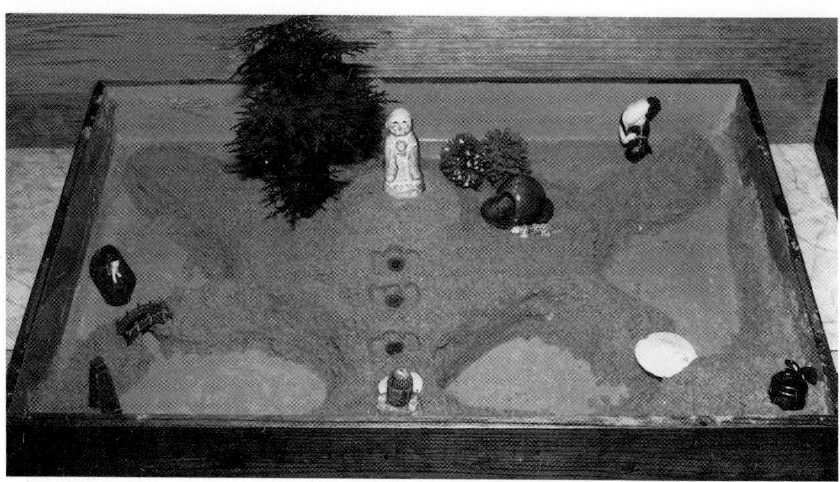

Figure 31.5

it should be. A series generally should not stop with a "Self tray." The energy released needs to be grounded or integrated in some way before the sandplay therapy is terminated.

The little bear cub from Ilsa's first scene (Figure 31.1) is now on a raft left center which can float nearly any place in the tray. All the water is connected except for the bottom center, where the stream was blocked in the first scene. All of the land is connected too, the two lower corners by bridges. The bridge on the left is the one she used in the initial tray to connect the threatening masculine with the warm feminine. The bridge on the right is a sand dollar. Sand dollars, with their star design, are symbols bringing together the sky and the sea.

The leopard by the oven from the first scene reappears as do the two gods from the second tray (Figure 31.2). The Japanese Jizo and the Central American god now face each other; they are connected by three steps. Ilsa saw the pathway between the pair of gods as representing a new relationship, perhaps between the East and the West, or between inner and outer worlds, the spiritual and the concrete.

On each step, Ilsa placed one gold coin, the treasure brought to her by the appearance of the Self. And Jizo is flanked by flourishing growth; a huge evergreen tree and two trees in bloom replace the autumn tree of the first tray. There has been a rebirth.

The base of the whole scene is a large turtle. After she saw the shape of the turtle in the sand, Ilsa told me that she used to collect turtles and thought of the turtle as a symbol which helped to ground her in physical reality, compensating for her superior intuition. In the preceding scene (Figure 31.4) the shape in the sand looked like a butterfly, a symbol of transformation. In this final scene, it is as if Ilsa has built a new more solid base for continued work in analysis and in life.

Soon after the completion of this sandplay series, Ilsa made a journey to the Orient and later told me of a deep spiritual experience she had there. She felt that her journey in the sand helped to prepare for what happened within her during her outer journey.

Ilsa's case illustrates the possibility of doing successful sandplay work in unusual circumstances: a client who is in therapy with one therapist while doing a sandplay process with another, and who is limited to doing only a short-term process within a few sessions.

No problems resulting from the dual therapy became apparent. The sandplay process proceeded despite my knowing relatively little about Ilsa. I respected her primary relationship with her analyst, and found no need to question her further about her life. Ilsa volunteered some comments on herself and her immediate life circumstances from time to time, but the two processes mostly went their own separate paths. When the three of us later reviewed the slides, her analyst expressed her appreciation for the sandplay process and what reviewing the slides had done for her understanding of what was going on in the analysis.

My conclusion is that this kind of dual analysis is entirely feasible. It can work, especially when there is a sense of trusting collaboration between all three participants and a policy of "non-interference" which allows the sandplay to unfold without too much scrutiny.

When working within the confines of a limited number of sessions, I think that the level of motivation is the key. I do not think it would work if someone just casually wanted to try doing sandplay. There has to be a genuine need for it. In Ilsa's case, she felt stuck and she herself had initiated the effort to supplement her analysis with another form of therapy.

Four or five sessions must be viewed as a "mini-process." In instances in which a particular problem needs to be worked on, as here, mini-processes can be of great value, especially if they can both activate and contain the transformative powers of the deep unconscious.

Chapter 32

Irene: from sandplay into life

The making of sand scenes is a kind of active imagination. It invites the unconscious to participate in a conscious act. In making each sand scene, the client has the opportunity to integrate additional parts of their unconscious into consciousness. And with each such integration, the person moves forward in their growth journey.

In a series of sand scenes, one can see this movement, especially by following the use of miniatures that continually reappear, or by studying how major themes unfold, or by focusing on changes that occur in one or more significant areas of the sandtray. Watching for changes in specific areas of successive sand scenes can help in understanding what course the psychic growth is following.

In order to illustrate this kind of movement in actual practice, I am first going to compare the initial and final sandplay scenes done by a woman I call Irene. Then I shall talk about some of her intervening trays, how she got from here to there. Irene was a single career woman, a nurse, in her 20s.

Irene had already made a few sand scenes with another analyst prior to meeting with me. She started her first scene with me (Figure 32.1) by placing a large piece of driftwood in the middle of the box of dry sand. She then crossed four red arcs – segments from a circus ring – over one another on the left, put a girl on a post in the center and a witch on a higher post to the left. Later she said that she could acknowledge both the young girl and the old witch as parts of herself, but that the only feminine side of herself she could usually recognize was the witchy side. She then added trees, an oriental man and woman, a dog, and a boy on a horse on the right side, and an open oyster shell at the center front. She said she liked the trees and animals, but did not know why she selected the oyster shell.

When I was studying the scene later, I came to realize that it reflected Irene's unresolved conflicts about her femininity. The circle, her feminine totality, is broken. And the negative feminine in herself currently

Figure 32.1

Figure 32.2

dominates the scene; the witch is on the highest pole. Yet the open shell, another feminine symbol, suggests that she does have other feminine qualities which can be developed, which may be just emerging from the unconscious. The trees also show a potential for further growth, although they are fenced in at this stage and cannot spread. And her liking of the animals suggests a respect for her instinctual side.

In Irene's final sand scene (Figure 32.2), the broken-up circus ring from the initial sandtray is put back together to make a complete circle. Two channels cross through the circle and the ring is balanced on the top in the center. All the figures in the channels are heading towards this center. After making the scene, Irene looked over the shelves and finally selected the witch she had used in her initial scene, tied a string to her and attached her to a pole set in the sand. She said,

> The witch was a final thought. All the rest are coming in there to decide what to do with the witch. The witch is the bad part of me. This seems like regression in a way, and in other ways it seems like pulling it all together. The other figures represent different facets of myself that I have dealt with.

Irene made eight sandtrays in between these initial and final scenes over the course of six months of therapy with me. The witch, who played such an important role in both the initial and final sand pictures, did not appear in any intervening sand scene. But the circus ring, which was broken up in the initial scene and formed a perfect centered whole in the final scene, frequently reappeared. Segments of the circus ring were used in five of the middle eight trays. First they appeared as three upright arcs, then as two separated half circles. Next the arcs were brought together in a complete but uncentered circle. Then the whole circle was centered and partly covered. Later the circle was placed on edge and located in the back of the tray. So Irene continued to use parts of the ring in varying combinations in many of her intervening sandtrays, leading up to the centered circle with the channels going in and out of it in her last scene. It is as if her psyche kept experimenting with the symbol of wholeness until it arrived at a final centering.

The development of a deepening relationship to the feminine, and between the masculine and feminine, was equally significant in Irene's process. In an early scene, a woman is sitting on one of the upright arcs; a man is going to rescue the woman and take her to a garden which contains a shell. Here the masculine is playing a protective role and is helping her find her secluded feminine side. Then a woman is sitting on a shell in the center. In the following two scenes a man and woman are side by side, but not interacting. Next a man and woman are journeying toward a bridge together. There is danger, but there is also a light to guide them. Then a man and woman are seated together in the center with the shell between them on a table. Next a man coming by boat is going to climb the center pole to get to the shell on top and take it to the woman standing by the well; they can then put the shell into the well where "it will be safe." And in the final scene, there is an intermingling of many feminine and masculine figures who all share in the task of dealing with the witch.

At the visit before her final sand scene, Irene said she had, for the first time, been able to tell the man she was living with that she loved him, and she had truly meant it. She was married a few months later, and terminated therapy.

For Irene the witch, the negative feminine, played a significant role. Irene identified the witch as internal, within herself, and needed to become stronger in order to handle this fierce feminine power. From a place of imbalance and fragmentation, she moved in her sandplay scenes towards becoming more balanced and centered in herself. She also made a clear-cut separation between the masculine and feminine in her earlier trays which were then able to interact cooperatively in the later scenes. Concurrently, she allowed a real-life relationship to evolve; her "break-through" came when she was able to express positive feelings to her fiancé.

Sandplay provides us with a permanent visual record of her journey and provided her with a way for living out her journey, first in imagination and then in life.

Chapter 33

Rhoda: seeking the spiritual

Given the limitations of brief time-limited therapy, the psyche sometimes responds by generating a complete sandplay process. I do not for one minute think that a whole therapeutic healing happens in this short a time. The full healing and individuating response of the psyche may take many months or years to come into being. But it is as if the sandtrays lay down a kind of psychic blueprint which can then be used for further construction.

The limitation has to be a real one, not just a "Let's see if we can do it in five sessions." But when people come from out of town with only a short time to stay, or when I was about to retire, for example, the sandplay process can take an amazingly short time. It is encouraging to find, in these days when insurance companies so often require short-term therapy, that sometimes a sandplay process can indeed be completed within a limited number of visits.

From the outset, Rhoda and I both knew that we had only a short time in which to work; we agreed on a total of five sandplay sessions. We met monthly or every other month for a period of eight months. And, five years after she had done her final tray, we met together one last time to review the photographs of her scenes.

At the time Rhoda first came to see me, she was in her late 30s. She had been living with her woman partner for several years and had had a baby girl conceived through artificial insemination. She was working in a helping profession.

Rhoda felt her mother had been a good mom, but she had had only limited time to be with her because she was busy with her three other children. She had never felt comfortable with her father. Rhoda was the youngest of four children, and had been closer to her brother than to either of her sisters.

Her parents divorced when she was in her early teens and she stayed with her mother until going to college. Each of her parents had married again after twenty-five years of being single. Although Rhoda's father was Jewish she had been raised as a Quaker. She later left the Quaker religion and described herself at our first meeting as more interested in "pagan" religions.

In Rhoda's initial tray (see Plate 7), the dominant feature is the row of four black horses in the upper right corner. Rhoda said that the clear crystal and blue glass sphere on a double silver coil in the corner behind the horses represented the spiritual side of life. She felt that the horses were guarding this spiritual place.

I wondered why she needed so much power lined up to protect the spiritual. Were these horses guarding the spiritual for her or from her? Perhaps they represented an unyielding animus that had in some way been preventing her from getting more related to the deeper Self. Rhoda commented that the spiritual was always there for her, but that she had not been deeply in touch with it. Her energy had been too much taken up by the requirements of everyday living.

The abalone shell next to the crystal and sphere holds broken pieces of egg shell and an acorn. In the review, Rhoda said that the shell fragments were mistakes that she had made in her past. At the time she made the tray, she felt that she was a failure, she had not realized her potentials. But the acorn within the pearlescent abalone shell suggests that there may be some new growth to come within the feminine.

An athlete stands in the upper left corner beside a crying baby. Rhoda saw the baby as her own little daughter who at that time was demanding, difficult and subject to tantrums. The athlete represented the strength she needed to wrestle with the baby. In the review, she added that the proportions of the figures were just right; the baby girl had seemed very big to her and she had felt very small. It was apparent that there was a conflict going on in their relationship that was verging on a power struggle.

In the review Rhoda said that the dark mask below the baby was her own rage. She explained, "At that time I was just discovering my rage. I had always had trouble with anger. I was feeling like I had to do too much in taking care of the baby and the house."

Rhoda thought that the mother polar bear below the mask was protecting the baby seal. But, knowing that polar bears prey on seals, I wondered if she had some ambivalence about wanting at times to protect her baby and at times to punish her. In the later review, she said that the bear was also her adult self and the seal her child self. She was able to see that her inner child and her outer baby were related, a helpful insight for mothers.

Next she put a tree in the tray. Perhaps its plant energy could help to mitigate the powerful animal energy of the blockading horses. Lastly, she put a little partly formed figure into the canoe. She said that this was herself going on a journey without being sure of where she was going. But the bridge that leads towards the spiritual is there. And she could see that the person in the canoe could get to the spiritual area by crossing the bridge and going around the horses.

The bridge connects the spiritual, which she has been too busy for, with mothering, which is causing her problems. How can the bridge unite these two sides? The strength which she needs to have to handle her daughter is currently being turned against her, and barring her direct access to the spiritual. She has to go around through the open and receptive feminine. How will this occur?

We can watch how this happens by following the changes in these key areas in her next four sandtrays:

1 The power of the masculine softens.
2 The feminine becomes stronger.
3 The mother–child relationship, both inner and outer, becomes more joyful.
4 She gains more access to the spiritual.

Rhoda stood for more than ten minutes looking at the objects on the shelves and picking up different ones before she started to make the next scene (see Plate 8). She then built a high mound in the sand and put a temple on top of it. In the review, she said that this temple was a center point or an access to what was to come. Already she is getting in touch with more of her spiritual self.

This sequence – of a bridge relating opposites in the first tray followed by a centering in the second tray – is the same sequence that I had observed in my earlier study on bridges. I did not notice this sequence of bridge followed by centering in Rhoda's series until I started writing about her trays. It is always amazing to me that each time we go over the pictures of a sandplay process, we see something new!

Rhoda saw the five blocks coming into the circle of figures in the lower right as stepping stones into her sandplay series. The block that had fallen down was the initial session that she had already had and the four standing blocks represented the four remaining sessions.

The stepping stones lead into a circle of figures which starts with a terra cotta image surrounded by pieces of obsidian. Both these materials are born from fire, the terra cotta from the ceramicist's kiln and the obsidian from volcanic fire. Next there is a water grouping: a fish, a mermaid and two whales, one black and one white. Then there is a house with a naked woman leaning over it. The circle ends with an Eskimo mother and child; there is an animal bone behind them and a snake in front.

Rhoda said the terra cotta figure was struggling and in pain; the five jagged obsidian pieces represented the hurts. At that time she and her partner had purchased a new house and Rhoda was concerned about the cost, the added work of keeping it going, and lots of things that were wrong with it. She felt, as she said, "pushed out of shape," exactly like the figure.

The mermaid and the pair of whales are separated by a piece of tree bark. She said the bark was a tunnel going between the mermaid and the white whale. In the review, Rhoda indicated that the upper whale represented her mother, whom she saw as all good, and the lower whale represented her father, whom she saw as all bad. The bark tunnel which connects her mermaid self with the whale/mother looks partially broken, like the egg shells in the initial tray. But at least there is a passageway. She went on to say that her life task had been to come to terms with who *she* was. Being the youngest child, she had had a hard time of it.

The nude woman bending over a house looks as though she is both being supported by and hovering over it. New life, the flowering tree and the acorn, are nearby. This grouping, which suggests a more positive relationship between woman and home, is on a diagonal from the "bent-out-of-shape" woman. It is in marked contrast to the worry and anger about her new house which Rhoda had expressed when she talked about the suffering terra cotta figure. I have learned to pay attention to objects that are on a diagonal from each other. Often they indicate the two sides of a conflict or a relationship that is currently being worked on.

The Eskimo mother and her child represented collective mothering to Rhoda. "It goes way back to the beginning of time. It gave me a feeling of re-uniting with all that. It was both a personal mother, [I] and my child, but also the universal mother and child." The objects on the diagonal from these are the mermaid-tunnel-white whale grouping which represented her connection with her own mother. The experience of this kind of "mother-line," from a mother to her daughter and from that daughter as mother to her daughter, is very important for women. Here it helps Rhoda to strengthen and deepen her connections with her own daughter.

The overall impression of Rhoda's next scene (see Plate 9) is more chaotic. Rhoda did notice some order in the arrangement that comes from the four white horses, one in each corner, that have replaced the four black horses lined up in a row in her first scene (Plate 7). And the horse in the upper left is drinking water from a shell, getting nourishment from the feminine.

The pink tree at the upper right is near what she had called the spiritual area in her first scene. Rhoda said that there was a feeling of cosmic energy about the tree. And that it had been a relief to put in the white pyramids; they seemed more solid than she herself had been feeling at the time. The pyramid, with its three triangles and single apex at the top, is often seen as representing the masculine. Her positive feeling towards the solid white pyramids may indicate the beginning of a transformation in her, up to now generally negative, feelings toward men.

The snake goddess in the upper left of center is in the same location where the athlete had been in the first tray (Plate 7). In that initial scene, the smaller athlete had been barely up to handling the angry child. Now this powerful earth goddess brings real feminine strength into that area. The armless Venus, the sky goddess of love, is on a diagonal from the snake goddess in the lower right. Another part of her feminine self may have been feeling helpless and crippled at that time.

The last objects she put into the tray were two mirrors, a double one reflecting the snake goddess on one side and the peacock on the other, and a single mirror reflecting Venus. When she was making the tray, she said that the relationship between the two goddesses was what the tray was all about. In the review, she told me that the goddesses represented alternating aspects of herself – perhaps power and love – and that the mirrors indicated her attempt to reflect on both these two sides.

The black male gorillas in the left center were fighting. Rhoda said they represented her anger, and the coins scattered around them were her worries about money. The gorillas were arguing, talking it out. They were in about the same location as the angry mask in her first scene; the undifferentiated impotent rage of the mask all by itself has become more differentiated into a dual confrontation between equal partners.

The baby turtle hatching from an egg in the lower center is being born alone on the rough surface of a piece of coral. Does she sometimes feel like she would like to get away from her baby? Or feel guilty that she often *is* away?

In the lower left corner are eggs in a nest; a death figure stands nearby. Perhaps some old attitude has to die while something new is being born.

There are a number of "rounds" in this tray: the nest, the metal sphere, the zodiac circle, the mirrors, the shell. There are also many squares and cubes scattered here and there throughout the tray. Both rounds and squares are connected with wholeness. Rhoda made no comment on these geometrical figures. Apparently she was not deliberately or consciously picking these shapes; they were an unconscious part of her process.

Rhoda started her next tray (see Plate 10) by making a mound on the left and placing a castle, the Grail castle, on top of the mound. In the review, Rhoda called this center the magical world of children, and of her own child, the positive fairyland that young children live in for a while. The baby with the teddy bear standing almost in the center of the tray is smiling and happy. She is quite different from the crying tantruming child in her first tray (Plate 7)!

The men in the "fairy tale area" are artists: a flute player, Swiss horn player, jester and dancer. The male apes arguing among the scattered coins who were in this area in the previous scene (Plate 9) represented the more traditional masculine values of aggressiveness and monetary worth; all of the masculine figures in this area now are more related to beauty and to play. Rhoda said that the black runner with the torch below the dancers was bringing more energy and vitality to the arts and to the playing that was going on there. The light of the torch brings more consciousness to her little girl side without destroying the magic of it.

The castle takes the place of the temple in her second scene (Plate 8). Rhoda said that the castle was more real than the temple, that one could "live in a castle." A castle is an androgynous symbol. As a place to live in, it is a feminine image; as a fortress, it is a masculine image. So that a bringing together of the masculine and feminine happens in this scene for the first time.

There are four clusters of figures grouped around the central castle: a diving girl surrounded by five figures (lower right); five women doing "women's work" (upper right); four penguins around a large marble egg (lower left); and a mother and baby kangaroo (lower center).

Rhoda identified the diver in the lower right as herself. She is surrounded by demons who are closing in on her. She said that she felt trapped, that she wanted to dive deeper to find her unused potentials but there were obstacles preventing her from doing this. The obstructive signs around her read: "School," "Red Cross," "Slow," "Danger," "Stop."

The women in the upper right are all engaged in traditional feminine caretaking or nurturing activities: woman shouldering a jug; Native American woman preparing food on a plate; squaw carrying a baby; girl scattering grain; and farm girl carrying a pail of water or food for the animals. For Rhoda, these women represented working life as contrasted to the more imaginative artistic life of the fairy tale area. But the farm girl is pointing towards the castle, connecting or "bridging" the two areas of work and play with her gesture. And the baby, too, seems to be looking in her direction.

The four penguins in the lower left bring the colors of black and white together. First Rhoda had separated black and white sequentially (black horses in Plate 7 followed by the white horses in Plate 9). Then she had separated them simultaneously (black whale below white whale in Plate 8). Now she unifies these opposites. Rhoda thought the penguins were guarding the large marble egg. The union of opposites helps to keep the potential for future development secure.

The kangaroo with a baby in its pouch in the lower center is in the same area where mothers and babies had been portrayed before: the mother polar bear and baby seal; the Eskimo mother with a baby in her arms; the lone turtle hatchling. Rhoda, in our review, saw the kangaroo as herself holding her baby and caring for her. Initially in her first scenes she had been looking for the spiritual in some higher more abstract place. Now she realized that for her the spiritual could be found in motherhood and in sharing the magic with her baby.

The color red stands out more in this scene than in any previous sandtray (two red objects on the left side and two on the right). Perhaps at this point Rhoda was allowing herself to go more with her feelings regardless of whether they came from the joyous fairy tale side or the frustrated achieving side. The number "five" is also frequently used in this tray (five demons, five nurturing women, five male figures in the center). Five often suggests a coming to the "quintessence," to wholeness.

Rhoda placed the two spiritual treasures from her first scene on each side of the center in her last tray (see Plate 11). She put the crystal on a coiled snake on the right and the blue sphere in a pool on the left. She said that the crystal within the amber circle surrounded by four pieces of rose quartz was solar, fiery energy. She added that the blue glass sphere in the blue pond on the left was lunar, cooler, balancing the fiery side. Both energies, she thought, were within her.

The little red-and-white boat livens up the cool blue side and the blue egg brings some softness to the fiery red side, somewhat like the yin/yang symbol with its dot of black in the white and dot of white in the black. And again there are many rounds in this tray: the white spider web in the upper left, the thatched roof at the right, the two circular areas of spiritual energy, the cup of the chalice on the mirror in the center. Both the yin/yang and the circle may be references to wholeness.

Between these hot and cool energies there is a central line of figures: the Grail chalice on a round mirror; an open mussel shell; and Kwan Yin with a unicorn. The chalice carries the image of the Self, both in the Christian sacraments and in the stories of the Holy Grail. The open shell immediately above the chalice represents the receptive feminine. And Kwan Yin here replaces the snake goddess of Rhoda's earlier tray; compassion replaces power. And the unicorn beside her represents, according to Dora Kalff, the mystical experience of the union of opposites.

The big and little starfish on the lower right were her final placements. She saw the two starfish as mother and child. After having experienced the mother–child unity in previous trays, Rhoda is now able to be separate from yet close to her baby. The two starfish also suggest the association of her Self and her baby's Self. It is a beautiful ending to her series.

Rhoda reaches her goal of connecting with the spiritual in this final tray through connecting with her child, who had been so hard to get along with initially. There is a message here that is familiar to students of alchemy: the treasure lies in the *nigredo.*

Looking back, we can briefly trace changes in the four themes identified in Rhoda's first tray as important for her further development:

1 The Masculine
Plate 7: four stallions block the way to the spiritual
Plate 8: her father, the lower whale, is all-bad
Plate 9: angry male gorillas argue over money
Plate 10: men are both artists and bringers of light

2 The Feminine
Plate 7: the feminine abalone shell holds broken hopes
Plate 8: the "bent-out-of-shape" vs. the hovering woman
Plate 9: the powerful snake goddess vs. the crippled goddess of love
Plate 10: the achieving/failing vs. the nurturing feminine
Plate 11: the goddess of compassion

3 The Mothering
Plate 7: the little athlete struggles with the big baby's rage
Plate 8: she connects with her own mother, the white whale
Plate 10: she appreciates the magic of childhood
Plate 11: like the starfish, she can be with, yet apart from her child

4 The Spiritual
Plate 7: the way to the abstract spiritual is blocked
Plate 8: a temple gives more access to the spiritual
Plate 10: she experiences the living spiritual in mothering her child
Plate 11: the chalice, the Grail is found

At our review, I learned from Rhoda that soon after her final tray she had gone into personal therapy for herself. She had expanded her work in her profession. She and her partner had separated, but she reported continued pleasure in being with their daughter, now 7 years old. And she had returned to the Quaker Society and become active again in her religion.

When Rhoda was looking at her final tray at the end of our review, she said, "I like seeing this final scene. It makes me happy." She continued,

> I felt a resolution because it was the last one I would have with you, but also I must have felt a resolution of the things I had been struggling with. It was a balancing of all these different elements. They were feeling more balanced and in harmony with each other. I feel that I have access to all the things that are here. I was looking for peace and balance and energy. I lose it sometimes but I do have access to them. The whole scene seems complete, like an arrival.

Chapter 34

Ursula: ten trays in fifteen years

Ursula's sandplay series demonstrates the continuity of the sandplay process even when there are long spaces between trays. Ursula made just ten trays in fifteen years of work with me, with more than three years between some trays. And yet, they all hang together. We are increasingly finding that a sandplay series remains cohesive whether it is brief or scattered over a long period of time.

Ursula's turtle tray was included in the earlier chapter on the symbol of the turtle. It is a Self tray. I am including the rest of her series here partly to show what happens after the Self appears. Her last five trays demonstrate the strengthening of the ego that typically occurs after the manifestation or constellation of the Self.

Ursula came to me for analysis at the age of 50 years. She had been in analysis previously between the ages of 20 and 30 years, until her analyst moved out-of-state.

Ursula's father did not think women should get a college education. Women should become teachers, secretaries or wives. Ursula became both a secretary and a wife. Her mother was critical of her and never fully accepted her. She had two older sisters who married and had children. There was much rivalry between them. They were never companions.

Her husband was the only person in the family with whom she had a long good relationship. He was an achiever himself and prized her intelligence as well. She and her husband both came from upper-middle-class families.

She could not have children due to hormone difficulties, so they adopted a two-month-old baby girl. Ursula had many problems with this daughter after she reached the age of 2 or 3. They just did not "get along." Much of her verbal therapy was taken up with talking and crying about this relationship.

Ursula herself was very bright. But she seldom received credit for her brightness or for anything she did. Since she could not have children, she felt that she was a failure as a wife. She had hoped adopting a child would

Figure 34.1

mitigate this feeling. After many years of conflict with her daughter, she felt that she was a failure as a mother as well. She had no severe pathology but her ego was weak.

She was very critical of herself and she could not accept any of the good things I said about her. At first, I did not realize that my trying to counteract her negative image of herself in this way was not helpful. The conflict that should have remained in her became a conflict between us. Later, I learned to stay with her, not reinforcing her self-criticism, but just accepting it as the way she felt. This was better.

In Ursula's first tray (Figure 34.1: "The problem and possible solution") there are three orientals carrying loads. One man on the left is carrying his burden on his head, the other on his back. The man on the right is carrying a pole with pails over his shoulders. On the left is a pelican; on the right, a goose. A bridge spans a small stream in the center.

Dora Kalff looked at this tray and, with almost no supplementary information to go on, said:

> This woman takes burdens on herself. She is under the domination of her negative animus which goads her to be the good daughter, the good wife, and the good mother. And what about the bridge? Burdens are carried on both sides. So what is to be reconciled by bringing the two sides together? Perhaps the birds on the two sides of the stream will give the answer. The pelican on the left is the only bird who feeds its young from blood taken from its own breast. It is the symbol of self-sacrificing motherhood. The goose on the right is a symbol of stupidity, servility. The goose girl in fairy tales is servile. So perhaps the bridge suggests the possibilities of reconciling the image of the perfect mother

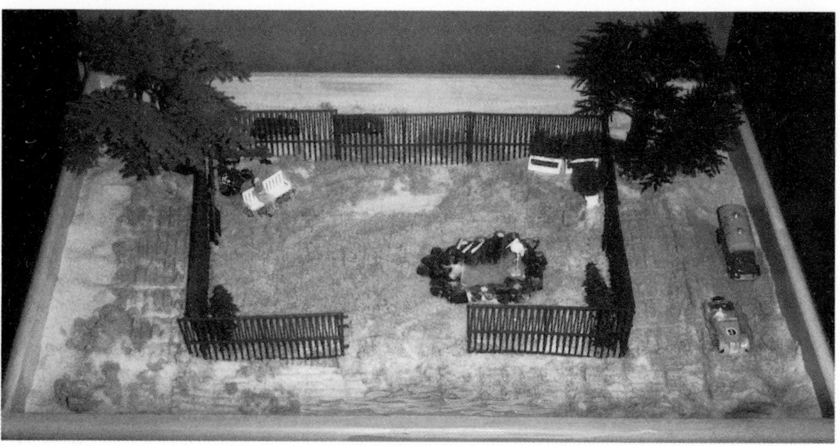

Figure 34.2

> and the feelings of worthlessness. At this point it would seem that her animus is telling her she must be the perfect mother at the same time it is telling her that she is worthless. A reconciliation would seem to be finding something in between perfection and worthlessness.

This is the kind of intuitive skill that Dora Kalff had in "reading" trays.

In Ursula's next scene (Figure 34.2: "Letting things happen"), a woman is resting on a bench and a boy is sitting quietly near a stork by a pool which is inside an enclosure. The enclosure is open to the outside where cars and trucks are busily driving by. There is plant growth both inside and outside the enclosure; both inner and outer aspects of herself are growing.

In the review five years after the completion of her final tray, Ursula said, "My only recollection [of this tray] is of an older woman resting. . . . There's an enclosure but one can get out of it. . . . It's like giving up the struggle and letting things happen."

Ursula's third scene (Figure 34.3: "Getting along with her instincts") was done more than three years later. It could be classified as an animal–vegetative scene. There are no humans in it at all, only plant and animal life. It looks like a jungle. Ursula appears to feel comfortable with her animal instincts. She provides a shell with water for the hippo, rhino, bear and deer (lower left).

After she made the tray she commented, "They all get along together. Even the king of the jungle is no danger. The other animals will cope with the potential threat of the lion [lower right] by walking away and leaving the water hole to him." The animus is no longer attacking her. Indeed, a positive animus, the bull elephant protecting his family, appears

Figure 34.3

Figure 34.4

in this scene (center). There is an animal mother–child unity, the giraffe pair.

During the review, she said that she liked elephants. "They are strong but gentle. They only attack as a defense. They form a circle to protect the children."

During the session when Ursula did her next tray (Figure 34.4: "Focusing on the feminine"), she talked more about feelings – angry, fearful, erotic – than she had in previous sessions. In the scene she made, she focused on the feminine. In the center she placed a shell with water in it, like the one she had used in her last tray (Figure 34.3). Then she built up an ocean scene around it. The pelican mother from the first tray

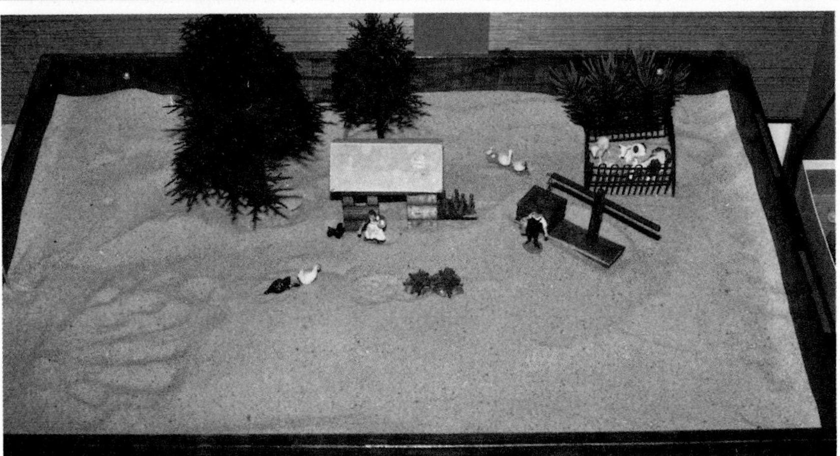

Figure 34.5

is still in the picture but the goose has been replaced by two doves, birds of peace.

In the review, she remarked, "There are three birds in a triangle – not competing. It's the same way it was with the animals in the previous tray. There's no competition for anything."

Her next scene (see Plate 4: "Turtles climbing to a god") radiates the numinosity of a Self tray. Here the conflict presented in the initial tray has been transcended. A group of ancient turtles have left the sea of the unconscious and are climbing up the central mountain to pay homage to a masculine god. The father turtle leads the way. The animus is again positive, not burdening or attacking. And the redness of the carps suggests more activation of her feelings.

At the review when she saw this tray, she said,

> I love this. This was my flowering year. When I envisioned this tray in my mind, the animals were coming from a distance going over barriers. I envisioned fences that they had to climb to reach the center – climbing slowly. The design pleased me. But I am astounded there are no fences. The Fu dog is more than just a pet. He is the guardian of the Temple, guardian of this personage in the center. The circles are like water, back to timelessness. The ushering in of a good year, a creative year. This tray always meant something special. It gave me pleasure that I could do something so creative and lovely. It's more significant than I can define. It's cosmic.

At this time, Ursula reduced the frequency of her visits from once a week to once a month. I thought this might be her final tray. There was a two-year gap before she did another tray. During that time the relationship with her daughter improved. And she had two significant dreams which she reported to me. Both took place in a garden. In the first dream,

> There was fungus which had spread in the garden but vegetables were growing and a man handed me a pear from a tree that was identified as my tree.

In the second dream,

> The garden was being tended by someone else but it was now my responsibility to oversee the tending of the garden. It was a sunny place and I fed myself celery from it.

The first tray Ursula did after the Self tray is a farm scene (Figure 34.5: "Nurturing"). A man and woman are feeding and caring for the farm animals. Fire and water, the essential elements needed for life and for development, are both present (two bonfires in center; well at right). There are many representations of mother-and-child: sheep with lamb and cow with calf, in fenced-in area; rooster and hen with chicks (left); and duck with ducklings (top). The ceremonial Fu dog of the previous tray has become a real animal (by woman). After experiencing the archetypal power of the Self in her previous tray, Ursula returns to the everyday world. And now, in this world, both masculine and feminine can parent and nurture.

When Ursula reviewed this tray she said,

> Everyone is going about his own business. Each one doing his own job. There is a feeling of a path, of stages. If you could define these stages, those you must pass in therapy, then if one is found missing you would know it. Sandplay is a vision of these stages. The unconscious is doing the directing.

She summed up some of the most important elements in sandplay, which we had never discussed.

In her next tray (see Figure 23.7, p. 98: "Being judged"), Ursula's judgmental side is represented by an Aztec god who keeps her from going through the torii. She is the tiny submissive person, left center, who has her arms folded across her chest. Only the Greek mother goddess to her right is helping her. All of the other negative judging figures are under the influence of the mighty god who blocks her as unworthy to go through the sacred gate.

In this tray Ursula is able to concretize the experience of being adversely judged. And, more importantly, she identifies a part of herself, probably experienced initially in the co-transference with me, who is supportive of her.

In her next tray (see Figure 23.8, p. 98: "Release"), the torii is no longer blocked by the negative Aztec judge. The tiny figure in the center can now go through the gate. Two guardians protect her way. On the other

Figure 34.6

side of the torii there is a sacred temple. The passageway to the temple is available to her.

In the review Ursula remembered a feeling of release. She said that the little girl in the center "belongs to all of these temples and they all belong to her." She has access to what lies behind the torii and has accepted it. This is the middle way.

Ursula's next tray (Figure 34.6: "Towards the end of the race") is an all-male tray except for the girl with a dish of grain in the upper left corner. All the farm hands on the left are working to supply food. On the right there is music and dancing. A man carrying a torch leads a group of male runners across the center on a diagonal. A figure of the winged horse Pegasus follows.

Ursula said about this tray,

> The important thing now is that they have the torch. This represents pure energy; fire and running. It could be towards the end of the race. The dancing is like a celebration. None of the figures are in competition. They are doing their own things – the dancers, the runners, the farm workers. On both sides they are watching the runners.

At the end of her next regular session, which was a month later, Ursula said that she wanted to change the tray she had made at the previous session. But it was the end of the hour. I asked her if she would like an extra visit before her next scheduled session a month away. She was happy to accept this offer. When she came in, however, she decided to make a new tray rather than trying to reproduce the previous tray.

Ursula's final tray (Figure 34.7: "Completion") is similar to the previous scene. A herd of horses is galloping on a diagonal across and out of the tray. A blonde girl is riding the lead horse.

Figure 34.7

In the review she said,

> When I envision this, I envision a blonde girl with her hair flying riding a horse. It is a good feeling of rightness. There's no bridle, no saddle. She is flying down the road on her horse – clearly in charge. It's a wonderful feeling.

This was her final tray. After she had done the tray, she told me about standing up for herself on the phone with her daughter and not feeling guilty about it. This was a triumph for her. She came in only seven times during the following year. I announced at one of our appointments that I would be retiring in a year; she came in the following session and announced that she was stopping that day. Her ego was now strong enough so she could leave me before I left her.

In the review of the sand scenes she said, after looking at all ten trays, "It's interesting! I didn't know how much I was saying. And isn't it interesting how well I said it!" Finally, she was praising herself!

Chapter 35

Amy: feeling trapped, feeling angry, feeling strong, feeling free

In the early 1980s, I noticed a new phenomenon in my analytic practice. One woman after another came into my office saying, "I feel a kind of power I never felt before." It seemed to just suddenly start happening, and it kept on happening. They were excited by this power and afraid of it. What might come next? They had trouble identifying what this power was. It was not a desire to wrest power from another person. It was not destructive. It seemed like a special kind of "woman power" that had been waiting in the wings, a kind of freedom to be themselves, to feel anger and hate as well as caring and love. Women were finally claiming the full range of their affects, even the demonic affects of the dark feminine. And such experiencing brought with it a new feeling of strength and effectiveness.

I would like to briefly consider two differentiations: between hostility and anger; and between experiencing and expressing anger. Hostility is generally a chronic, unfocused condition, whereas anger is more acute and focused. A hostile person is a bitter person who may or may not become openly angry, whereas an angry person is, for the moment, or several moments, ready to explode, or actually exploding.

When Marie Louise von Franz was asked at a meeting in 1976 what *she* does, or what one *should* do about anger, she replied, "Measured expression." Anger should be *experienced* in full, but *expressed* in measured amounts. This is not easy. It is just because it is so difficult that anger is so frequently repressed, only to come out then in unconscious ways and sometimes without any control. Often anger has to be first expressed explosively or clumsily in order to be experienced within. When people I am seeing are going through this stage, and it is like a stage, I often pray that those around them will not punish them so severely in retaliation that they will turn off not only the outer expression, but also the inner experiencing, of the feeling. I liken it to going through the sound barrier. Once you are through it and have become more accepting of your own angry feelings, you can then develop the means to express your anger in the measured amounts which von Franz recommends.

This brings up the question of how to receive anger from another person. Receiving anger depends upon listening to the other. Really listening and hearing and trying to empathize. Trying to put yourself in the other's shoes. Trying to sense how they are feeling. Not just the anger, but all the other feelings leading up to the anger.

But receiving anger is not the same thing as ignoring it. Psychologists have often, at least in the past, recommended that parents ignore the temper tantrums of their children. In Zen Buddhism, they speak of transforming anger or hate into love. And the mutual development of two people depends on receiving anger from the other without punishing them for it.

But appearing to ignore anger outwardly only makes for increased inner anger. Often it helps to let the other know that their expression of anger has been effective, that you have felt it. Nothing is more infuriating or more demeaning than to try to hurt someone and have them be totally unhurt! Nor more frightening than to have the person you have tried to hurt totally collapse. Your humanness makes you feel the hurt; your strength keeps you from collapsing.

Now I have really painted myself into a corner! I have said that one should fully experience one's anger, and then I have said that instead of meeting another's anger with your anger you should listen to them and empathize. So let me say that I believe that a sense of strength comes with both experiences: the experience of fully feeling your anger with or without expressing it; and the experience of transforming your anger by trying to empathize. It sometimes helps to remember that anger often comes when there is a true caring for the other. And the accompanying, or consequent, feelings of strength can be used to help effect the changes one desires. One can get out of traps.

A woman I call Amy did a series of sand scenes that demonstrate this sequence of feeling trapped, feeling angry, feeling strong, and feeling free.

Amy was in her early 30s. She had graduated from college when she was 21 and had married her husband a few years later. At this time, during a physical examination, the doctor had found a malignant tumor. The cancer was successfully treated with surgery and had not recurred.

Amy came up to the Bay Area for a few weeks to do some sandplay with me while briefly interrupting her therapy with an analyst whom she had been seeing for over two years. We arranged for twice weekly visits for three weeks.

It was while working with Amy that I first began to realize that following the sequence of items placed in the sandtray can be particularly meaningful. This discovery led me to develop what I call "sequence analysis." To illustrate how this works, I shall discuss the figures she used in the same order that she put them in the tray.

Figure 35.1

At her first sandplay session (Figure 35.1: "The struggle"), Amy touched and stroked the sand in both the wet and dry sandtrays and commented, "Both feel neat." She put a single piece of turquoise in the lower center of the dry sand and went on from there.

A woman in black with bowl fragments (lower left):

Amy said that the figure reminded her of a dream she had:

> A woman was seated near some bowls. The woman told her the bowls contained something. When Amy asked her what they contained, the woman refused to tell her, saying that it was for her to find out. Amy then angrily smashed one of the bowls.

The figure of the woman in the tray is looking quietly at the bowl fragments she has picked up off the ground. Amy said that the woman was being patient about Amy's impulsiveness in smashing it. This is an example of receiving anger. Amy needs to vent her anger and to have it received by the other, both the other outside herself and the other within herself.

White coral pyramid (left center):

The pyramid with its three triangles and common apex is a strong solid masculine symbol. Its white snow-like quality suggests coldness, masculine coldness, while its size and solidity suggest masculine strength. The sequence of old woman followed by white pyramid suggests a kind of compensatory process, moving from the feminine to the masculine.

Fire (by woman):

The warmth of the fire is the opposite of coldness. So here is a second compensatory sequence, moving from cold to hot.

Small black obsidian (lower center):
This piece is opposite in size and color to the large white pyramid made of coral from the sea, but it is equally cold and hard in appearance. It is of volcanic origin; its hardness was made by fire. So we have more opposites: fire vs. water, and earth vs. ocean.
Demonic figure (center of tray):
Amy asked me the story of this figure, how I had obtained it, and I told her. Perhaps she needed this sharing as a kind of tangible reaffirmation of the therapeutic *temenos* after placing this sometimes disturbing figure in the tray.
Ceramic turtle (right of center):
After our verbal exchange she seemed more relaxed. She made a pool of water by pushing the sand away to display the blue floor of the tray and put a ceramic turtle in the water. The turtle goes between water and land, so represents a connection between the two.
White horse with gray Mayan god (lower right):
The white horse is on a path which goes between the turquoise and obsidian stones. It is headed towards a god, as if it is beginning a spiritual journey. Amy said the horse's head was bowed "in reverence to the god."
Two wrestlers (upper left):
On a diagonal from the god figure, Amy placed a clay sculpture of two figures wrestling. She said it reminded her of when she was struggling with something early in her analysis. According to Dora Kalff, figures placed at the opposite ends of a diagonal often represent a current problem that the person is struggling with. Here, Amy seems to be struggling with her anger – which is bad – and her longing for the spiritual – which is good.
Kali (lower left):
The Hindu goddess Kali both creates and destroys. Amy said, "She represents anger and strength." When Amy feels angry she feels strong.
Trees (upper right):
She added these in the corner opposite Kali. She commented, "You don't have any real trees – no real greenery. I'm going to have to fix that." She was gaining sufficient strength to be critical of my material.
Girl with arms up (left of center):
Amy said, "She is the opposite of Kali. She is good but weak."
Glass dragon hidden in the forest (upper right):
Something with primitive power is available in the unconscious.

The constellation of the terrible goddess who is strong, followed by feelings of growth (trees), allows her to express hostility (criticism of my collection). This is followed by the appearance of the good girl who is weak. Anger is strong but bad; good is weak. Amy is struggling with these

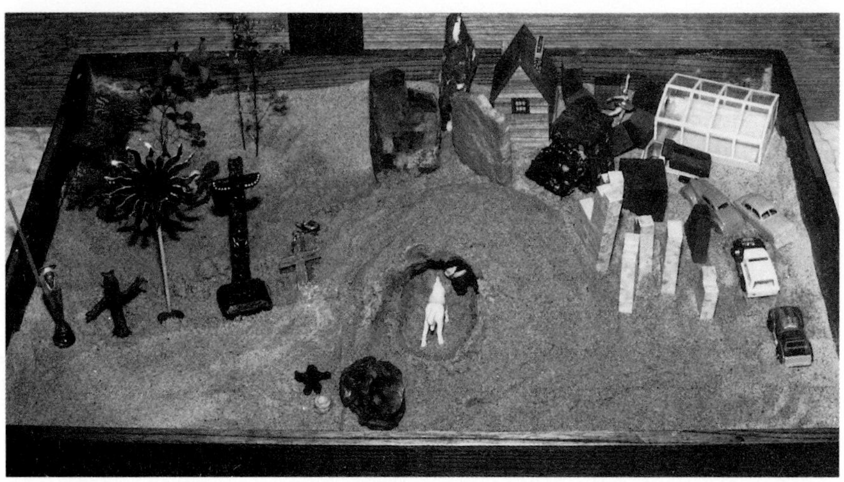

Figure 35.2

contradictions: she wants to be strong, but not bad; she wants to be good, but not weak.

Amy started her next tray (Figure 35.2: "Feeling trapped") by making a semi-circular ridge around a center cavity with a small pool.
Cave (center):
Amy described this formation in the sand as a "cave with water and an escape hole."
Old woman with bowl fragments (in cave):
She put the figure from the dream into the cave by the water. After adding rocks she said, "This is a lesson for me in using what's available instead of wishing for what is not here," another expression of negativism toward me.
Glass greenhouse (upper right):
This is where protected growth can take place, but it is empty.
Enclosed female dancer (upper right)
She told me later that she felt trapped and suffocated by living in the city. She had grown up among orchards.
Grayish mass (lower center):
She said that this was a symbol of her tumor. She later noted that the mass was the same size and shape as the entrance to the cave. She felt that the removal of the cancerous mass had opened up the way to her inner resources.
White horse (entering the cave):
Amy said he was "carrying the energy of the journey."
Five religious symbols (left center):

This group of sacred symbols included the Madonna, a tree goddess, the sun, a totem pole and an engraved gold cross.
Figure with one leg broken off holding baby (behind religious symbols):
Amy commented, "This is a good place. It's protected, but they can look out even if others can't look in." The religious symbols hide the figure with the broken leg and the baby and protect them from intrusion.
Foliage:
She had picked this herself that morning. It was reddish, like a blossoming tree.
Black bear with blue eyes (left of center):
This was for her a "helpful fetish figure," perhaps a source of magical power.
Jewelled turtle (left of center):
The turtle was going into a hole on the left side of the cave. She called this a "fetish with a self symbol, the jewel on top. He hides by drawing inward."
Cars, ambulance, dump truck (right side):
These all were "to get the dancer out."
Marble posts:
She used six different posts to represent the skyscrapers of the city that enclosed and trapped the dancer, and herself.

In this scene, her feminine spontaneity is confined and trapped. Yet the tumor, when removed, opens up a way of escape from the cave; and the rescue vehicles, magical fetishes and divine white horse are all ready there to help her. A death, or at least a crippling, is juxtaposed with a birth; both are held and protected by the spiritual.

Amy asked, as she started her next scene (Figure 35.3: "Feeling angry"), "Have you added things?" reversing her earlier critical remarks about my collection.
Dried foliage:
Again she had picked the foliage that morning.
Molded sand (center):
She made a hole through the sand, something like the exit hole from the cave. She then made a second hole and troughs going from each hole to top left and lower right corners.
Toothy animal with top hole (center):
This object looks like an animal vase or candle holder with a tail handle. She said it was "mysterious, primitive." This is one of my most used objects. One woman said that for her it represented rage combined with a feeling of inner emptiness. The value of this particular toothy animal object is that the inner emptiness is accompanied by the baring of the angry teeth. The anger at the emptiness is made manifest.

Figure 35.3

Clay figure with fangs (left of center):
Amy described this as a "spontaneous child-like boogie man."
Woman with baby (upper right of center):
She said, "I feel sad doing this. I feel there ought to be a man here, but I don't see one that fits."
Gangster-like boy (initially placed in lower left, then moved to right center):
When she added a figure of a boy holding a bomb she initially positioned him in the lower left. She said, "I feel stuck. He's angry. He wants to blow up the world." She associates her own anger with maleness and strength.

When people say they are stuck, I have come to know that something important is in the process of happening. Amy started to leave, then stopped. She looked back and said, "I want a man who is strong and wise." She moved the boy to the right center and replaced him with the sequined elephant in the lower left. She added, "I can't just get rid of him." And she is right! She cannot just get rid of her anger, no matter how afraid of it she is. She did not bury the boy with the bomb, or repress the anger. He is still there, but now he is not so central, he is more off to one side.
Female Dancer (upper right):
She put the dancer, who earlier was trapped in the city, near the angry boy with the bomb.
Stream (along right edge of tray):
Water is flowing. She is getting unstuck, untrapped.
Bridge (upper right):
This is the first time she has used a bridge. Connections are being made.

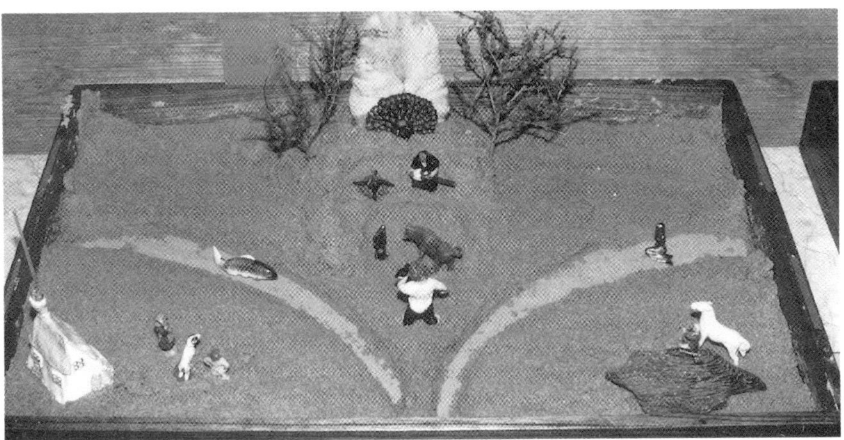

Figure 35.4

Flowering tree (upper right):
"That's pretty good, a cherry tree!" She is feeling better.
Frog with crown (upper right):
The frog often symbolizes transformation. Biologically tadpoles transform into frogs, and in fairy tales the frog transforms into a prince.
Bronze crusader (by boy with bomb):
The heroic masculine is facing away from the trickster boy who carries the explosive anger.

There is more continuity and more flowing in this tray. There is room for the potentially explosive masculine anger of the boy and feminine anger of the empty animal/woman who shows her teeth. The woman who carries the baby is no longer crippled. The dancer no longer trapped.

When Amy started to do her next scene (Figure 35.4: "Feeling strong"), she complained that there was not enough sand in the tray. I tossed in some sand from the other tray. She said, "I can pretend with less sand, but it would be better with more." I replied, "Do you know that if you really wanted more, I would get it for you?" Later, I thought that I should have let her complain without trying to make it better. But in review, Amy said she had felt my response showed that her complaint could be heard and be effective for change. Just as the wise old woman had not denied or judged the breaking of the bowl but had accepted the girl's anger and held the pieces before putting them back together.

Streams (from sides to center):
She molded the sand and made streams going from each side to the lower center.

Oval white coral (top center):
Amy initially put the masculine white pyramid made of coral in the tray again, but then replaced it with this other piece of coral. Often people think this coral figure is shaped like a vulva. This sequence suggests again a compensatory movement going from the masculine to the essential feminine.
Peacock (against the coral):
The peacock is often seen as a symbol of transformation. In mythology, the peacock transforms poison into healing medicine.
Bull (near center):
The bull is another powerful masculine symbol, which again is moved off center in the tray.
Girl with bird (bottom center):
Amy associated this figure with nightmares she used to have as a child. She would be shut alone in a large room and would imagine a huge bird flying in the window. She remembered feeling both scared and angry. Her current fear of being entrapped is thus associated with a similar childhood fear, and both are related to anger.
Woman with broken bowl fragments (top center):
This figure appears for the third time. Again the warming energy of fire is nearby.
Bronze crusader:
This heroic figure had been placed near the boy with the bomb in the previous tray (Figure 35.3). "He has to confront the bull," Amy said, and she turned the bull to face him.

We have a quaternity here: the crusader who represents the archetypal masculine hero; the bull who represents instinctual male energy; the seated woman with bowl fragments who represents the feminine archetype of the "wise old woman;" and the fire which represents an elemental, perhaps feminine, form of energy. The masculine is not being developed at the expense of the feminine; both are being developed in balance with each other.

Boy with the bugle and white horse (lower right):
Amy observed, "The horse and boy need to be together." The spiritual/instinctual quality of the white horse needs to be together with the positive masculine feeling of the young boy musician. The masculine is becoming more differentiated. It is no longer associated only with anger and power.
Bronze mermaid (center right):
The mermaid is part human and part fish; she combines the human and the instinctual. She may be related in some way to the crusader, who is also made of bronze.

Girl in red dress with teddy bear (lower left):
"I used to have a teddy bear." This positive childhood memory contrasts with the negative childhood memory of the nightmares.
Cornwall ceramic house (lower left):
"It looks warm." Again she expresses a positive feeling, here towards the sheltering maternal.
White dog by house (lower right):
Amy said the dog "just had to be there" beside the house. The instinctual energy of the dog has to be related to the feminine warmth of the house, like the instinctual/spiritual energy of the white horse has to be related to the masculine feeling of the boy bugler.
Little girl with hand on hip (lower right):
"She wants to be here too. It is my impatient self, wanting to have the wise old woman tell me more so the process will go faster." My not interpreting was frustrating to her, but she was coming to understand it. And she was learning that the impatient part of herself is not necessarily negative; it can lead to assertiveness, and hence to strength.

In this scene, there is an intermingling of masculine energy, both heroic and instinctual (the bugle boy with the white horse; the bronze crusader; the bull) and feminine strength (the oval coral; the mermaid; the old woman; the impatient little girl; the girl in red). And Amy feels strong enough to confront some of her childhood fears in the tray (nightmares) and to challenge me in the transference.

The center of this tray looks like a bud opening.

Amy again began her last sandtray (Figure 35.5: "Feeling free") by molding the sand.
Water area (left bottom):
She opened up the sand to make a water area and built an island mound at upper right.
Bone owl with blue eyes (top center):
Owls are traditionally associated with wisdom. Later she added a lantern representing consciousness combined with wisdom.
Dark person holding light baby (top center):
She called the dark person a "dying old man, a yogi, who is protecting the baby." So the sequence of figures who were holding the baby across these several trays is: crippled person; woman; and dying Yogi.
Brass incense pot (lower right):
She lifted the lid and put the fire into it. The fiery/angry energy is now contained in a sacred pot. It can be warm and comforting without being dangerous.
Girl in blue (upper right):
This was the same defiant figure who had wanted to know more in the preceding tray.

Figure 35.5

Priest (left of upper center):
The priest is another religious figure. The Mayan god came before him; later in this tray he will be followed by the Kwan Yin and a Greek goddess.
Two white horses and two blue horses (upper left):
Amy said that the horses are following the priest. "They are on a journey together," recalling the white horse in her initial tray (Figure 35.1) who was journeying toward the Mayan god.
Tiny girl in yellow dress (upper right):
The little girl is a small human representation of the good feminine.
Kwan Yin (lower right):
Kwan Yin is a divine form of the good feminine, the oriental goddess of compassion who is a protector of children.
Bronze Greek goddess (lower left):
This goddess represents the western spiritual feminine, just as Kwan Yin represents the eastern. The figure is partly hidden, as if the spiritual feminine is only beginning to come out of the unconscious.
Cedar wood (lower left):
Amy had carved this piece of wood a little and had brought it in. She said it was "a queen with a bishop's hat," combining in one image the regal feminine with the religious masculine.
Clay boat (center right):
Amy asked for clay and modelled it into a boat. In her earlier dream she broke the bowl because she could not get the information she wanted from the old woman. Now she asks for something and it is given to her. She can make her own container.

Here the energies of anger are available but are contained by the sacred. Amy's own small human strength is backed up by the power of positive feminine deities. She can go over the bridge to every place on the land and she can go in the boat to every place on the water. She is no longer confined; she can independently come and go as she pleases. She is truly free.

The whole form of this final sandtray looks like a swan with the head and beak at the upper right and the tail at the lower left. The swan is androgynous (its long neck is phallic and its body is rounded and feminine); it represents a union of masculine and feminine. Amy has brought together these previously disparate parts of herself. She can be strong without being a bad boy; she can be feminine without being a weak good girl. The baby, the new life, has gone forth into life from the arms of the dying old Yogi. The eighth and final stage of yoga is release.

Chapter 36

Emmy: the co-transference

In sandplay therapy we have a unique opportunity to observe the co-transference in the sandtray, with miniatures standing in for the human patient and therapist. The actual interchange of feelings between the client and therapist is, however, also important and not to be discounted. The playing out of the co-transference in the tray and the experiencing of the co-transference in the room are both essential parts of the process.

As therapists, it is sometimes easier for us to remain empathic when patients use the tray rather than words or actions to express some of their feelings towards us, since our own arousals and defenses are not as apt to intrude. And it may also, at times, be easier for the patient to express, and to experience, both positive and negative transference in the safety of the tray.

To illustrate the interplay between the co-transference and the sandplay scenes, I would like to present a series of trays done by a woman called Emmy.

Emmy was in her late 40s when she came to see me. Her sons had grown up and left home. She was divorced and living alone. She had been in Jungian analysis with a man for a few years. They had decided together that she should come to me for sandplay while at the same time continuing her analysis with him.

I felt an immediate liking for Emmy. She reminded me of my favorite aunt. I consciously recognized that this was a repetition of feelings I had had in my childhood, a true transference on my part.

When Emmy started with me, I told her that I would be retiring in eight months. So we always worked within this time limit. She did her twelfth and final tray the week of my retirement. Nearly a year after this final tray, I met with Emmy and her analyst to review the trays together.

In the center of Emmy's first tray (Figure 36.1: "The gathering place of women") is a well. An old woman with a large head is on the left side of the well and a mother with her child is on the right. There are four

Figure 36.1

figures in the lower half of the tray: a kneeling Native American woman with a plate of grain; a woman with a jug on her shoulder; a male hiker; and a girl in a red dress holding a small branch up to the hiker. The Cretan snake goddess stands in the upper left corner behind some trees. Merlin the Magician is below her near two stones. A stream goes from the trees at the top down past the well and off to the right.

When Emmy put the first woman into the tray, she said, "I feel attached to the old woman." And she asked, "Does she have a whole body?" Then she immediately added the mother with her child. I was a thinking type; Emmy was predominantly a feeling type. So perhaps the woman with the large head represented me, the "thinking" or more "head" woman; and the mother with her child represented Emmy, the "feeling" or more "body" woman. In the review, we also noticed that the large-headed figure was presiding over the well, much like the therapist who presides over the emergence of contents from the patient's unconscious.

This tray, which Emmy called the "gathering place of women," brings together aspects of the feminine which she had within her but had not yet fully lived. Her analyst pointed out during the review that the snake goddess represents chthonic female strength and power. The figure was dark and partly hidden by the trees. He added that Emmy at that time had not yet found her own strength. The women on either side of the stream are providing nourishment, both grain and water. The girl is reaching out towards the male hiker. And the large-headed woman is often seen as a representative of the wise old woman. All these various possibilities of woman – as strong, nourishing, related to man, wise – are gathered together in this initial tray.

Figure 36.2

Merlin is the only man in the scene besides the hiker. Emmy must have felt the need for some magic in her process, too, some masculine magic. Merlin may represent her transference view of her male analyst at the time; perhaps she wanted to bring him with her into this new experience.

After finishing most of the scene Emmy said, "This corner needs something" and casually tossed two stones into the lower left. Stones and rocks are often seen as the dwelling place of the gods. Peter was said to be the "rock" on which the Christian church was built. Emmy may have felt an unwanted, and hence partly repressed and denied, need to live out a more religious or spiritual part of herself.

In the review, Emmy recalled that one month after this tray she had attended a Bach festival; this was the beginning of her search to find a renewed connection with a church. And the year we were reviewing her scenes, Emmy had gone to an Easter service for the first time since her mother had "threatened her with religion" when she was a child.

Emmy's second tray (Figure 36.2: "Facing the judges") was done six months after her first. Emmy was going to be evaluated by a board of interviewers for a promotion which she was very eager to obtain.

The old woman with the large head from the first tray is at the top center. Four men stand in a semi-circle in front of her. The kneeling Native American woman, also from the first tray, is below them in the center of the scene with one black and one white baby lying in front of her. The flowering tree to her right nearly hides a small Buddha. An Etruscan goddess or priestess stands near the Buddha. A Japanese monk is playing a flute in the lower left.

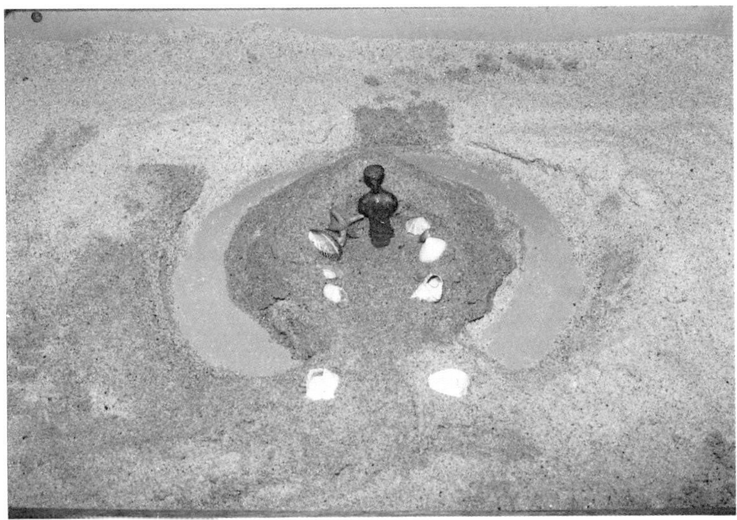

Figure 36.3

After finishing the tray, Emmy said the old woman reminded her of me watching over the scene, and that the kneeling woman with the two babies was herself going before the board. The monk blowing on his flute was "announcing himself." She knew that this particular kind of monk does not beg but plays his flute so that people will know he is there and come out to offer him food. The kneeling woman with her babies and the flute-playing monk are dependent figures who elicit care-giving from others. Emmy was able to add the four judges only after placing these figures who expect to receive care into the tray. Only then could she tolerate the experience of being judged. And finally, after commenting that she did not want to be too humble, she put the small Buddha in under the flowering tree.

In the review Emmy realized that she *had* been too humble when she came before the board. She should have had the empowering snake goddess from the initial tray with her when she was being interviewed. Her analyst agreed that she had needed the strength and energy of that fiercer feminine side to help her hold her ground.

Emmy's next tray (Figure 36.3: "Reconnecting with the deep feminine") is focused on a Greek mother goddess on top of a central mound surrounded by shells and a starfish. There are two additional shells further down where the sand meets the water.

This watery scene devoid of human beings represents a psychological descent; Emmy has had to "drop down" into a less conscious part of the psyche after the stress of going before the panel of judges. She needs to replenish herself by elevating and valuing the great earth mother goddess

Figure 36.4

and reconnecting with the ocean, both symbolic of different aspects of the deep maternal unconscious.

The number "five" recurs in this scene in both the five-pointed starfish and the five shells going down each side of the mound. Five sometimes refers to the human body (one head and four limbs; five fingers; five senses). The formation in the sand reminded us both of body parts; I saw it as a head and she saw it as a womb. In her first tray (Figure 36.1), the central figures were a woman who was mostly head and a woman who had given birth to a child. In that scene head and body, thinking and feeling, logos and eros, were clearly separated into opposites. In this sand-tray, they come together in this single sand image that is simultaneously both head and womb.

In our joint review, Emmy told us that although she did not know at this time that she had failed to get her promotion, she had felt diminished by the interview experience and had appreciated my talking with her at length about it during the session. A positive transference which was based on her actual experience of our verbal interchange was constellated; previously the positive transference had been based more on her projected expectation that I would be like the "wise old woman" archetype than on the reality of our current experience together.

The week before Emmy made her next tray (Figure 36.4: "The hero and the dragon"), we had a misunderstanding about the scheduling of our appointment. Emmy came at a time in the morning when I could not see her, and I was left later in the day with an unfilled hour. And then at the beginning of the session when she made this scene, I was about ten minutes late.

Figure 36.5

After entering the sandplay room, Emmy stood before the dry tray looking at the shelves for fully ten minutes before taking down the white dragon and placing it on the left. She added a small bonfire and a crusader brandishing a sword near the dragon, and put a treasure chest in the cave above him. Then she placed another group of figures in the lower right corner: a queen with her dog, a flowering tree, and two other small trees.

Emmy had waited for me for about ten minutes. She then stood in front of the shelves for about ten minutes before she started placing any objects in the tray. I think this was an unconscious retaliation, a getting even. She could punish me, and she could do it in kind. She had to wait; I had to wait.

Emmy then for the first time put aggressive figures into the tray. The white dragon she chose is the more benign Eastern dragon, not the fire-breathing Western one, but it was a beginning. And there was fire nearby, along with the soldier and the treasure. Emmy needs to have this heroic masculine energy with her when she has to do battle with the dragon in order to win the treasure. After portraying this masculine drama, Emmy could experience more gentle feminine feelings in the tray, including tenderness (the queen and her dog) and generativity (blossoming plant life).

In our review, Emmy told us that she did not know what to make of this tray at all. After I reminded her of the misunderstanding about the previous appointment time and then of my being late, she recalled the occurrences, but had no conscious memory of feeling angry. But in the sandtray sequences, at some unconscious level, she seemed to know that if she could make use of the strength of her anger she could find the treasure partly hidden in the cave.

Figure 36.6

At the beginning of her next session, Emmy talked about her sister and their struggles with each other. In response, I referred to my own sister, and Emmy and I complained about them together. I had not talked about personal things with Emmy before. Perhaps I was trying to make up for having been late to the previous session.

Then Emmy put the kneeling woman into the sandtray (Figure 36.5: "Treasure obtained"). She again commented, "She always seems the most like me. I don't know why." She opened the small treasure chest that she had used in the previous scene and was delighted to find that the coins and crystal she had put in it were still there. She felt that I had honored them. She removed the crystal from the box and put it and the chest in the center by the woman. She very carefully threaded a gold chain through the key to the chest and then around the woman's neck and around the open chest and crystal.

Lastly, Emmy added the tree goddess over on the left. This figure is associated with transformation. In one story, a tree is transformed into a goddess; in another myth, a goddess is transformed into a tree.

During the review, Emmy's analyst commented that sometimes you have to hack your way through to get valuable things and sometimes you have to receive what is given to you. Emmy had experienced both these ways of obtaining the treasure in her sandplay scenes: fighting the dragon for it, the masculine aggressive way; and being given the key she needed to open it, the feminine receptive way.

Emmy made the scene of fighting for the treasure when she was mad at me, when she was having more negative transference feelings. She made the scene of receiving the key to the treasure when she felt more intimate with me, when she was having more positive transference feelings. I certainly did not plan that – one doesn't, one can't. This kind of sequence is an example of the co-transference and how it operates naturally in sandplay.

Emmy's final tray (Figure 36.6 "Energy for life") came a few days before the date of my retirement. A stream runs from the upper right to a central pond and then to the lower right. There is a stone in the center of the pond. Nearby the girl with the branch and a gnome are talking together. A flowering tree and a house with a water wheel are on the right; a cow and calf with a row of green trees are on the left. Green foliage and trees border the water.

A stone, like the ones she had casually tossed aside into a corner in the first scene (Figure 36.1), is now in the central position in the pool; the religious feelings that had been denied are now in the place of honor. And, when she put the girl and gnome in the tray, she said "I felt they needed to chat." Her dialogue with the unconscious is ongoing. She has greater access to the Self.

The human mother–child image from the initial scene is now experienced on a deeper, more instinctual level in the cow and calf. And the free-flowing stream from the first tray has been put to work, turning the water wheel by the house, bringing productive energy into life.

Emmy's series began with mutually positive co-transference feelings. Emmy and I liked each other. I transferred my positive feelings for my aunt onto her. She felt attached to the old woman in the initial tray, perhaps in part perceiving the archetype of the wise old woman in me. And Emmy represented our different typologies – thinking and feeling – as separated opposites in the tray. Then I supported her during the stressful period of being judged by the board, which deepened the positive feelings she had for me. And in the next sandtray, she was able to bring together and unify the opposites of thinking and feeling which had been separated before.

Then we had the misunderstanding about the appointment, which caused us both feelings of guilt and resentment: "I had it wrong; no, she had it wrong." Then I acted out, I was late. Emmy retaliated by making me wait. In the tray she played out this negative co-transference with an aggressive scene and caught a glimpse of the partly hidden treasure. Next we talked about our sisters, our shadows. This brought us closer together again. In the following scene, Emmy received the key and opened the chest of treasures. Then, after she had experienced both positive and negative transference feelings in the protected setting of sandplay therapy, there was a release of energy. In the final tray, the flowing water in her life stream could be applied to the water wheel and used to produce work in the world.

Michael Fordham once told me that he did not like to use sandplay in therapy because he wanted the patient to see the witch in him in the transference, not in an object in the tray. But sandplay does not preclude seeing the witch in the therapist. Emmy saw me as both good and bad. She saw both angel and witch in me as well as in objects in the tray. And when the anger towards the witch is experienced in the safety of the therapeutic *temenos* in a way that strengthens and empowers, the treasure can be attained.

Chapter 37

Debbie: preparing to die

When Debbie called for an appointment, she said that she wanted to do sandplay with me because she had recently been diagnosed with lung cancer and had been told that she would live for no more than two years. She wanted to do sandplay in order to get ready to die. I found myself feeling frightened. I had read Jane Wheelwright's book, *The Death of a Woman* (1981), and I had been so admiring of Jane's "staying with" her patient Sally, who also died of cancer. Jane had been able to receive Sally's anger and rage, to feel with her sadness and despair, and finally to witness her withering away into death. I wondered if I could be with anyone in that way, if I could give in the way that would be required, would be demanded. I need not have worried. Debbie did not make demands. She gave more than she took.

At our first appointment, Debbie told me more about herself. She was 60 years old. She came from an intact family with a younger sister and brother. Her mother had wanted Debbie to be athletic like her sister, but she was not. She was "bookish;" she had loved school. Her brother also loved school, and her father proudly put him through college and graduate school and into a profession. But he thought girls did not need that much education. He put Debbie through high school and two years of what was then called "normal school." She graduated with a teaching credential.

Debbie taught school for a while. Then, when she was 21 years old, she fell in love for the first time and got married. It was not a happy marriage. They had very little in common and they could not get together sexually. Debbie thought their sexual problems were all her fault because, after all, her husband had been analyzed, so it could not have been his problem. She had bouts of depression, she smoked too much and drank too much, and once she took an overdose of sleeping pills. She knew she needed psychotherapy but her husband would not hear of it. He did not want his colleagues to know he had a wife who needed therapy, especially sex therapy. After twenty-five years of a bad marriage, after their sons were in their 20s, Debbie arranged for a divorce.

With some of the alimony money Debbie did get therapy. She went to a woman candidate at the C.G. Jung Institute for nearly four years. Then she stopped because, as she put it, she "ran out of money." She also thought that she was ready to stop. Many of her problems had cleared up. She had no more depressions and she had stopped smoking and drinking.

For the last several years, Debbie had been fairly content. She lived alone in her own home with lots of books and a garden. She wrote poetry. Although she had made no real relationship with a man since her divorce, she had many women friends. She was on good terms with her sons and their wives. The only thing that concerned her was that she was not working. She felt that she should be "gainfully employed," but nothing really interested her except writing poetry and, as she said, you could not make much money doing that.

A couple of months previously she had been getting ready for a vacation trip and had gone in to see her doctor about a lingering cough. He suspected lung cancer and recommended further tests, which Debbie postponed until she returned from her trip. The tests showed a cancer that had started in the right lung and spread to the left lung and the lymph nodes. The doctor told her not to expect a cure. They could help her with the pain, but she would die in about two years.

Debbie said she came to do sandplay in order to "get things together and get ready for death." When I asked Debbie about her religious beliefs, she said that she guessed she was an agnostic. She had been taken to a Protestant Sunday school when she was a child and had in turn taken her own sons to church, but Debbie never really "believed." She had, however, always had an awe of the universe.

I suggested that Debbie see a male psychiatrist and analyst for some sessions at the same time that she was seeing me for sandplay. I wanted to have this colleague as a back-up when I was away, and I also wanted to have someone I knew following her medical treatment. Moreover, this analyst had survived lung cancer himself. Debbie did not like the idea of seeing a man, but she accepted my referral and a satisfactory contact was made.

Debbie came for twenty visits during the twenty-one months that our relationship spanned. She chose not to come every week. It was clear to me from the beginning that she did not want to become too dependent. She made fourteen sandtrays in the twenty visits.

In discussing her trays, I am not going to try to identify all of the details nor to interpret the full tray. Instead, I will follow certain themes that presented themselves in the trays as we proceeded. In retrospect, I realized that these included:

1 Coping with the death sentence. She had already started by getting the therapy she wanted. But initially she showed almost no emotion when she discussed her cancer.

2 Transforming her negative images of her parents (who themselves had already died).
3 Becoming less resentful towards her ex-husband and their unresolved sexual problems.
4 Feeling less inferior as a woman towards men.
5 Relieving her guilt about not working.
6 Reducing her conflict about attachment/detachment (which she worked on in the co-transference).
7 Connecting with the next world in the absence of any organized religion to help her.

Looking at the overall impression of Debbie's first sandtray (see Plate 13), it is apparent that there is an inner area and an outer area. The inner area is populated by many trees and animals, while the outer perimeter is practically empty. Remembering that Debbie had come to do sandplay in order to prepare for death, I thought that the bustling inner area might be a representation of life. And the almost vacant outer perimeter might represent death. At the end of making this scene, Debbie placed the red bridge in the lower right corner, bringing the inner and the outer areas together. In this first tray it seems that she is attempting to make a connection between the known, life, and the unknown, death.

There are other connectors besides the bridge in this tray. The blue beaded snake at the lower right, which will reappear frequently in many of her trays, seems to be headed over the bridge as if it is to be the first to begin the crossing over from life to death. The starfish (not visible in Plate 13), which lives in the ocean and is shaped like a star, may also represent a connection between water and sky.

There are also two turtles in the tray, a ceramic turtle at the top straddling the water, and a smaller brown turtle on the right almost hidden by a tree. Turtles are apt connectors of opposites. Their bodies symbolically unite two pairs of opposites: male/female with the phallic head and neck representing the male and the round shell representing the female; and sky/earth with the rounded dome representing the sky and the square plastron underneath representing the earth.

Turtles are also long lived. It is not unusual for turtles to actually live a hundred years, and in Chinese lore they are said to live up to 3,000 years. This certainly approaches immortality. Perhaps Debbie, in using turtles in her tray, is trying to deny her mortality. Or, on the other hand, perhaps her use of turtles suggests an intimation of some kind of immortality.

We see several other images suggestive of spontaneous regeneration or healing which are consistent with a denial of permanent loss or with the sensing of some possibility of transformation. The snake on its way across the bridge often symbolizes renewal since it regularly sheds its skin and grows a new one. The peacock to the left of the snake is thought of as immortal in several cultures because its flesh is so slow to rot. Moreover, the peacock in both alchemy and early Christianity is a symbol of resurrection. The crab and starfish at the bottom of the stream both renew parts of themselves. The crab, which represents the sign of "Cancer" in the Western Zodiac, produces a new shell to accommodate its larger body as it grows and the starfish regenerates a new arm when one breaks off.

Just above the tops of the two tall slender trees in the center is a dark spinning wheel. To the right of the spinning wheel is a silvery castle and between the two is a girl in white. Debbie told me that this girl was Sleeping Beauty. I thought to myself that here was another association related to immortality. In the fairy story of Sleeping Beauty, a jealous old witch who was not invited to the party for the infant princess puts a curse on her: at the age of 16 the princess will prick her finger while spinning and will die. The king desperately bans all spinning wheels from the castle and even from the kingdom in order to protect his daughter. But at the age of 16 the princess finds her way to a room in the top of the castle where an old woman is spinning. The old woman encourages her to learn to spin and the princess pricks her finger and falls to the floor. But she does not die because one of the benevolent wise women had commuted the curse of death to a hundred years of sleep. At the end of the hundred years, a prince finds the sleeping princess, kisses her awake, they fall in love, get married, and live happily ever after.

While I was focusing in my mind on the fact that the princess slept rather than died, Debbie was focusing on the fact that the king prevented his daughter from growing up by not letting her learn to spin. When Debbie told me this, I became aware that in a sense Debbie's father had prevented her from growing up by not providing her with the education she needed.

The final item Debbie added to the tray was a Madonna in the upper left under a large tree. She said she had not wanted to include it because she felt suspicious of Christian symbols, but something in her had made her put it in anyway.

In Debbie's next scene (see Plate 14), an inner area and an outer area are again connected, this time by a causeway of wet sand rather than a ready-made bridge. Debbie constructed this herself out of wet sand; she is more actively attempting to unite the inner with the outer. And the outer area is no longer empty. There are a number of images there, including several trees, which indicate the possibility of growth on the other side.

Five of the items in the lower right have to do with religion and/or ancestors. Two of the black objects are totem poles. In the religions of some Northwestern Native Americans, the totem pole connects the tribe with their animal ancestors. Between the two totem poles is the head of a crusader. Crusaders fought in the religious wars of the Middle Ages. Behind them is a Kachina doll wearing a colorful garment and feathered headgear. In the religions of some Southwestern Native Americans the Kachina represents a mythical ancestor. The adjacent grey object is a Mayan god holding a baby.

There are fewer items now in the inner area. The same blue beaded snake used in the first tray is in the center. There are five sources of light in a circle around it: the sun, three glass bottle tops that are frequently used as lights, and a little lantern just above the head of a snail. The presence of light indicates an illumination, a greater consciousness which is now connected with the snake.

The snail appears to be coming in from the outer place. The snail is often seen as a union of the conscious ego on top (the hard outer shell) and the larger unconscious that the ego rests on (the soft under part). The snail is also seen as a spiritual symbol because of its spiral shell. It is as if the snail is slowly bringing something spiritual from the outer more unconscious area into the inner more conscious place.

The ballerina in the lower right corner was the last item Debbie put in. She said she herself had been interested in dancing at one time. She has put part of her life into the outer area, the place of death.

After Debbie finished making this tray, I did something which I seldom do. I asked her if she wanted to make another tray. Perhaps at some level I sensed she needed an opportunity to make a compensatory scene. She seemed happy at my suggestion.

Debbie started this second tray (see Plate 15) by putting a figure she said was "frightening" in the upper left corner. This figure is often seen as a diabolical representation of death (skull head not visible in Plate 15). Later she added the black bat below him.

In the lower left Debbie added five figures that she called "nightmarish." These are all bodhidharmas; they have truncated human bodies without legs or eyelids. Bodhidharma was the Indian sage who remained seated for nine years without eating or sleeping while waiting for enlightenment. During the nine years, his legs withered away. And, at one point when his eyes closed sleepily, he pulled his eyelids out in disgust with himself. These somewhat grotesque figures may reflect Debbie's fear of bodily deterioration which, in people with cancer, is often almost as great as the fear of death.

Debbie placed other frightening figures in the tray as well: a leering face, a ghoulish head, and a strange amorphous creature on the center mound. She put alligators around both mounds. Alligators devour. To the left, below the mounds, are mice. Mice gnaw. She may feel gnawed at and devoured by her cancer.

Beside the mice there is a witch, a negative mother image associated possibly with her own personal mother and/or with me. I was sitting near the left corner of this tray close to the witch. The five aggressively armed soldiers in the upper right corner may stand for her anger. So, both fear and anger are present in this tray. There is no more denial of her negative feelings.

I do not know if Debbie could have made this tray without having made the more positive tray first. Or perhaps she *had* to do this tray because the previous tray was too positive and there had to be a compensatory experience. In any event, she could concretize both her fear and anger in the sandtray, and could thereby experience them at a deep level in the safety of the co-transference. Debbie never talked directly at any point in the sandplay series about either of these emotions. Expressing and experiencing them in the tray was enough.

When Debbie added the wizard in the lower right corner with his magical crystal and the two butterflies – which are often thought to represent the soul – just above him, she said, "I've got to have my one good." I do not see hope as denial. Hope is essential nourishment when we are in despair.

When Debbie started her next scene, she took down a gold crown and a silver crown from the shelves. She said that the crowns represented the sun and the moon. She tried placing them in various parts of the tray but said they did not fit. She finally put them in the lower left, covered them with sand, and put two glass bottle tops over the spot. Apparently the crowns were important to her, but she was not quite ready to use them yet, so she buried them and marked the location so she could find them again for future use.

Debbie stretched the familiar blue beaded snake out on top of a large driftwood root, overlooking the scene. Just above the snake, she added the spinning wheel, a reminder of the relentless spinning of fate. Debbie told me again that the story of Sleeping Beauty was important to her, and again she connected not being able to spin with feeling guilty that she did not have a job. This was the closest she ever came to blaming her father for not providing her with more education.

Debbie added two wrestlers to the tray and commented on the fights she used to have with her sister. She did not remember what they fought about, but she knew that they were always fighting. Sisters are often shadows of one another; Debbie here is willing to wrestle with her shadow. If she can struggle with her shadow now she might feel more peaceful at the time of her death.

Debbie put a group of hang gliders in the scene, inserting their supporting wire into a bottle on the shelf behind the tray, and said, "They will fly down." At the time, I thought she might mean that they would fly down to rescue her. I realize now that this also anticipated the theme of a growing connection between heaven and earth, one of the themes that becomes important from this tray on.

In Debbie's next tray (see Plate 16), she differentiates between the masculine and the feminine. She put a collection of masculine items on the right: a tiny bronze crusader, a stag, a lion and a rhinoceros. And a group of feminine items on the left: a mermaid, the Venus of Willendorf, a recumbent cow, a squaw holding a baby, a Greek mother goddess and a woman/tree.

The overall scene has sexual overtones. Several groupings may make reference to woman's rejection of male impregnation. The massive snake from the masculine side is coming into the center as if to impregnate the feminine pool which is shielded by the blue beaded snake. The woman/tree in the upper left is reminiscent of the story of Daphne who turned into a tree to escape from Apollo's pursuit. The mermaid has a tail instead of a genital area. Perhaps in this scene Debbie is, in some subliminal way, acknowledging her part in her failed sexual relations with her husband.

A white male death figure holding a flower stands behind the mermaid. He is quite different from the scary dark death figure she used in her third scene (Plate 15). He almost appears to be bringing the flower to the mermaid, perhaps an early intimation of the coming of death as a *coniunctio*, a sacred marriage, a Liebestod.

There are also figures which suggest the possibility of new beginnings in this scene. In the upper left corner there is a large egg protected by dragons. In front of this biological egg is the cosmic egg encircled by a winged serpent. And Debbie once again added the Madonna. This nurturing, holding representative of the Great Mother may help her hold and experience the separation between and union of masculine and feminine that was going on in this tray.

There are more new developments in Debbie's next tray (see Plate 17) – the five tiny babies in the center. In the upper left there are several nurturing women: a squaw with baby by a warm fire, a Native American woman preparing food from grain, and a woman carrying a jug on her shoulder. A lion stands behind a tree in the center of the left side. The lion does not seem to be aggressive, but rather protective. Debbie is here experiencing both nurturing feminine and protecting masculine images; these positive images may help to compensate for the largely negative images she has carried of her actual parents.

In the lower right are many shells, representing the feminine in a more abstract form. The flying gulls represent the spiritual. And, since gulls live in sky, earth and water, they may also symbolize a connection between all three elements.

The blue beaded snake is encircling a tall tree in the upper right corner. There are four doves around it. The cosmic or universal tree is often depicted with a serpent encircling the base and with a bird, usually a dove, at the top. This cosmic tree was formed, according to the Bible, by combining the Tree of Life with the Tree of Knowledge. And it also unites three realms: underworld, earth and sky.

Debbie called the beaded snake her "signature snake" and said she needed it here. The coiled snake forms a ring which is penetrated by the phallic tree, representing in symbolic form another experience of the *coniunctio*, the sacred marriage.

Her next tray (see Plate 18) is filled with stars. Debbie made the large star out of children's building blocks and placed many other stars of various kinds on the left and right mounds. Debbie had first created her own bridge out of sand in the second scene (Plate 14), the concourse that connected the unknown with the known; now she builds her own star out of blocks. And by laying the star on the sand, she again joins together heaven and earth, unknown and known.

Debbie embellished the star that she constructed with twelve gold coins and protected it with two snakes: a folk snake and the beaded snake which she had identified as her "signature snake," her essential identity. The snake is poised, ready to ascend the right mound, going up from the earth toward the heavens. In her first scene (Plate 13) the beaded snake was starting to cross a level bridge between the inner and the outer; here it is beginning to climb up the mountain from earth to heaven. Again she is making a symbolic connection between the known and the unknown, between life and death. In the beginning the connection was made horizontally; now the connection has become vertical.

When Debbie came in the following time she announced, "I want to stop for a while. I'm stopping with Dr. [X] also. I feel I want to have a rest from all that." When I reminded her that I would be going on vacation in a month she said she had completely forgotten that I was going to be gone. By "forgetting" she could ward off the feelings aroused by my impending vacation, and by interrupting therapy herself first she could avoid the experience of being abandoned. She could leave me before I left her. We decided to make one more appointment to review her slides before I left.

Debbie then made her next scene (see Plate 19), which I see as a body tray. Debbie first placed a tower or pagoda on the left followed by a garden pond in the lower left center. At some level these may represent a phallus (the high tower) and a vagina (the round pool), thus continuing the masculine–feminine *coniunctio* theme from her earlier scenes.

Debbie then built up the right side into two mounds. After looking at them for a while, she made a third mound nearby. She told me later that she made the third mound to keep the others from looking like two breasts. She then made a fourth mound on the left and placed glass spheres on top of the right three mounds and an egg on top of the left mound. So she ended up with not just two or three breasts, but with four, each with an erect nipple! She next placed a mirror on the mound on the right and used sand to cover up some of the mirror, saying she wanted it smaller.

She did not *want* to want to be fed (the denied breasts). She did not *want* to want to be mirrored (the partially concealed mirror). She did not *want* to be dependent like a child on its mother. She was leery of personal attachments, especially at this time when therapy was going to be interrupted. Before she left, however, she very carefully threaded a gold chain and colored yarns among the mounds, along with the blue beaded identity snake, so that everything was connected and said, "I want everything attached."

In this session Debbie was struggling with her ambivalence, her dependency/independency, attachment/detachment conflicts. She began with "I want to stop" and ended with "I want everything attached."

The focus in Debbie's next scene (see Plate 20) is on the tiny infant in the inner area. Four blue horses surround the baby. The sky-blue horses seem to be providing spiritual protection for the baby and the two totem poles on either side of the baby provide ancestral protection. This central grouping gives the impression of a divine birth.

For Debbie, I think this scene was connected with the recent birth of her grandson. She had hoped to live to see this baby, her first grandchild. This scene may also be concretizing for her an intimation of immortality: from the ancestors behind to the new generations beyond.

The totem pole Debbie used in this scene is taller than the one she had used before. It is the tallest in my collection. She placed it on top of a mound, extending the mound up into the sky, thus again vertically reaching up to connect the below with the above.

Debbie placed especially symbolic figures in each corner of the tray. On the right there are two feminine symbols, a mermaid in the lower corner and a Greek mother goddess in the upper. On the left there are two masculine figures, the head of the crusader in the lower corner and a chacmool in the upper. The chacmool, in the Toltec religion, was the receptacle for the heart of a victim sacrificed as an offering to the rain god. This was part of a ritual beseeching the rain god to send rain to the newly planted seeds below so that new life could begin. Again there is this inevitable connection between sacrifice and new beginnings, between death and birth.

In the following scene (see Plate 21), fear is back – the five bodhi-dharmas reappear in the upper left. And the wrestlers are back in the lower left. The huge black whale and white whale facing the wrestlers from the water reinforce the impression of a struggle going on between them, between the opposites. Debbie's earlier struggle with her personal shadow may have extended now to the larger struggle of life with death, the shadow of life. Von Franz interprets the image of wrestling made by a dying patient as a wrestling with death (von Franz 1987: 22).

There are three babies in the opposite corner of the tray, on a diagonal from the wrestlers, one in a carriage and two on the ground. Dragons are guarding them. The cosmic egg sits beside them, the egg that gives birth to the universe.

In the lower right, on a diagonal from the fearful bodhidharmas, is a fuzzy bear, often seen as a warm mother, the strong father stag and an animal baby, a fawn. So in this corner an animal family of different species is represented. Both groupings on the right compensate for the negative images on the left. But here there is no bridge to connect the opposites. They are left to stand, as is.

After this tray in which fear reappeared, Debbie made a tray concretizing her anger. She placed a volcano, which expels the fiery energies of anger, in this scene and then an incense burner, which securely contains them. She was experiencing anger as both potentially explosive and as contained. This sequence parallels the movement in her third tray (Plate 15) where she also externalized first fear and then anger. At no time in her process did she ever verbalize her fear or her anger. She dealt with them only in the tray.

A large body of water occupies the center of the next tray (see Plate 22). A small central island emerges from the water. The sun shines on the island, and two babies lie under it, one wrapped in blue, the other in pink, a boy and a girl. It is as if the sun, representing consciousness, has come forth from the waters of the unconscious and, with this rise in consciousness, Debbie comes to experience the masculine and feminine as equals. In creating this image of equality between the sexes in the sandtray, she is transforming her inner image of women as being inferior to men. This feeling of the inferiority of women had probably been engendered in her by her experiences with her father, who had viewed girls as not meriting as much education as boys did, and with her husband, who had dismissed her needs as unimportant compared to his own.

A journey in the round surrounds the pool, a journey with no beginning, no end. It is a cyclic rather than a linear journey. The circling is in the clockwise direction, the direction of coming into consciousness.

The overall impression of Debbie's next scene (see Plate 23) is one of peace and calmness. Debbie called it a pastoral scene. Many animals are coming to drink from the water on the right. Debbie put in a farmer at top center who could "take care of all this." Then she placed a Venus of Willendorf in among the animals at the top left and added, "The farm is fertile." She put the Greek goddess next to the Venus and said that she had been thinking of her mother lately. "I recall her footsteps coming down the hall when I had a kidney operation when I was twenty-eight years old. You need a mother when you feel sick." Her images of negative parents have been transformed into images of caring parents. There is not only tranquility, but also nurturance and fertility in this scene.

Debbie's presence at this time gave the room a feeling of serenity. She was frail; she required a cane; she sat down to make the tray. But her voice sounded strong, stronger than it had for some time. I felt I was looking at a woman whose outer frame was weak, but whose inner core was solid. She said she felt tired, but had no more feeling that she had to do things. She no longer felt guilty for not having a job. "It just doesn't matter. It's a nice feeling. I don't have to be a certain way."

In Debbie's final tray (see Plate 24), the blue beaded snake is coiled in the center, wearing a golden crown. She had identified the golden crown as the sun when she buried it in her fourth scene. Here, when she places the sun-crown on the snake whose home is in the ground, she again unites, for the last time, the sky and the land, the unknown with the known. The gold crown can also be seen as an image of the Self and the snake as her own most essential being. The numinosity of the Self here unites with the final distillate of all her experience of life, and crowns it.

For the first time the snake is coiled in the counterclockwise direction, the direction that traditionally signifies going down into the unconscious. Perhaps Debbie senses that at death there is an inversion, an inversion of the known and the unknown. At death the known, the ego identity, the I, becomes the unknown; the personal ego-snake goes down and disappears into the unconscious. And the other, the up there, the unknowable, becomes, at death, the known.

The Madonna on the left is standing on a crescent moon which rests on the earth. So the moon returns with the sun. The silver and gold crowns that she had buried for future use before are now above ground. The glass bottle tops, which were circling the snake in the second tray and which marked the burial place of the crowns in the fourth tray, are at the bottom center in this tray. The glass marker lights could be set aside.

Several animals from previous trays witness this crowning. And there is one new item, an orange Medusa at the top just right of center. When she placed this figure in the tray, Debbie said, "She has lots of power. I think I need that. I need physical strength." And the Madonna is giving her spiritual strength.

And, finally, Debbie placed two butterflies above the crown and snake, the same butterflies that she had used in her third tray (Plate 15) to represent hope.

Debbie was too weak to come to the office after her final tray. At my suggestion, I brought the slides of all her sandplay scenes to her home and we viewed them together. She lay on the couch and made appropriate, sometimes even lively, remarks as we viewed them. As she finished looking at the slides, there seemed to be a sense of closure for her. She seemed ready to die, not with any fanfare, or resignation, but just ready.

Each week, on the day that had been her appointment day, I telephoned her at noon and asked her if she wanted me to stop by at the time of her appointment, which was the last appointment of the day. Sometimes she accepted my offer and sometimes she did not. She always expressed appreciation for my call. One time Debbie said she knew she was dying, but that it did not feel that way. She added, "Of course, how would I know. I never died before."

A few days before I was again to leave on vacation I called to see if she wanted me to come over to her home. She was too tired, but she had had a dream the night before that she wanted to tell me. At the end of telling me the dream, Debbie said that she liked the dream, and that it made it more real for her to tell it to me.

This was our last contact. When I returned, I learned from her son that she had died. She died peacefully, with no pain until the last evening when her doctor was called in to give her pain medication. A month before her death she had celebrated her grandson's first birthday, and a week before, her sons and their wives had come to her bedside to say their farewells.

In closing I want to tell you the dream that was our last contact. Debbie dreamed:

> I was in a beautiful setting in the country with a white Victorian house in view. It had white railings around large porches. It was an old-fashioned house like the one we lived in when we were first married and my husband was going to graduate school. It was rolling land and very green. A couple of fields away I saw a crowd of people. They seemed to be digging. I think "They are digging my grave and this is my funeral." It is a lovely place. If I could choose a place to be buried, this is the place I would choose.

Appendix

What I look for in final case reports

First, what I look for in a final case report to show me that the applicant has absorbed the basic principles of doing psychotherapy and values them:

1 Acceptance of the client/patient and respect for his/her uniqueness.
2 Respect for the relation to the unconscious.
3 Empathy and appreciation for the process as it occurs.
4 Respect for self-healing in patients.
5 Non-intrusiveness in the client's process.
6 Respect for and some knowledge about orientations different from one's own, including religious, cultural, and sexual.
7 Understanding of differences in life tasks at different ages and for the different genders.
8 Sufficient knowledge regarding acute and chronic physical and psychological conditions to refer to other professional persons at appropriate times. Attention to drug and incest problems.
9 Ability to cope with emergencies.
10 Ability to recognize substantial amounts of co-transference and to respond appropriately. Awareness of when to seek consultation.
11 Understanding the need to respect boundaries between therapist and client. Observance of those boundaries with appropriate distance and warmth.
12 Meticulousness about confidentiality and other ethical issues.
13 Discipline and care in keeping records.

Since I cannot expect to see all these aspects in a single report, I look for the applicant's not having lapsed in any of them.

Second, what I look for in the case report, in addition to the above, to indicate that the applicant is ready to be recognized as a qualified sandplay therapist:

1 Evidence that the client has profited from the therapy, and that the use of sandplay has contributed significantly to that improvement.

2 Ability to understand objects in the tray in terms of:

- the personal life experience of the client
- the culture in which the client was raised
- archetypal meanings
- the appearance of the same object in previous trays
- the order in which it was placed, e.g., first, last
- the sequence in which it was placed, e.g., what came before, and what comes after
- its location in reference to the position of the therapist in the room
- the immediate personal meaning to the client, often not known until the review.

3 Ability to see how the client is using objects in the sand scene to express anger or love or other feelings towards the therapist, and to realize what the therapist's role is in this.
4 Understanding the sandtray series as it progresses, including attention to the molding or smoothing of the sand, use of three dimensions, changes in boundaries, inter-relation of objects, dry vs. wet sand, active vs. static arrangements, landscaping, chaos vs. harmony.
5 Ability to make connections between the sandtray scenes and other data such as dreams, outer life, past experiences, family problems, co-transference and physical condition.
6 Grounding in Jungian theory and other basic theories of psychological development such as those offered by Neumann, Fordham, Winnicott or Klein.
7 Correct use, if used, of such terms as archetype, symbol, shadow, animus, anima, self, Self, mandala, transcendent function.
8 Understanding of at least some of the other often used frames for interpreting sandplay and dreams such as alchemy, chakras, fairy tales and myths. Clearly bridging from these conceptual frames to the clinical material, the flesh-and-blood person.
9 Correct references to the fairy tales, myths, and other literary sources with integration of these primary sources appropriately into the text and avoidance of references which do not significantly relate to the case.
10 Avoidance of dependence on cookbook interpretations, including multiple references to and dependence on symbols books.
11 Ability to summarize the sandplay process so that it makes sense as a meaningful inner process.
12 Brevity.

Finally, what I note but try not to let influence me too much:

1 Clarity of photos.
2 Clear and consistent labelling of photos.
3 Clarity of writing, grammar, spelling.
4 Accurate listing of references.

Lines from Kay

Know your fear
Grieve your sorrow
Cherish your hopes
Respcct your wants

Share in giving
Use your courage
Preserve your awe
Be gentle toward failings

Own your hate
Explore your envy
Speak your anger
Cry your hurts

Live your love
Be your joy
Treasure your life
Revere death

Bibliography

Allan, S. (1991) *The Shape of the Turtle: Myth, Art and Cosmos in Early China*, Albany, NY: State University of New York Press.

Amatruda, K. and Simpson, P. (forthcoming) *Sandplay – The Sacred Healing: A Guide to Symbolic Process*, Boston, MA: Sigo.

Ammann, R. (1991) *Healing and Transformation in Sandplay*, LaSalle, IL: Open Court.

Beebe, J. (1992) *Integrity In Depth*, College Station: Texas A&M University Press.

Bolen, J. (1984) *Goddesses in Everywoman*, San Francisco: Harper & Row.

Bradway, K. (1978) "Hestia and Athena in the analysis of women," *Inward Light* 41, 91: 28–42.

— (1979) "Sandplay in psychotherapy," *Art Psychotherapy* 6, 2: 85–93.

— (1982) *Villa of Mysteries: Pompeii Initiation Rites of Women*, San Francisco: C.G. Jung Institute of San Francisco.

— (1985) *Sandplay Bridges and the Transcendent Function*, San Francisco: C.G. Jung Institute of San Francisco.

— (1987) "What makes it work?," in M.A. Mattoon (ed.) *The Archetype of Shadow in a Split World*, Einsiedeln, Switzerland: Daimon Verlag, pp. 409–14.

— (1990a) "A woman's individuation through sandplay," in *Sandplay Studies: Origins, Theory and Practice*, Boston, MA: Sigo, pp. 133–56.

— (1990b) "Developmental stages in children's sand worlds," in *Sandplay Studies: Origins, Theory and Practice*, Boston, MA: Sigo, pp. 93–100.

— (1990c) "Sandplay journey of a 45 year old woman in five sessions," *Archives of Sandplay Therapy* 3, 1: 68–78.

— (1991) "Transference and countertransference in sandplay therapy," *Journal of Sandplay Therapy* 1, 1: 25–43.

— (1992a) "Sandplay in preparing to die," *Journal of Sandplay Therapy* 2, 1: 13–37.

— (1992b) "Sun and moon in sandplay," *Journal of Sandplay Therapy* 1, 2: 47–9.

— (1993) "Sandplay toriis and experiences of transformation," *Journal of Sandplay Therapy* 3, 1: 32–43.

— (1994a) "Sandplay is meant for healing," *Journal of Sandplay Therapy* 3, 2: 9–12.

— (1994b) "Sandplay of 'home' and 'career' women: initial and final scenes," *Journal of Sandplay Therapy* 4, 1: 36–45.

Bradway, K., Signell, K., Spare, G., Stewart, C., Stewart, L. and Thompson, C. (1990) *Sandplay Studies: Origins, Theory and Practice*, Boston, MA: Sigo.

Bustard, R. (1973) *Sea Turtles: Their Natural History and Conservation*, New York: Taplinger.

Campbell, J. (1974) *The Mythic Image*, Princeton, NJ: Princeton University Press.

— (1983) "The way of the animal powers," *Historical Atlas of World Mythology*, 1, London: Summerfield.

Carr, A. (1967) *So Excellent a Fishe* [*sic*], Garden City: Natural History Press.

Cavendish, R. (ed.) (1983) *Man, Myth, and Magic*, 5, New York: Marshall Cavendish.
Cram, R.A. (1966) *Impressions of Japanese Architecture*, New York: Dover.
Dieckmann, H. (1986) *Twice-told Tales: The Psychological Use of Fairy Tales*, Wilmette, IL: Chiron.
Edinger, E. (1985) *Anatomy of the Psyche: Alchemical Symbolism in Psychotherapy*, LaSalle, IL: Open Court.
Fordham, M. (1969) *Children as Individuals*, New York: Putnam's Sons.
— (1978) *Jungian Psychotherapy: A Study in Psychology*, New York: John Wiley.
Freud, S. (1915) "Papers on technique of psychotherapy," *Standard Edition of the Complete Psychological Works of Sigmund Freud*, 12: 97–157, London: Hogarth.
Gassner, S., Simpson, H., Weiss, J. and Brunner, S. (1982) "The emergence of warded-off contents," *Psychoanalysis and Contemporary Thought* 5, 1: 55–75.
Gillmar, J. (1994) *Beauty as Experience and Transcendence*, Ann Arbor, MI: UMI Dissertation Services.
Goodheart, W. (1980) "Review of Langs' and Searles' books," *San Francisco Jung Institute Library Journal* 1, 4: 2–39.
Gordon, R. (1993) *Bridges: Metaphor for Psychic Processes*, London: Karnac.
Graves, R. (1957) *The Greek Myths*, 1, New York: George Braziller.
Jung, C.G. (1928) *Contributions to Analytical Psychology*, New York: Harcourt, Brace.
— (1953) *Psychology and Alchemy, Collected Works*, 12, New York: Pantheon.
— (1954a) *The Development of Personality, Collected Works*, 17, New York: Pantheon.
— (1954b) "Psychology of the transference," *The Practice of Psychotherapy, Collected Works*, 15: 164–340, New York: Pantheon.
— (1956) *Symbols of Transformation, Collected Works*, 5, Princeton, NJ: Princeton University Press.
— (1961) *Memories, Dreams, Reflections*, New York: Pantheon.
— (1963) *Mysterium Coniunctionis, Collected Works*, 14, New York: Pantheon.
— (1967) *Alchemical Studies, Collected Works*, 13, Princeton, NJ: Princeton University Press.
— (1969a) *Psychology and Religion: West and East, Collected Works*, 11, Princeton, NJ: Princeton University Press.
— (1969b) *Structure and Dynamics of the Psyche, Collected Works*, 8, 2nd edn, Princeton, NJ: Princeton University Press.
— (1971) *Psychological Types, Collected Works*, 6, Princeton, NJ: Princeton University Press.
— (1973) *C. G. Jung Letters: 1906–1950* (ed.) G. Adler, Princeton, NJ: Princeton University Press.
— (1976) *The Symbolic Life, Collected Works*, 18, Princeton, NJ: Princeton University Press.
Jung, E. (1957) *Animus and Anima*, New York: Analytical Psychology Club of New York.
Kalff, D.M. (1980) *Sandplay, a Psychotherapeutic Approach to the Psyche*, Santa Monica, CA: Sigo. A revision with a new translation of (1971) *Sandplay: Mirror of a Child's Psyche*, San Francisco: Browser.
— (1991) "Introduction to sandplay therapy," *Journal of Sandplay Therapy* 1, 1: 7–15.
Kawai, H. (1992) "The sun and moon in Japanese mythology," *Journal of Sandplay Therapy* 1, 2: 39–46.
Kenton, E. (1928) *Book of Earth*, New York: William Morrow.
Kohut, H. (1984) *How Does Analysis Cure?*, Chicago: University of Chicago Press.
Kotschnig, E. (1968–9) "Womanhood in myth and in life," *Inward Light* 31: 16–30; 32: 5–23.

Langs, R. (1981) *Resistances and Interventions*, New York: Jason Aronson.
Lowenfeld, M. (1969) *Play in Childhood*, Portway Bath, UK: Chivers. (Originally published 1935 London: Gollancz.)
— (1979) *The World Technique*, London: Allen & Unwin.
Menaker, E. (1974) "The therapy of women in the light of psychoanalytical theory and the emergence of a new view," in V. Franks and V. Burtle (eds) *Women in Therapy: New Psychotherapies for a Changing Society*, New York: Bruner/Mazel.
Mitchell, R. and Friedman, H. (1994) *Sandplay: Past, Present and Future*, London: Routledge.
Miyanoshita, H. (1964) *We Japanese*, Yokohama: Yamagata Press.
Neumann, E. (1959) "Psychological stages of feminine development," *Spring* 563–97.
— (1973) *The Child*, New York: G.P. Putnam's Sons.
O'Connell, C. (1986) "Amplification in context: the interactional significance of amplification in the secured-symbolizing context-plus field," unpublished PhD dissertation, California Institute for Clinical Social Work.
O'Flaherty, W. (1975) *Hindu Myths*, Harmondsworth, UK: Penguin.
Rogers, C. (1942) *Counseling and Psychotherapy*, Boston, MA: Houghton Mifflin.
Romer, A. (1956) *Osteology of the Reptiles*, Chicago: University of Chicago Press.
Rudloe, A. and Rudloe, J. (1994) "In a race for survival," *National Geographic*, 185, 2: 94–120.
Rudloe, J. (1979) *Time of the Turtle*, New York: Alfred A. Knopf.
— (1995) *Search for the Great Turtle Mother*, Sarasota, FL: Pineapple Press.
Ryce-Menuhin, J. (1992) *Jungian Sandplay: The Wonderful Therapy*, London: Routledge.
Searles, H. (1965) *Collected Papers on Schizophrenia and Related Subjects*, New York: International Universities Press.
Shuell, M. (1996) "The theory of sandplay in practice," unpublished PhD dissertation, California School of Professional Psychology at Alameda.
Signell, K. and Bradway, K. (1995) "Some answers to Skamania questions," *Journal of Sandplay Therapy* 5, 1: 16–35.
Spencer, M.J. (1977) "Mirror: as metaphor, as symbol," *Professional Reports, Fourth Annual Conference of the Societies of Jungian Analysts of Northern and Southern California*, 72–115, San Francisco: C.G. Jung Institute of San Francisco.
Stewart, L. (1992) *Changemakers: A Jungian Perspective on Sibling Position and the Family Atmosphere*, London: Routledge.
Thompson, C. (1990) "Variations on a theme by Lowenfeld," *Sandplay Studies*, San Francisco: C.G. Jung Institute of San Francisco.
von Franz, M.L. (1972) *Creation Myths*, Zurich: Spring Publications.
— (1987) *On Dreams and Death*, Boston, MA: Shambhala.
Watson, J. (1992) "Pulling turtles out of the soup," *National Wild Life* April–May: 19–24.
Weinrib, E. (1983, 1992). *Images of the Self: The Sandplay Therapy Process*, Boston, MA: Sigo.
Wells, H.G. (1975) *Floor Games*, New York: Arno. (Originally published 1911 in UK. First US edition 1912, Boston, MA.)
Wheelwright, J.B., Wheelwright, J.H. and Buehler, J.A. (1964) *Jungian Type Survey: The Gray-Wheelwright Test Manual* (16th revision), San Francisco: Society of Jungian Analysts of Northern California.
Wheelwright, J.H. (1981) *The Death of a Woman*, New York: St. Martin's Press.
Williams, C. (1976) *Outlines of Chinese Symbolism and Art Motives: An Alphabetical Compendium of Antique Legends and Beliefs, as Reflected in the Manners and Customs of the Chinese* (3rd revision), New York: Dover.
Winnicott, D. (1971) *Playing and Reality*, New York: Basic Books.

Index